Praise for the first e<

"*Bashert* is the engrossing story of Andrea Simon's search for her roots, her re-engagement with her grandmother Masha, who journeyed from Volchin to Brooklyn, to Woodridge, to Israel, to Berlin and back. It is the story of the past that once was and never again will be—Volchin, a Jewish town whose population was decimated. . . . Simon's writing makes us care about her, her grandmother, her town and her self-discovery. Pilgrimage is the most ancient of religious rituals, a journey forth that is also a journey into self and *Bashert* is an admirable account of Simon's pilgrimage. We learn as she learns, we engage, we remember, we cry out and we even at times laugh. **Perhaps the first—or at least one of the first—of a new genre of Holocaust writing** that will become more familiar and more urgent as the survivors are no longer with us and their descendants are forced to uncover from history what they once could encounter directly from memory."

—**Michael Berenbaum**, Director, Sigi Ziering Institute: Exploring the Ethical and Religious Implications of the Holocaust and Professor of Jewish Studies, American Jewish University, Los Angeles, California; former President of the Survivors of the Shoah Visual History Foundation

"Makes a significant contribution to our understanding and perception of the Holocaust in eastern Poland (Belarus). . . . Balances impressions of life before and during the Holocaust in eastern Poland with other fragments of family life in the U.S. and other parts of the world from roughly 1915 to the present day. This has the welcome effect of demonstrating the quality, beauty and despair of those lives that were destroyed. . . . The very personal approach and the attempt to reconstruct fragments of the quality of life . . . give it a special and enduring quality."

—**Martin Dean**, U.S. Holocaust Memorial Museum

"*Bashert: A Granddaughter's Holocaust Quest* delivers something much more than a story about the author's kin. It carries a message that transcends all cultures, races and generations. . . . Ms. Simon's memoir whispers a warning to all who read it: do not let the past become the future."

—**Melanie McMillan**, *The Litchfield County Times*

"*Bashert* is an emotional roller-coaster ride. I laughed heartily at some of the family anecdotes, and I cried bitterly at the description of the horrific executions of innocent men, women and children whose only crime was being Jewish. I *kvelled* with Andrea when I learned of her family's bravery and courage . . . and I mourned the senseless loss of so many loved ones. *Bashert* is essential reading. . . . While we are all aware of the horrifying misery that confronted Jews and other minorities in the concentration camps . . . much of what occurred in the smaller and often unknown villages inside Czarist Russia remains unreported. *Bashert* opens our eyes to the personal story of a strong and determined young woman, who lost her home and family . . . and found a new life in America. Masha will take a place in your heart as she did in her granddaughter's and mine and create a pocket of warmth and pride that will forever remind you of how the strength of one person can change the destiny of an entire family. I urge you to read *Bashert*, but please be sure to have a hanky at hand."

—**Michael D. Fein**, editor, *The Gantseh Megillah*

"Based on interviews, memoirs, historical accounts, archival documents, and family anecdotes, Simon undertook what she describes as a 'spiritual search' for her family members killed in the Holocaust. . . . In her quest for the truth, Simon has written a loving eulogy to her lost family."

—**George Cohen**, *Booklist*

Also by Andrea Simon

Historical Fiction
Esfir Is Alive
Floating in the Neversink

Bashert

Andrea Simon

Vallentine Mitchell / *London*

Bashert

A Granddaughter's Holocaust Quest

WITH A FOREWORD BY DR. CLAIRE LE FOLL

VALLENTINE MITCHELL
LONDON • CHICAGO, IL

Published in 2019 by Vallentine Mitchell

Catalyst House
720 Centennial Court
Centennial Park, Elstree WD6 3SY, UK

814 N Franklin Street
Chicago, Illinois
60610, USA

www.vmbooks.com

Photography (cover & page vii) of Ester Midler, courtesy of Ray Brooks
First published in 2002 by University Press of Mississippi

British Library Cataloguing in Publication Data:
An entry can be found on request

ISBN 978 1 912676 15 6 (Paper)

Library of Congress Cataloguing in Publication Data:
An entry can be found on request

Printed by 4edge Ltd, Hockley, Essex

Dedicated to the memory of Iser Midler, Bashka Midler,
Ida Midler, Sara Midler, and Ester Midler;
Masha Midler Lew Miller Hiro;
and Norma Lew Simon, who would have been so proud.

Contents

This book, and indeed my search itself, could not have been possible without the loving support of many people from all over the world. To help me thank them, I have divided these "assistants" into categories.

For research assistance, thanks to the YIVO Institute for Jewish Research and the late Dina Abramowicz, reference librarian; and to Sarah Ogilvie, United States Holocaust Memorial Museum.

For translation assistance, thanks to: Dov Bar (Hebrew); Lisa Degtyar (Russian); Shmuel Englender (Russian to Hebrew); Miriam R. Goldberg (Hebrew); Katia Ioannides (German); Ilanit Kamin (Hebrew); Shoshana Lew (Hebrew); Michael Livshits (Belarusian, Russian); Miriam Osman (Polish); Naomi Rappaport (Yiddish); Eytan and Marcia Rubinstien, EDUFAX Translation Services (Hebrew); Julian Tokarev, Web Ideas International Company (Russian); and Daniel Vogel (German).

For editorial advice and encouragement, thanks to my writing group: Patricia McMahon Barry, Jane Gardner, Pam Leggett, and Sanna Stanley. For extra help on the manuscript, thanks again to Pam and to my daughter, Alexis. Other "readers" included: Clare Palmieri, Joan Katz, and Karen Mann, who each gave an enthusiastic thumbs-up. Valery Lanyi presented supplementary material. Leonid Smilovitsky, Diaspora Research Institute of Tel Aviv University, was generous in sending relevant research. And Martin Dean, United States Holocaust Memorial Museum, reviewed my book with constructive and invaluable suggestions.

Acknowledgments

For publishing assistance, thanks to Craig W. Gill, editor-in-chief, University Press of Mississippi. Without his acceptance and guidance, this book would probably still be in my closet. I also owe a debt of gratitude to Ellen D. Goldlust-Gingrich, copy editor; Anne Stascavage, editor; and to the other professional staff at the University Press of Mississippi.

For the generous sharing of memories and photos, thanks to my family: the late Dina Bronitsky, the late Ray Brooks, the late Gerson Lew, the late May Lew, Shoshana Lew, Barbara Reich, the late Sara Spindel, and especially, to my mother, Norma Simon, who died on September 8, 2000, at the age of 83, for all of the above. And, for all the *kvelling*, thanks to the *gantseh mishpocheh*, including my husband, Andreas Neophytides, and my daughter, Alexis Zoe Simon Neophytides.

For pointing me in the right direction, thanks to Jewish Federation members: Lily Guterman, Rosanne Lapan, Stuart Mellan, the late Louis Pozez, Ruthann Pozez, and Sara Sanditen. My participation in the Eastern European trip would not have been possible without the patient knowledge of tour leader and friend Miriam Osman; my meeting with the Israelis would not have occurred without Sara Sanditen; and the memorial to Brona Gora would not have happened without the inspiration of Louis Pozez. Special thanks to Rosanne for staying the course.

For unconditional support about Volchin, thanks to the late Dov Bar, the late Esther Bar, the late Shmuel Englender, the late Hanna Kremer, the late Mike Kremer, Drora Schwartz, and Hannah Williams. Without Shmuel's relentless interviews and priceless memories, without Dov's tireless research and dedication, and without Hanna Kremer's unselfish "gift," this book would have remained only an unfulfilled idea. My debt is immeasurable.

For help on the paperback edition, thanks to Timothy Pew for his expert typesetting and design. Thanks to the super team at Vallentine Mitchell Publishers: Lisa Hyde (editor), Toby Harris (sales and marketing), and Jenni Tinson (design and production). Thanks also to publicist Rachel Tarlow Gul for her kindness and expertise. Finally, my extreme gratitude to Dr. Claire Le Foll for her magnificent Foreword.

Bashert was based on a variety of materials, including audiocassette-recorded and videotaped interviews, memoirs, historical accounts, personal observations, archival documents, family anecdotes, reference books, and newspaper articles. Many of these sources contained eyewitness testimony, recorded either shortly after the Holocaust or more recently. A great deal of the source material has never been released in published form; much certainly has never been translated into English. It's safe to say that this book contains the most extensive information to date on the Brona Gora and Volchin massacres, although, as writing this book has taught me, even that could change at any moment.

As can be expected from such a work, the material has come to me in many styles and languages, including Yiddish, Hebrew, German, Polish, Belarusian, and Russian. This has required the use of several translators. Different translators sometimes worked on materials about similar events. By the time I received certain eyewitness testimonies, they had been translated and retranslated, for example, from Russian to Hebrew to English.

Each language presented its own spelling of cities, towns, villages, and even people's names. Within the same language, different texts had different spellings, often as a result of changing nationalities and fashions. Most alphabets had no English equivalent other than a phonetic interpretation. With patronymic Russian names, I have kept to the style of the translator, occasionally referring them as surnames, even though English and Russian

usages place them as middle names. Dates, numerical accountings, and events were often contradictory. And given different sensitivities to culpability, facts, such as ethnicity and perpetrators' names, were often omitted altogether. Some archival documents, including eyewitness testimonies and commission investigations, were recorded in Soviet times and contained gross gaps and distortions; German documents were also sketchy. Added to this "Tower of Babel," was the basic subjectivity and *Rashomon* character of remembrance.

I often used the spelling of a town or name that was the most familiar to me, even though it may have been a Yiddish or Polish version. For example, I used the Yiddish village names of *Volchin* and *Visoke* since these are the ones I have heard all my life. Although the longer name of the massacre site is *Bronnaya Gora* (and a contemporary road sign reads *Bronnaya Gara*), I chose the shortened *Brona Gora* to coincide with the spelling used by the United States Holocaust Memorial Museum and in various prestigious publications. The German name is *Bronnaja Gora*. I used the name *Belorussia* when discussing preindependent times and *Belarus* for modern usage. Mostly, I used the name *Brest* for that city, although it has had other names, depending on national identity at the time. I was not as careful with other place names as it became too confusing. Instead, I chose the most popularly used versions.

Finally, I have come across documents with differing accounts of the same event. I have often included repetitious material to add to the historical record, to show the predilections of the source, to maintain consistency in narrative flow, to portray the reality of such a search, to reinforce the atrocity unfolded, or to present emotionally difficult material in smaller, easier doses.

While I have been devoted to uncovering this material and filling a significant gap in Holocaust literature, there was no way to get the exact facts. For a perfectionist such as myself, this was difficult to accept. Given all these concerns, it is my sincerest wish that I have done justice to those whose stories needed to be told. For in the end, this is all that matters.

Bashert is an extraordinary book. One might think: why do we need another book on the Holocaust, another memoir of a survivor's relative seeking their roots? We would be wrong. This book is much more than that.

First of all, it was one of the first memoirs published on the so-called 'Holocaust by bullets'. Unlike memoirs by Holocaust survivors written in the decades following the war, exemplified by Elie Wiesel or Primo Levi, that made of Auschwitz the symbol of the destruction of the Jews during the Second World War, *Bashert* unveiled the brutal reality of the Holocaust in Soviet territory, well before the media buzz generated by the works of Pere Desbois and Timothy Snyder later in the 2000s, to name just the most famous. Published for the first time in 2002, the book is one of the first to describe precisely the massacres of Jews that happened in the territories occupied by the Wehrmacht after June 1941. As now better known but was ignored for a long time, a large proportion of the Jews who were then living in the Soviet Union were exterminated before the 'final solution' to the Jewish question was formulated in January 1942. They were killed in particularly brutal and traumatic conditions: gassed in trucks, or more commonly shot in the head or in the heart and then piled in mass graves in forests near their villages and towns. Andrea Simon has produced a remarkably well documented historical account, drawing on a variety of primary sources. Using German archives, reports from the Soviet Extraordinary State Commission that investigated Nazi war crimes starting from 1942, regional archives, and also personal testimonies, memorial publications and interviews she conducted herself, she gathered a wealth of material to trace the fate of her own family but also that of other Jews in the region of Brest (Belarus). She also raised important historical questions about the passivity of the Jews, the collaboration of local populations, the difficulty of making sense of incomplete and contradictory testimonies and the impossibility of memorializing these events in the former Soviet Union. More than 'bashert' (pre-destined), this book and the encounters with other survivors or survivors' children who share with her the results of their own research bear testimony to her determination and inquisitive character, at a time when internet and social media did not exist.

Bashert is not only a book of history; it is also and foremost a captivating piece of literature that artfully interlaces the personal story of Andrea and her ancestors with history. Half-way between a detective novel and the tale of a spiritual quest, Andrea keeps us on tenterhooks. We surprise ourselves by awaiting with the same fear and excitement the translation of the latest document in Hebrew or Russian that she received in her mail, to learn more about the fate of the Midlers and other Volchin families. The anecdotes about her flamboyant grandmother Masha and her other relatives, the accounts of encounters with other Volchin descendants, the interviews and exchanges with eyewitness and survivors make this quest all the more fascinating and profound. By telling us about the 'behind the scenes' aspects of this quest and her questioning about her own identity and the fate of the East-European Jews who died, escaped or emigrated, Andrea Simon succeeds in touching us and making us think.

Bashert's reedition is important, even though the mass killing of Jews in Nazi-occupied Soviet Union has entered the historical narrative of the Holocaust since its first publication. The book's focus on a specific region, Western Belarus, is unique in itself, and offers a necessary counterbalance to a historical narrative on mass killings that focused in its initial stage on Ukraine and the Baltic states, with Babi Yar and Ponary becoming symbols of the Holocaust in the East. The implacable and meticulous description of the still rarely remembered Brona Gora massacre, during which 50,000 Jews were killed in 1942, reminds us that some parts of this history still need to be uncovered and studied. The recent discovery of 1,214 skeletons on a building site in the centre of Brest and the persistent reluctance of local officials to acknowledge the uniqueness of the Holocaust makes the reading of *Bashert* particularly timely and urgent.

The long silence about the Nazi mass killings on Soviet territory and the marginalization of Polish and Soviet Jews from the memory of the Holocaust are a consequence of the Soviet refusal to recognise the specificity of the Jewish genocide. The post-war official narrative that promoted Soviet heroism and a united memory of 'peaceful citizens' brutalized by the fascist enemy prevented Soviet Jews from remembering and commemorating this past. The collaboration and silent eye-witnessing of the massacres by Slavic populations were also taboo. The collapse of the Soviet Union has only partially changed this situation. It has allowed survivors and their descendants to visit the places where Jews lived and died, as Andrea Simon did with an American group in 1997. It also made possible research by local and foreign historians and resulting publications. However, the memorialization of the Holocaust, especially in Belarus, remains problematic. The memorial complex opened in June 2018 on the site of the extermination camp of Maly Trostinets near Minsk in June 2018 still commemorates the mass extermination 'of people'. It would not have mentioned the word 'Jew', if not for the inauguration in 2019 of a monument funded by the Austrian government to commemorate the fate of thousands of Austrian Jews deported and killed in Trostinets. In the absence of official memorialisation, the memory of what happened is left to the initiative of individuals, like the Belorussian woman in *Bashert* who takes her children and grandchildren to Brona Gora, or the director of the Kobrin museum of history who not only saved Jews but also collected information and wrote about their fate. Andrea Simon's book is all the more important not only to 'never forget', but also to question our certitudes on what, how and why things happened.

Dr. Claire Le Foll, Associate Professor of East European Jewish History and Culture, Parkes Institute, University of Southampton, 29/04/2019

July 1997

My grandmother's spirit haunts me still. "*Mamaleh*, it's not over," she calls from her grave. Her croaky voice, heavily layered by cigarettes, bitterness, and the fractured intermingling of Yiddish, Polish, Russian, Hebrew, and English, reaches through my skin, pinching my heart. "Bless your *pupik* [navel]," she bellows in an imitation of herself, "there's more work to do."

I know she's right, because even now, shortly after my trip to Poland, Belarus, and Russia, I learn more about my lost family. I'm happy—thrilled—to make new contacts, to discover what seem like facts. But I also know that these facts are as elusive as the scattered ashes of my massacred relatives—ashes that lined village ditches, ashes that clung to crematoria walls, ashes that blanketed forest floors, ashes that have dissolved into nothingness.

Descendants of Abraham Isaac Midler

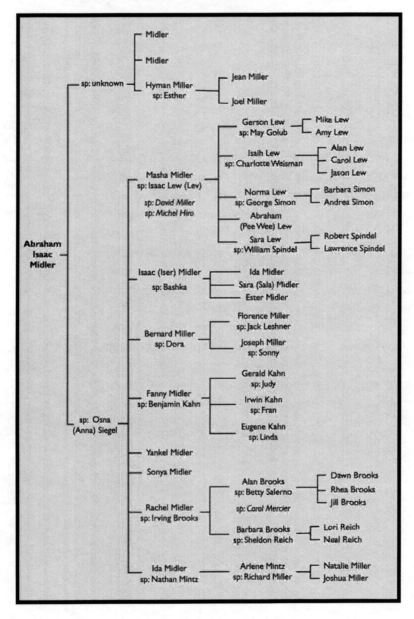

Descendants of Isaac Lew (Lev)

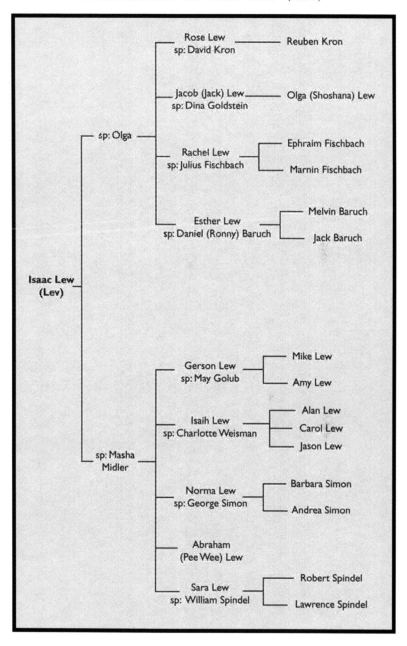

Chapter 1

January 1997

Frigid blasts seem to belch from New Jersey smokestacks, catapult like cannonballs across the Hudson, gathering momentum through the narrow branches of barren linden trees, and burst through my poorly sealed Riverside Drive windows. As always, my fingertips are the first bodily parts to feel the cold, and I'm tempted to put on gloves as I sit at my computer, facing what I often think is the windiest spot in the world. I flex my fingers, trying to restore normal circulation, and lay them in proper position on the keyboard; and as I begin to write, a voice—that voice—comes to me like another gust of icy air.

"Such a village," my grandmother Masha croons about her birthplace, Volchin, "a place like no other—a real paradise."

"But Gram," I protest as I always did as a child, eager to hear every morsel about her early life, "then why did you leave?"

"What do you mean? Everybody wanted to run away from Europe. They killed the Jews. Pogroms and pogroms and pogroms on the Jews. Oy, how we suffered."

"You left family there?"

"Yes, my brother Iser and his wife and daughters."

"Why didn't they leave?"

"Why? Why, there was always a reason. We all sent him money, many times. We made out the papers. He used the money for this reason and that reason, for school, for another thing."

Bashert

1

"And what happened to them?"

"Killed like every other Jew."

My fingers stiffen again, and I stare at my computer, startled that this conversation appears on my monitor, seemingly verbatim from more than 20 years ago. Then, I remember clearly, I didn't press the issue. I took my cue from my grandmother, who, for once in her life, looked like she couldn't say more.

As if out of respect for Masha's silence, the words stop on my screen as mysteriously as they began. I long to continue but become increasingly uncomfortable from the chill and go into the kitchen to make a cup of tea. When I return, I open my desk drawer and pull out a plastic box with six 90-minute audiocassettes, interviews I taped with my grand-mother over a two-year period beginning in 1978. At the time, I was a 33-year-old freelance writer, wife, and mother of a toddler. According to her citizenship papers, Masha was 85, although several other documents made her younger.

During our sessions, we generally sat at the round table in Masha's eat-in kitchen on Ocean Parkway in Brooklyn. With the sun filtering through the sheer white curtains behind her, illuminating the rivers of wrinkles throughout her pink baby-soft face and the white strands in her thick, almost-black, lion's mane hair, she'd tell me her "stories," good-naturedly stopping often to find a photo or open a letter. She'd take advantage of my presence and have me set her hair in big wire rollers enclosed by a dangling pink hair net (and thereby save herself money at the beauty parlor), or make a *glasseleh* tea with a used tea bag browning a spot in her sink. Sometimes, my mother, Norma, then a little over 60, sat across from us, holding my squirming two-year-old in her lap, playing "This Little Piggy Goes to Market" on my daughter's chubby fingers.

There we were, four generations of women: my mother, still classi-cally beautiful, although, to her dismay, she didn't inherit her mother's luscious hair; my daughter, Alexis, a brown-banged bundle of antics; me, a long-haired ex-hippie; and my grandmother, adjusting her horn-rims with magnifying circles engorging her cataract-spotted brown eyes, tugging the dropped earrings in her LBJ lobes, laughing, cursing, exag-gerating, calling everyone "bastards" or "princes," and loving her place as the center of it all. Whatever her story, she'd drift back, with dreamy nostalgia, to her childhood.

I load and reload my portable tape recorder, rewinding and fast-forwarding, trying to locate those earlier memories.

I hear my voice, nasal and insistent: "But when you lived in Volchin, what was your house like?"

"It was beautiful, the nicest. You could eat off the floor."

My mother and her older brother Gerson, both as cantankerous as their mother, agreed about Volchin. As young children, they often traveled there from Warsaw and other Polish towns. To them, whose lives were uprooted by war and persecution, the Volchin house was idyllic.

"I remember a huge tile stove in the kitchen—white tiles. It heated the house. In the winter, we used to sleep on the top of the stove," my uncle Gerson recalled during a recent family meeting.

"To me," my mother interrupted with a similar look of longing, "it was a tremendous mansion, because in Warsaw, all of us nine children and our parents lived in one room, separated from another family by a sheet. The Volchin house had an attic with dried fruit of all kinds. My cousins used to throw apples to us from the roof."

Whenever my family got together, the talk invariably reverted to my grandmother Masha, and arguments—the same arguments—over exact ages and names, were always as vehement as if they were brand-new. Was she still a young teenager when her teacher gave her special tutoring? And did this teacher, as Masha claimed, eliminate an important reference from the teaching certificate that would have severely restricted her opportunities—the fact that Masha was a Jew?

When this happened—she was about 17—Masha heard about a distant relative, Isaac Lev (later changed to Lew), who lived in Warsaw, where he was the headmaster of a Jewish school. In his 30s, Lev was a distinguished religious and secular scholar and a new widower struggling to raise four children in a large house.

I locate this episode on one of Masha's taped interviews and listen as she explains their complicated relationship: "I didn't know him, but I knew he lived in Warsaw and he's a big, big shot in a big city. He was related to my mother. His father married my grandma. My mother never saw him. He was her stepbrother. He put an ad in the newspapers: he needed teachers to take care of the fourth, fifth, and sixth grades. He didn't mention female teachers. So I hollered to my mother, 'I want to go to Warsaw.' My mother, she wanted to kill me. But I knew, I stuck to my father. I was to my father like an angel. If I wanted something, I got it."

And so she did.

Not only did Masha become the first female teacher at Lev's school and an asset with her proficiency in four languages, but she insinuated herself into his household. "I never dreamt ever he'd look at me," she says with uncharacteristic humility. "There was a governess for the children. . . . I was crazy for the kids. I felt so sorry for them without a mother. They wanted to be with me, so I went with them."

From her own "modest" account, Masha was beautiful, with long braids, tall, and dynamic. She made quite an impression on Lev's children, who ranged in age from infancy to about seven. And her charms were not wasted on the master of the household: "He started to bring me presents and take me to the biggest theaters that I never dreamt to see in my little village where I came from, and every night we went in another place to dance."

Masha's mother opposed the relationship and ordered her daughter to return home. Lev, a master of diplomacy, took Masha and his children to Volchin and presented his case. As far as he was concerned, he argued, Masha had a mind of her own and no one could dissuade her from what she wanted. Masha's father was impressed by Lev, who was handsome, a linguist, pious, and, by their standards, prosperous. Masha's mother, however, saw beyond these outward trappings to the responsibilities before her young daughter.

Later on, when Masha married, the "troubles" began. It is unclear from her stories where and when these events happened, but they seem to have occurred in or around Warsaw when she had very young children, about 1920. This coincides with the Red Army invasion of Poland's eastern frontier, when the Cossacks wreaked violence and destruction throughout villages and cities.

According to Masha:

The Russian soldiers were looking for women. I put white flour on my face to make myself like an old lady. . . . My grandmother, my mother's mother, had put all over the living room, whiskey. The soldiers liked whiskey and got drunk. By my bedroom, she put on long curtains and a sign, "Don't come in. This is quarantined. There's a woman with children, and they're all infected." I was already jumping out the window. I took a chance to be killed. The soldiers asked a neighbor, "Where is that woman with the long hair and the beautiful face?" She answered, "That woman is not here. You see, the children are all sick, and she is somewhere dead outside. Go and give a look." So then, they went away.

Twice they came with pogroms. In Warsaw, we bought a wagon with a horse, and we started to go. . . . I figured we'll take a chance. . . . And we went around like this, the whole year [stopping] wherever there was a place to find a little water for the children. . . . [Through] the woods, like this, we traveled. . . . The kids were all blown up from malnutrition. My mother stayed in Volchin with her children. She didn't know whether I'm alive, and I didn't know whether they're alive.

Through the years, I heard various versions of those stories and pieced together my own truth. But, certain facts were irrefutable: Masha always made the best of the situation. "From Warsaw to Volchin," Uncle Gerson said, "she would flirt with all the officers on the train. When the First World War broke out, we went from town to town as the German army advanced." Then, there were the years of hiding, in the woods, always on the move.

There were many examples in Masha's life, but one—from her later years in New York's Catskill Mountains—had a tight grip on me. My aunt Sara, my grandmother's youngest child, recalled, "When all the children were gone, and I was the only one left, my mother said, 'Saraleh, pack a bag.' With two valises, we walked out of our 17-room boardinghouse and left everything. She never looked back." I couldn't imagine doing such a thing.

In the 1950s and '60s, when I was growing up in Brooklyn, I often visited Masha in the Brooklyn apartment she rented, on and off, for 40 years. It was a magical place—I can still remember the layout of each room, the position of each *tchotchke* (trinket). From the hallway, past the coat closet, there was a spacious rectangular living room dominated by an enormous kelly green sectional couch with gold-braided trim. On one side of the wall stood a tall mahogany secretary; the top drawer opened into a desk with slatted secret compartments. Near her Magnavox television, where I loved to watch "Picture for a Sunday Afternoon," overshadowing an end table, was a large crystal globe filled with roses preserved in filmy brown water. The walls were covered with artwork, mostly cheap copies of Van Gogh and Picasso, except for a large expressionistic portrait of two women, painted by my Israeli cousin, Shoshana.

It was in the living room my grandmother managed to clear space and open a long table when she had guests for Passover seders, Chanukah parties, or impromptu family dinners. It was where my great-aunt Rene would invariably fall asleep with food in her mouth, where Uncle Ronny would unveil his strawberry shortcake, where Uncle Richard would peek at my cousins' romance magazines, where everyone would argue about everything, and where there was basically one and only one focus of attention—Masha.

When my grandmother would tell her stories, she, of course, appeared preeminent. From the voyage to America in 1923, to struggles in Brooklyn, life in the Catskills, her profession as a nurse, the murder of her second husband, the deaths of two children, worldwide travels, her third marriage to the debonair owner of a Berlin cabaret—all these adventures and tragedies were fodder for my childhood imagination.

As an adult, I often wrote about my family. Masha, in her egotistical and colorful way, always managed to overtake my characters—as she does again so many years later on this arctic winter day. It's time to write her story, to let her run wild. But before I can do justice to her life and era, I have to go back to the beginning, to a little town in what was Poland, then Russia, and Poland again, a town called Volchin.

And so I begin my search. Does this town still exist? Can I trust my remaining relatives, who say it was near Bialystok? How can I be sure when I can't find it in indexes of books on the Holocaust and Eastern Europe? How can I be sure when I can't even find it on the map?

I call my friend Miriam. As a travel consultant, she often arranges Eastern European missions for the United Jewish Appeal. I ask if there is a way I can get to this village. She says perhaps I can go to Warsaw and then hire someone to drive me. Then she sends me an encyclopedia entry, translated from Polish, that locates a town called Wolsztyn in the western part of Poland, closer to Germany than to Russia.

"No, this can't be," I say. "From everything my family told me, it was on the eastern side, near the Russian border." My voice falters. How can I be certain this isn't the place? So many things my grandmother said were exaggerated; so many things my aunts and uncles remembered were contradictory.

I open my computer and turn to the Web. I'm new to the Internet; this is my first professional search. I type Volchin, Poland, and get pages of irrelevant references. I finally locate a man whose organization provides information about scores of towns, including Volchin. I'm excited, but I expect the material to be about another place with a similar spelling. I click on his name, explain my quest, and press "send." My first e-mail.

Incredibly, he responds: "Volchin is 10 versts (about five miles?) south from Vysokoye, the latter being more of a town, whereas your Volchin appears to be not much more than a large village. Vysokoye had a station on the railway between Bialystok (and points north) and Brest (and points south). Volchin is right near the Polish border, near the town of Janow Podlaski. The Bug River is the border at this point."

This is the town, I know it!

I go to the Jewish Division of the New York Public Library. In a reference book, I find: "Volchin, Byel.; Voltchin, Wolczyn. pop. 180. 189 km w of Pinsk." Yes, this must be it. But "Byel." must mean Byelorussia (Belarus), not Poland. From another reference, I read census figures: "1766, Jews, 402; 1847, Jews, 886; 1897, general population, 617, Jews, 588."

Then I visit New York City's YIVO Institute for Jewish Research, the preeminent repository for library and archival materials on the history and culture of Eastern European Jewry. I pore through catalog cards. There are listings for everything imaginable relating to Yiddish culture and Polish/Russian life. There's no entry for Volchin. I'm overwhelmed by doubts. Who am I to write about a life I know nothing about? How can I ever do justice to this part of Jewish history, when so many before me lived the life? I rush out of YIVO, shivering in sweat.

At home, lying in bed, I hear my grandmother speaking. Am I dreaming?

"Go back," she says. "So many times, you wrote about things you didn't experience. And you made it your own."

"But Gram," I say, about to fall into familiar insecurity. "Gram?" The next sound I hear is my alarm clock going off.

Returning to YIVO, I'm determined to speak, to risk revealing my ignorance. A petite, elderly woman with short white hair huddles with a man over a reference volume. I recognize her from a newsletter photo. She's Dina Abramowicz, a librarian from the only functioning library in the Vilna ghetto; miraculously, she's still active. I wait until she sits at her cluttered desk. I tell her about my grandmother's town, Volchin. She nods politely, registering no recognition.

Without warning, she almost jumps out of her seat. Just as suddenly, she scurries about the small, airless room, skillfully maneuvering around and under extended card catalog trays, down aisles clogged with chairs, sliding books off shelves and flipping pages. Finally, she finds a volume of interest and motions me to a table.

"This is something about Belorussia," she says. "It's in English. You can read and take notes."

I obey, although I can already tell by the short listing that there'll be no reference to Volchin.

After five minutes, Dina returns with another volume. She turns pages. "Ah," she says. "I will translate." I open to a clean page in my notebook. "Wolczyn, river Pulva, tributary to Bug," she says matter-of-factly. Yet there is a glint in her eyes. I grip her hand. She continues, "End of 19th century: 102 houses, including 5 brick. Residents: 804, most Jewish. Two Russian orthodox churches, 1 synagogue, 1 elementary school, 14 little shops, flour mill. Fairs three times a year—Jan./Apr./June. Jews, small commerce. Tailors, seamstresses."

She closes the book. "This is all," she says. But she's not finished with me. She guides me to the other end of the table, where huge, plastic-covered maps lie in a heap. I help her lift several until she locates the one she wants.

Both of us bend and squint. I find Brest. And then, just a little farther up and to the left, I see in the tiniest type: Wolczyn. "That's it! Volchin!" I yell.

"Yes," she says and with her fingers traces the line from Brest. "About 20 miles northwest of Brest," she says, patting my hand, a gesture she had performed for countless before me.

I leave YIVO, unconscious of my trip home. I must have walked to Columbus Circle; I must have descended the escalator; I must have boarded the uptown subway. But if a friend testified that instead I hailed a cab, and we sped to my apartment on the Upper West Side, I wouldn't have protested. All I know is that what seems like minutes later, I have the phone in my hands, and I'm dialing Miriam, my travel agent friend.

After explaining the dangers of going to Belarus, a totalitarian country, she gives me the address of a guide in Poland who can arrange the trip over the border. While waiting for his reply, I receive a call from Miriam. "There's a group," she says, "the Jewish Federation of Southern Arizona. They're planning a 10-day trip to Poland, Belarus, and St. Petersburg. It'll be exhausting."

This group, she explains, is being organized by a Brest-born American who had recently learned of a Jewish massacre site called Brona Gora, located in a forest between Brest and Minsk. It's the first mission of its kind to this region. Many of the participants had donated money to help the remaining Jews of Eastern Europe. Included in the group are Holocaust survivors and others wishing to locate their roots.

"I must go," I tell Miriam. "My mother was born in Warsaw. My grandmother and other relatives were born in Volchin, near Brest. And my great-grandfather traveled to St. Petersburg. This trip was made for me. It's fate." Before long, I'm on my way. Destination: Volchin, Belarus.

June 1997

On the plane to Frankfurt, where I plan to meet the delegation and change planes for Warsaw, I close my eyes and go over the itinerary, worrying about a possible plane delay preventing my transfer. The plane lurches and rights itself. A ping announces the seat belt sign, and, during a few minutes of turbulence, I blink back my fear. Snippets of recent family interviews bump into each other behind my caked eyelids. My distant cousin "informing" me that my grandmother was Hungarian. "Yeah," my sister said, "she was one of the lost Gabor sisters." On first hearing about my trip, my mother, whose well of anger is deep, said, "Why would anyone want to go to Volchin?" But, then, closer to my departure, she admitted, "I wish I had the physical stamina to go with you."

I hear the voices. My grandmother's soars above them all: "Don't listen to the others. You must make your way."

In my mind, she is no longer as she was toward the end of her life. Instead, she is the Masha of my earliest memory and the earliest photo I have of us together, with my sister and my other grandmother Sarah, standing in front of Sarah's building on Beverly Road in Brooklyn. It is 1948, and I am three years old, bundled in a front-zippered, quilted snowsuit with a drawstring hood. Next to me is my sister, Barbara, four years older and considerably taller. Behind my sister, Grandma Sarah stands, hands on Barbara's fur collar. Sarah must have been in her 50s, but she looks older, as women did then—white hair, full face, prominent glasses, and a double strand of pearls. Masha stands behind me, 5 feet 8 inches tall, a good head taller than Sarah. Masha wears a long, patterned silk scarf, stylishly draped around her neck, a large leather pocketbook hanging from her arm. Her coat is slightly opened, her Joan Crawford-padded shoulders jauntily slanted to match the French beret framing the left side of her dark hair. Even though Grandma Sarah gave me more money for my birthdays and spent many hours sewing my clothes, I was so proud that Masha was standing behind *me*. She was like no other grandma I knew.

Before we land, my seatmate, a Turkish man going home for a wedding, returns from the bathroom reeking of cigarettes. In a confidential tone, he mumbles, "They caught me smoking in the bathroom. They want me to speak to the captain when we land. What will they do to me? You know, they're Germans."

"Don't worry," I say. "It's just a warning."

As we say good-bye, and I look into his fearful face, I can't help but feel sorry for him. But I need to forget about smoking, about plane crashes. Here, in the land of my people's slaughterers, I need to forget it all.

It's my first day in Warsaw, and we barely have time to check into our rooms at the Marriott Hotel before we begin our tour. On the bus, I begin to hear the group members' stories. There's Lidia from Athens, who tells us that Greece lost 89 percent of its Jews during the war and that she spent those years hidden by Christians. There's Lily, born in Brest, who hid in a Polish friend's attic and was one of an estimated 11 of the city's Jews to survive. These women, I remind myself, are the lucky ones.

The modern capital passes in a blur, and I spot one skyscraper, non-descript thoroughfares, and indistinct passersby. A poster affixed to a street lamp advertises Sprite; a billowy sign threaded across a shopping plaza headlines "Robert," then promises something in words filled with consonants. The familiar crosses the unfamiliar, but I have no time to sort out the difference.

We stop at the old Jewish Gesia Cemetery, where we pass the graves of Poland's illustrious Jewish past. Under a display of black-and-white photos of children, there's an inscription: "In memory of one million Jewish children murdered by Nazi German barbarians."

To the side, a plaque contains a poem, "The Little Smuggler," dated Warsaw ghetto, 1941, by Henryka Lazowert. Midway, it reads,

> *Do not weep for me mother;*
> *do not cry*
> *Are we not all marked to die?*

She has only one remaining worry:

> *Who'll care for you tomorrow*
> *Who'll bring you, dear Mom,*
> *a slice of bread.*

That evening, we meet for a buffet in the hotel's private dining room, a simple and tasteful space with white-linen-covered tables and red leather chairs. After chitchatting, we go around the room and share our reasons for coming on this trip. As my turn approaches, my heart-beat races. I'm eight years old, terrified that the teacher will call on me, paralyzed that I will be derided for my awkward speech. Over and over, I wonder, "What can I say?"

I listen to a second Miriam, Miriam Lichterman, a petite, snub-nosed, formally dressed woman with auburn hair. Born in Warsaw, she survived life in the ghetto and several concentration camps. After the war, she married another multiple-camp survivor, Cantor Jacob Lichterman of the renowned Nozyk Synagogue, the only Warsaw syna-gogue to withstand the bombing. Starting a new life in South Africa, the Lichtermans had two sons, who also became cantors. Both are on this trip. Their dream is to sing in the same synagogue as their late father.

Why did she come? Miriam answers, "For me, it's a pilgrimage."

A few people clear their throats. Next is Louis Pozez, the mission's organizer. A short, well-spoken man, bald with white sideburns and bushy black eyebrows, Louis is casually dressed and has the open smile of a simple workingman, not the demeanor of the very successful business tycoon that he is. Louis left his native Brest when he was 17. Twenty-three members of his family, including his parents and younger brother, remained and were killed at Brona Gora. He had found out about the 1942 massacre only a few years earlier, when he learned of a list record-ing Jews over age 14 living in the Brest ghetto. The list came to nearly 500 pages—names, names of parents, dates of birth, and signatures of 12,260 people. Proof for so many of so many.

Those from the list, and about 9,000 children under the age of 14, were transported to Brona Gora and massacred.

Louis explains that this large-scale atrocity appears to be one of many little-known mass shootings that occurred in the former Soviet Union territories and that certainly have received less attention than the Germans' other methods of extermination.

Sketchy eyewitness reports from Brest and other regional ghettos tell a similar story. Awakened at dawn, the Jews were rounded up and surrounded by SS soldiers with dogs. Led to the railway station, the bewildered crowd was loaded onto airless cattle cars—each car packed with 200 people. By the time they arrived at Brona Gora, 65 miles from

Brest, the weakest were already dead. There in the forest, all the Jews, including young children, were killed, row by row. The total number was staggering—50,000 human beings. Many of those from Brest were murdered in one enormous *aktion* beginning on October 15, my birthday.

Louis is here, he says, the deep-set bags under his eyes seeming to sag even further, to share with his wife and daughter a memorial service at the site.

My mouth loses its moisture. I'll never be able to form a coherent sentence. How can I be so presumptuous as to stand with these people? And then a voice insinuates itself among my mental clutter. "You got a reason," my grandmother says. "You got a good reason."

Others speak, others like myself—younger, removed from the horror by a generation or two, those who wish to see their ancestral town, visit the remaining Jewish population, just be there. "For me, it's a privilege," one woman says. Another says, "To walk the walk." And another simply utters, "Ditto."

Finally, it's my turn. I look around at the group. Most are from Arizona, most are conservative Jews. I'm a New Yorker, a nonobservant Jew. I grew up with virtually no religious instruction except to study the Bible as literature. Each December, my rebellious mother shocked her Orthodox family by positioning a fake green Christmas tree, complete with Santa and elves, next to the Chanukah menorah. What am I doing here?

"I was born in Brooklyn," I begin, certain they already know this from my nasal accent. "I'm a writer and photographer," I continue, also aware that admitting this leaves me vulnerable. "I'm planning to write a book about my grandmother's life. She was born in a small town near Brest. My mother and her brothers and sisters spent a lot of time there before the Cossacks wiped out their childhood. Unfortunately, they can't come here themselves. I have come for them." A woman at my table clasps my arm. I'm not sure if it's a gesture of compassion or pity.

The more I talk to these people, the more I discover coincidences. Essie, a tiny, attractive woman about my age who also has ancestors from the Brest region, grew up in my same Brooklyn neighborhood and then moved to her family hotel in a Catskill town. "Where?" I ask excitedly.

"Woodridge," she says.

"I can't believe it!" I yell. "That's where my grandmother had a boardinghouse. That's where I spent all my summers." From a shtetl in

Belarus to a shtetl in the Catskills. There's that fate again. The world of shrinking Jews becomes smaller and smaller.

The Catskills is where I first became obsessed with my grandmother's stories. My father's family also moved to Woodridge, where they owned two houses. During the summers of my youth, if Masha wasn't renting a bungalow, she'd stay with my family, sleeping on the convertible couch in the living room, whose wall abutted my bedroom wall. Although Masha said she never slept, her rumbling, guttural snores nearly rocked me out of bed.

One day when I was about nine, my cousin Michele and I were in the dining area of my small cottage, looking at old photos of Masha. She was in the kitchen, stirring a pot of stuffed cabbage, and we kept interrupting her for a spoonful and for identifications of people in the photos. After a while, Michele and I got bored and put on a show. Before long, Michele announced, "Masha Lew, from a tiny village in Russia to the shores of the Atlantic, *this* is your life!—Da, da da da, da da."

Then I came out of the bedroom wearing my father's jacket, stuffed with a pillow, his hat, and a thin, black mustache I drew with Maybelline eyebrow pencil. "How is my darling wife?" I asked.

"Oh Isaac, you look so young," Masha said, sitting back on the couch, enjoying my impersonation of her first husband.

"And you're still beautiful," I said as Isaac.

"Too bad you got divorced," Michele said as I ran back into the bedroom, changing clothes to be someone else from Masha's life.

Over the next few years, whenever Masha came to visit, Michele and I gave my grandmother another version of her life. She loved every minute of it.

But in Warsaw, where my grandmother experienced many "This Is Your Life" episodes, I am as restless as Masha used to claim she was. I go to sleep with heightened expectations. Only two days to Belarus. Only three days to Volchin. Everything else is extra.

———

During the two-and-a-half-hour train ride to Cracow, I look out the rain-spotted window. Open fields, farmhouses, wildflowers, mini mountains of hay, dense-leafed orchards. Peaceful, even bucolic, country-side. Can this be the same route taken by thousands jammed into cattle cars? Are these farmers, are these children, descendants of those who watched, those who jeered and cheered, as our own ancestors passed?

My companions—all Jews fully prepared for possible starvation—pass each other plastic bags loaded with hard candy, dried fruit, even cheese and crackers. I politely decline. My stomach churns in tune with the wheels.

In Cracow, as in Warsaw, we have little time to observe the city. We hurry from the train to a bus and chug through traffic. The driver parks in the Jewish section, a square of assorted old houses joined by a wide cobblestone plaza. There's little left of the living; instead, we visit a museum and a cemetery, where metal roofs hang over the tombstones to protect them from acid rain, we are told. Another example of what humankind has wrought.

We board the bus to the worst horror of them all: Auschwitz. I can get through this day, I tell myself, as I rush for a seat by the window. Despite the rain, which is getting heavier, I plan to photograph as much as I can. I need to remember the towns, the trees, the houses. I don't trust my memory. I can't even remember what we did the day before. I close my eyes, wait for the voice, wait for my grandmother to say something, anything. She is silent.

Inside the bus, my companions have bursts of talking. Garrulous and urbane Jerry tells about his grandfather in prewar Russia, jailed seven years for possessing something he never had: gold. Athletic and handsome Bruce describes his journey a few days earlier to a small town in the Ukraine where his great-grandfather lived. There, he met an old man who had a photo of the grandfather of Bruce's wife. The story of his day's adventure reeks with portents and coincidence. I recognize the phenomenon. It's like when a pregnant woman sees other pregnant women wherever she looks. If you want to see connections, they appear before you.

As we park in the lot opposite the State Museum, Auschwitz-Birkenau, I'm immediately struck by how close we are to the train tracks. Of course, we have to be close. There was space only for Mengele to order those who could work "to the right" and the old and infirm, the pregnant women and the children, "to the left."

Rows of redbrick barracks flank a narrow street and, if I forget the barbed-wire fences, I almost believe I'm at a normal military base—until I go inside. A white plastic model of the line "to the left" shows people descending into the underground changing area, where they strip and enter the gas chamber. Later on, we stand in the middle of that chamber, much smaller and darker than I imagined. Silently, the group looks up at the vents where gas spewed out. I hurry out, suddenly overcome by suffocating claustrophobia.

There are rooms with remains: piles of netted and twisted eyeglasses; a mass of intertwined artificial limbs, crutches, and prosthetic devices; a sea of blue, green, and red crockery; overlapping, named and addressed valises; a swarm of shoes; and the worst for me, huge clots of something that looks like it belongs on the ocean floor. It takes a few seconds to realize what it is: human hair—grayish, slate, almost colorless masses, as if trapped in midstage aging.

Dark, airless rooms; concrete tubs designed for four standing humans; metal pulley compartments, steel sheets for the dead, rolling into the ovens.

Do we have a right to stand here and gape? To focus our lenses and adjust our flashes? There's a thin line between voyeurism and compassion.

The two-kilometer road to Birkenau is also lovely, with open green fields, though I'm unprepared for the enormity of the place. I always heard of Auschwitz; Birkenau seemed an afterthought. But here, more than 40 one-story barracks, more primitive than those at Auschwitz because they were built expressly for the prisoners, seem to stretch beyond the horizon. Inside the barnlike structures, bunks of wooden slats face brick walls and concrete floors. Though the only light comes from a tiny four-pane window at the very end of the corridor, I can make out a dark shape below the window and another on the floor. They look like the silhouettes of human beings begging to escape. I feel their desperation; I absorb the stench, the acrid, animal odor—the aging concoction of wood-soaked urine, embedded fecal matter, water-less tears, burning flesh.

Outside, we gather around a collapsed thatched roof enclosing mounds of human ashes. We walk to the memorial, where we recite prayers and intone songs. Suddenly, the sky darkens and the light rain becomes torrential. Are all those lost souls weeping? Mutely, I read a nearby monument's inscription: "To the memory of the men, women, and children who fell victim to the Nazi genocide. Here lie their ashes. May their souls rest in peace."

It is estimated that between 960,000 and 2,500,000 people were killed at Auschwitz-Birkenau.[1]

On the return train to Warsaw, I reconstruct the previous night's conversation with Auschwitz survivor Miriam Lichterman, who had refused to accompany us to Cracow. Asked if she'd ever return to the camps, she answered, "I won't go back. I'd never go back."

That night, the camp's images replay and insomnia rules; finally, a reprieve comes in what seems like minutes before my wake-up call. This day is devoted to Warsaw, the city of my mother's birth.

For the Lichtermans, there's a greater mission, one we're privileged to witness. We enter Nozyk Synagogue for Shabbat services. As I climb to the women's section, I can still smell the fire from a recent bombing. We're joined by a handful of the city's remaining Jews and some tourists. The cantorial singing begins with the older Lichterman son, Joel. His brother, Ivor, echoes and then sings on his own. I don't watch their mother; I can only imagine her emotions.

Afterward, we walk to Miriam's old apartment building. In the courtyard, in the middle of a flower bed, there's a three-tiered monument housing a Madonna painting. Above the monument is a cross. Not the symbol of Miriam's youth.

Stupidly, I ask her if Warsaw has changed much since the war. "Yes," she says. "It used to be teeming with Jews. Now, it's teeming with Poles." I'm stunned with sadness but simply nod.

We tour the rest of Jewish Warsaw. And I remember. I have an old photo, taken in Warsaw around 1913, of a class in Isaac's school. There are about 30 children, boys and girls, three adults (presumably teachers, including one female), and in the center is Isaac, slightly balding with a prominent mustache. To his left is Masha, large-boned and zaftig in a V-necked blouse, her hair parted in the middle, directing attention to her open face. She stands out from the other somber-dressed people in her ostrich-feathered wrap, certainly not the demure wife of a religious man.

I try to reconstruct her life. I try to find the school, the well-appointed apartments, the crowded tenements and narrow courtyards of my mother's memory. I read modern tourist books with little mention of the Jews; I search maps; I question the guides. No one recognizes the street names. Have they been distorted by years of living? Or, more likely, have the names, like the houses and streets, been destroyed like all the rest of Jewish Warsaw?

That evening, I'm heartened. We sit down for a Yiddish State Theater production of *Fiddler on the Roof*. My grandmother attended the Yiddish theater. Of this, I'm sure. In the production, there are only two Jews. The company is amateurish, without charm. I feel inconsolable.

What is left of the Jews? An imitation of art; a slab of ghetto wall; a few stone memorials; a corner of the Umschlagplatz, where, in 1942–43, more than 300,000 Jews were driven to Treblinka. These numbers pile on my heart. I can't think about it too much. I just can't.

Before we leave Poland, we stop at the colorful and quaint Old Market Square. A group member asks our guide, a Polish intellectual, about the education of the country's children regarding the Holocaust. "It's part of the regular history lesson," he says. When pressed to elaborate, he seems torn. "Well," he admits, "now they are mentioning it more than they used to. After all, they are Poles." A rare moment of honesty.

Another mostly sleepless night. After an early breakfast, I board the bus with an iron vise clenched around my heart. This is the day I've been waiting for: we will be entering Belarus by lunchtime. I try to lift my spirits. I think of what's ahead. But my body belies my mind. My eyes burn beneath their sockets, only matching the fire lining my esophagus. I take baby sips from my water bottle. I'm so tired—so utterly, completely, bone tired. I can collapse later. I have a lifetime to sleep.

About 10 miles from the border, lines of trucks clog the lanes. We learn that they sometimes wait up to three days. There are endless searches. The customs clerks, we are told, are "in no hurry." The left-overs of the Soviet system have regimentation in their blood; they see no point in encouraging trade, in changing the rules.

As we park by the border, awaiting our passport check, a local bus stops to our side. A cluster of overweight women smiles at us, window through window. Their gold-capped teeth glisten. I lift my camera and point to it. The women continue to beam. I point to it again, wanting to be certain that it's okay to take their picture. They seem amusing to me, but I don't want them to see my smirk. I'm ashamed yet intrigued. They gather around each other, arms reaching out, and grin. I depress the shutter release. Though I hate posed pictures, I'm only too happy to comply.

Our entry into Belarus is unremarkable. Unlike the globe of my childhood, the country doesn't change from sky blue to lipstick pink. The distant fields look no different from Poland's. This should be no surprise. After all, western Belarus had been under Polish control at various times, most recently from 1921 until 1939.

The first river we pass is the Bug. My God! I consult my notes. It says, "Volchin (Wolczyn), river Pulva, tributary to the Bug." The river that goes to Volchin. Before long, I can see apartment buildings, and we approach the bleak skyline of Brest. A woman behind me, once a New Yorker, says, "It looks like Co-op City in the Bronx." We are all limited by our frames of reference.

Across the aisle, Sara, from Oklahoma and born in Brest, glances at her mother, Lily, who signs to her deaf brother, Nechamia. This is their first time in Brest since Sara was a child. Sara watches them as silently as her uncle's flying fingers, knowing they're remembering sensations from their hiding: inhaling the hay piled around them, feeling the coarse spikes spearing their raw skin, tasting the dry bile of fear.

"I've been wanting to talk to you," Sara whispers to me. "I got a call from a New York woman a few weeks ago. She was planning to come on our mission but dropped out at the last moment because her husband was recuperating from surgery."

I nod, waiting to see the relevance to my story.

Learning of Sara's strong connection to Brest, the woman had called about her hometown. "It was Volchin," Sara says. "Your Volchin."

"Really?" I shout. "There's a Jew alive from Volchin?"

"Yes, she escaped."

"Do you know her name, anything more about her?"

"No, but I think she knows someone from the Israeli delegation. They'll meet us in Brest. We'll ask then."

When the bus stops in front of Brest's Vesta Hotel, we're greeted by two armed guards who maintain grave expressions. At the door of my room, I struggle with the lock. Instantly, a woman appears, snatches my key and opens the door. I hear similar exchanges with my fellow travelers down the hall. The hotel must provide people to assist the helpless Americans with their keys. It would have been a lot cheaper and easier to install better locks.

Once in my room, I'm struck by its plainness. One twin bed, its thin gold-and-white bedspread supplemented by a coarse, folded blanket; a short tabletop chest; a Formica bureau with a TV. The decor of a 1950s thrift shop. The entire hotel, one of the city's finest, makes me feel as if I'm in a time warp. This must be basic Soviet-style luxury.

I drift toward the window, seeking light. The officers huddle with the bus driver. Beyond them is a house with a roof of corrugated tin, the ancient wooden walls painted drab green, the window trim an even drabber brown. Chickens and roosters parade back and forth. I turn around and take in my cold and unadorned room. Suddenly, I long to be in that pre-Soviet house across the street. I long to lie atop a large, soft bed, piled high with feather-filled quilts—*perinehs,* as my grandmother called them—soothed by the aroma of fork-poked apple pies, their finger-pinched crusts sticky with drizzled sugar paste, baking in the oven.

I once tried to get Masha to record her recipes, which she perfected after years of cooking for her family and then for her boarders in Woodridge. The most specific she got was, "a pinch of this," or "a *shtikeleh* [tiny piece] of that." She never made anything the same way.

Turning off my thoughts—and my senses—I stretch out on my hard bed and read about Belarus from my research notes, gathered in New York primarily from the *Encyclopedia of the Holocaust* and on the trip from tour guide information. At the time of the German invasion in June 1941, there were about 670,000 Jews in western Belorussia. Many were murdered in pits near their hometowns. This first wave of mass murder lasted until December 1941. The second wave began in the spring of 1942 and ended with the total annihilation of the Jews of western Belorussia. By the end of 1942, an estimated 30,000 Jews remained in Belorussia.[2]

There are currently between 80,000 and 100,000 Jews in Belarus. At the turn of the century, more than half of the population of the capital, Minsk, was Jewish. Of the estimated 100,000 Jews living in the Minsk ghetto during the war, some 90,000 were killed in various "actions." Now Minsk contains 20,000–30,000 Jews out of a total city population of 1.7 million.

In 1897, Brest, then called Brest-Litovsk, had over 30,000 Jews, more than 75 percent of the city's population. Today, the city has a paltry 600–1,000 Jews, mostly old and sick. Though the remaining Jews are generally needy, there are signs of rebirth with help from the world-wide Jewish community. Yet the basic question haunts many: Should Eastern European Jews be encouraged to live where their ancestors died, to struggle in a hostile land, or should they move to Israel and join those who made the voyage before them?

The next day is June 22. Our bus stops at the Brest Fortress, an enormous system of fortifications and a memorial complex where between 7,000 and 8,000 heroic Soviet soldiers and ordinary citizens held off the Nazis for one month in 1941. Most of the defenders were killed, died of starvation, or taken prisoner. Today is the anniversary of the German invasion of Russia. Another coincidence.

As I move under the arch, fashioned into a star, and proceed down the immense walkway, I hear someone shout, "Where is Andrea Simon?" Walking alongside my friend Miriam, the tour guide, I turn my head and see our mission leader, Stu, waving his hands. "Andrea Simon, come here," he yells. Miriam and I follow his beckoning hand.

"These are people from the Israeli delegation," he says, with his arm around an unfamiliar man. "They're from Volchin."

"What?" I ask as if I don't hear.

"From Volchin, your town."

"Volchin? But?"

"They were looking for a woman from Volchin who was supposed to come on the trip and canceled," Stu continues.

I remember Sara's story of the New Yorker who called her. But who are these Israelis? I'm in a heightened state of confusion—only aware that many people are gathering around us.

"My name is Dov," an attractive gray-haired man says in Hebrew-accented English. "I was born in Janow Podlaski, a town close to Volchin. My mother and much of my family were from Volchin. I spent my first two years there."

"Oh my God." I'm unable to summon anything more intelligent. "You mean the same Volchin?" I keep saying.

Then he introduces me to his wife, Esther, an ash-blond, pleasant-looking woman; and Drora, his buxom sister with frizzy, red hair. She is, he explains, younger and was born in Israel, where his family migrated. Suddenly, I'm being hugged by these women; automatically, I return their embraces.

"Wait. We have someone else," Dov says. From the crowd emerges an elderly man, though evidently spry in his bouncy white sneakers. Looking confused, he tugs the rim of his cap. "He doesn't speak English," Dov explains. "His name is Shmuel Englender. He is from Volchin. He lived there until 1941, when he left for the Soviet army. He's about 78 now."

Dumbfounded, I think about my great-grandfather. Despite my family's conflicting versions of his profession, it's clear he was a man of stature. Surely, Shmuel must have heard of him.

"Abraham Isaac Midler," I say, totally unaware of my warped time reference.

He shakes his head from side to side.

"He had a very nice house, at the edge of town," I say. "He was in the lumber business, or maybe tiles, but anyhow, he had land and looked after others. Maybe . . ."

Shmuel continues to shake his head.

"Your family name?" Dov asks. He notices my desperation. He'll help me.

"Midler, Midler, later it was changed to Miller. Oh, and my grandmother's husband, his name was Lev, later it was Lew."

If Shmuel was born around 1919, that would make him too young to have known my great-grandfather, who died shortly before Shmuel's birth. What was I thinking?

"Iser Midler," Shmuel says, tears welling.

"Iser! Yes, Iser! That was my grandmother's brother, my great-uncle." My heart races. I won't survive another minute. Yet I'm still not convinced. This cannot be. It cannot be that in the middle of this fortress, I should meet someone who knew my relatives.

I look for Miriam, who is usually circling her charges with maternal supervision. I need someone I can believe in. There she is, off to the side. She is weeping.

"Iser, he was a sewing machine salesman," I say, remembering my uncle Gerson's description.

"No," Shmuel says through Dov's translation. "He had a bicycle repair shop."

I knew it. I knew this was all a mistake. This Iser couldn't have been my uncle. But then I remember all my family's memories, the contentious *Rashomon* versions. Who knows? Maybe at one time, Iser was a sewing machine salesman. Maybe he never was. But how many Iser Midlers could there have been from this tiny village? I look into Shmuel's watery eyes. And through my own pools, I nod, unable to speak. Finally, I say, "Iser, yes."

We walk a few feet and stop. My head vibrates with noise. I can make out one thin, doglike trill. I know what it must be. The sound of my grandmother sobbing.

Leaning against the monument wall, I watch the men speaking Hebrew.

Dov translates for Shmuel: "Iser's wife was Ziba. And there were two daughters. The older was Nahoma."

"That was my mother's name before they anglicized it," I say, surprised—but not really. How can I be surprised any longer? The Brona Gora massacre of Brest's Jews began on my birthday, meeting these Volchiners in this place, and now my mother's name. I'm about to say, "No, it can't be. Jews don't name their children after living relatives," but I don't have the heart to protest.

Shmuel was Nahoma's friend, I don't doubt that. When he left Volchin, Nahoma was 15 or 16 he thinks. She was beautiful, Shmuel says over and over, as if remembering an old crush.

"What was my great-uncle like as a person?" I ask.

"He was very tall, slim, nice-looking, good-natured. He lived at the highest level."

"What do you mean?"

Dov continues to translate: "He received money, from America."

"Money, yes." I remember the stories from my grandmother, my aunts and uncles, how they had sent money, filled out forms, wrote letters, begging him to come to America. Always, there had been a reason: his wife's parents, his daughter's education. And always with the conviction that nothing could happen to them in their isolated village with kindly Polish neighbors.

"They had a big orchard. Iser used to sell fruit—apples, pears, cherries," Shmuel says.

Oh, my aunt Ray Brooks, Iser's sister—why hadn't I listened more carefully to her stories? "Every morning," she had said, "we went outside and got apples, peaches, anything you wanted."

As the groups tour the Brest Fortress, Dov, Shmuel, Esther, Drora, and I stay behind. My questions come so quickly, I take out my pad to jot down notes. Yet I can't keep up with the flow of information. Esther soon interrupts with her knowledge. Then Drora tells her versions. They had been to Volchin the day before, and Shmuel had to take three Valiums to get through the ordeal. He was practically comatose.

I piece together the story. Around Yom Kippur of 1942, two Nazis, with villagers' help, murdered all 395 Jews remaining in Volchin. Shmuel tape-recorded evidence of this massacre, one from a non-Jewish former classmate of Hanna Kremer, the woman now living in New York.

I can't bring myself to ask, but as we board our respective buses, making a date to visit Volchin together the next day, I say to Dov, "Ask Shmuel what happened to my family."

"They were killed that day, in that massacre. Everyone but Nahoma. She went to work outside the village. Nobody knows what happened to her."

On the bus, the lump in my throat seems to enlarge, blocking my swallowing. It takes me a while to realize that my seatmates are talking about my discovery.

"I'm happy for you," Stu says.

"It was *bashert*," says Ruth, a woman with family ties to Bialystok.

"What?" someone asks.

"You know, *bashert*," Ruth explains, "it's a Yiddish word. How can I translate it?"

One by one, I hear the answers: "coincidence," "more like destiny," "fated, fate." Yes, I think, it's *bashert*, it's fate.

That afternoon, at the Jewish Agency Youth Club, we sit on circular benches surrounding a primitive wood arena. Belarusian children, in colorful country costumes, welcome us with folk music and dance, including Jewish selections. Local TV crews patrol us. For the first time, I feel enveloped by native warmth. This is not Poland, I think. These people are simple; they have been shunned by foreigners. We're one of the first groups to visit them, and they are showing their gratitude.

In the evening, as we Americans dine with the Israeli contingent, I greet my newly discovered Volchiners. "You know," I say to Drora as we try to pick through bland and unrecognizable food, "all my fellow travelers are calling you my Volchin family."

"Well," she says, "it was such a small place, and everyone married a relative. I think we must be relatives, too."

I look at her rounded cheeks, at Dov's straight nose, at Shmuel's soft, crinkly eyes, and I know she's right. Each is my landsman, my family.

Following dinner, we stop at another site, an original cattle car that took the Jews to the Brona Gora station. Fittingly, the rain begins, and, before I know it, someone ushers me under an umbrella. Drora. The rest of "my family" clings to my other side. We stand silently as a cantor says Kaddish, the prayer for the dead.

June 23. The day we're going to Volchin. I'm supposed to meet my family at their hotel for lunch, and then we'll split into two cars. I awake to an unsettled stomach and severe cramps. Even if I get sick, I know one thing for sure: Nothing will stop me from going to Volchin.

Before my family rendezvous, our group tours the former Brest ghetto. Brest-Litovsk, the birthplace of our mission's organizer, Louis Pozez, and his friend, the late Israeli Prime Minister Menachem Begin. Now, the Jews here have no synagogue, no community center. This morning, at our hotel, we had the first minyan, the quorum of 10 male Jews, in more than 50 years.

The bus stops at a Catholic cemetery called Trishan. Jerry, a successful businessman, normally in control, shouts, "Trishan! I don't believe it!"

"What?" our guide asks.

For years, Jerry had been searching maps and books for the neighborhood of Trishan. Trishan—where his family was from. Now, by chance, we're here. Chance, maybe. I know better. It's *bashert*.

There's a memorial stone at the cemetery. It marks the place where the remains of 5,000 Jewish men from Brest were buried.

Another group member born in Brest, Paula, an elderly, frail, and private woman who left the country at the age of 17, walks ahead. She and her daughter, Judith, light *Yortzeit* (anniversary of someone's death) candles and lay flowers by the memorial. Paula grips the edge of the headstone. She can't seem to take her hand away. It's all she has left of her father. Her mother's resting place is elsewhere. Paula examines a passed-around list of those taken to Brona Gora and recognizes her mother's signature. "Now I know for sure," she says.

At the museum, we see a census report for Brest. It says that on October 15, 1942, there were 16,934 Jews. A different number than on Louis's list, but still substantial. For October 16, that figure is crossed out.

Though I'm emotionally riveted by the morning's activities, I'm preoccupied. I worry about my threatening stomach, the threatening weather. At Volchin, I must be able to walk around, see everything, photograph everything.

In the car, on the way to my family luncheon, I check all my paraphernalia: my tape recorder, my pad, pens, two cameras, flash, batteries, umbrella. I can't forget anything.

My family waits for me in the hotel lobby. They introduce me to their driver, a professor of physical-mathematical science and department chairperson. A Jew, he makes so little money at his profession that he must supplement his income any way he can.

At the hotel's restaurant, a poorly lit, cavernous space, the waitress makes it clear she's not happy about serving our party an hour before the rest of the diners. When she sees that our driver joins us—a surprise occurrence—she discusses the situation with her fellow workers. Looking perplexed, they scurry around for an extra chair, an extra setting, all the while shaking their heads. Dov repeats that he will gladly pay for this man's meal or for any inconvenience, but it's clear that money is not the issue. The unexpected. Change. A frightening concept.

I dig in my bag for my pocket-sized tape recorder, which I keep on my lap. I'm hesitant about this interview. Can I ask questions, such personal and painful ones, while we eat? In fractured English, the driver quizzes me about New York. I struggle to answer. I can't tell if he's genuinely interested in American life or has a more selfish motive. I resent his intrusion. Normally oversensitized to other's concerns, I must abandon this role. I came all this way for something else.

The soup comes. Several pieces of onions, a definite threat to my stomach, float among the vegetables. I take one polite spoonful and sit back.

Esther immediately asks, "Why are you not eating your soup?"

"I will," I answer.

Then the fish comes, covered in clumpy cream sauce. I move my fork around the plate for effect. Dov now joins Esther in concern over my finicky taste. They look at me as if I'm too thin. I look at them with love.

Finally, I check with Dov. "Are you sure it's okay to ask Shmuel more questions now?"

"Yes," he says adamantly. "Yes, of course."

I learn more about the story of Volchin. Before the war, there were about 500 Jews from approximately 70 families. In the early war years, Jews, including Shmuel's father, were tortured and killed for no reason. On the day of the massacre, all 395 remaining Jews, starving and close to death, were instructed to dress in their finest clothes. They were told they were going to a better ghetto in nearby Visoke.

Then, from the first homes in the Jewish section of town, not far from my great-uncle's house, they began the death march. With one Nazi in front and one behind, they walked about two kilometers. They passed the Jewish section, the old Catholic church, and reached the end of town. There, they were ordered to undress. Locals confiscated their clothes. Naked, the town Jews descended the sloping field into a ravine. One teenage girl, the same age as Nahoma, clung to her mother. She wanted to stand in front of her mother, to protect her from the bullets. She was wrenched away and pushed aside, to die without her family. The Nazis machine-gunned everyone. Then they stomped on the bodies and covered them with dirt.

People from another village came to help the Nazis. Throughout all this, many eyes watched, eyes that belonged to former friends, former neighbors.

The massacre happened by day. At night, the empty houses were ransacked. Many were later occupied by Germans. Land was taken for field crops. My great-uncle's orchards didn't go to waste.

After lunch, I get into the car with Esther and Drora in the backseat. We follow the professor's car with the men inside. As we get farther out of the city, the rain increases in intensity, punctuated by bursts of thunder and zigzags of lightning. I express my alarm.

During each flash of lightning, Esther repeats, "You must be an optimist. The rain will stop."

Though I'm watching every change in scenery, I'm able to absorb the women's stories. Drora and her husband had owned a hotel in northern Israel, in Nahariya. Since it's close to the Lebanese border, the tourist trade dwindled after the Lebanese War began in 1982. Resourceful, Drora and her husband converted the hotel into a home for the elderly. Now, they have 100 residents. With a small staff, Drora's family does everything.

"It sounds like very hard work," I say.

"Yes it is," she answers.

Esther tells me about her children and her life in Ramat-Gan, a suburb of Tel Aviv. I reply that my aunt Dina, born in a small town not far from Volchin and the wife of my mother's half-brother, lives in Ramat-Gan. Another coincidence, perhaps. A skeptic and nonbeliever, I nonetheless begin to see *bashert* everywhere.

The scene out my window blurs. I see only gray, streaks, and rain spots. I'm determined to photograph this route, the route that my grandmother must have taken many times, though by train and cart. My great-uncle Iser, and possibly even my cousin Nahoma, on her last trip outside Volchin, must have come this way by car. In a moment of clarity, I snap photos of the empty road ahead, the metal-roofed houses, the omnipresent slender-limbed birches and pines. Nothing remarkable. Through a smear in the fogged glass, I make out a stand of emaciated cypresses, and I think again, this must be a portent, a marker that things are changing. Objects appear and disappear. There are cows in fields, ducks crossing before us. A reddish-clay dirt road, then a paved one again. Open fields. Sheep. Haystacks.

As we get closer, the three of us shout at every signpost. "Does it say Volchin?" We know our driver doesn't speak English, but we're sure he can understand "Volchin." Finally, the road narrows and the driver stops by a sign.

"Volchin," he says.

I open my window and depress my shutter. The Russian letters are incomprehensible. It looks like BOY4blH.

We drive onto the street, and the rain streams like a waterfall. I wipe my window with a tissue, accomplishing little. The main street is narrow, flanked by wood fences. The houses are small and wooden, with those same corrugated metal roofs. There are many trees, linden I think. I wish I knew more about nature. Nothing like what I had imagined. Nothing like a shtetl, nothing like an impoverished, ransacked town. It looks like any pretty, small village, anywhere.

We stop at a house in the beginning of the village. It belongs to the district police officer. We will rest here awhile, hoping to wait out the rain.

As we get out of the car, Dov tells me, pointing down the road, "The main street is about two and a half kilometers south to north. The north is toward Visoke, the south toward Brest. Before the war, the south (known as Old Volchin) was occupied by the Russian Orthodox, the middle section (Volchin) by the Jews, and the north (New Volchin) by the Polish Catholics. In the Jewish section, which began near the church and went on until the Pulva River, there was a synagogue. Now it is a technical school."

A slim, mustachioed man in his late 30s, dressed in casual clothes like a jogging suit, greets us. His wife, a curly haired woman, motions us into the kitchen. Young children scurry into the bedroom. I shake the couple's hands. They make no effort to speak to us. Through a beaded curtain, the police officer, looking sleepy or hung over, leads us to the living room—a small, square space, with wall-hung Oriental carpets, heavy drapes, and upholstered couches, resembling the 1950s style of our hotel lobby. Everything, including a huge forest-scene mural, is somber brown and gold, blending into the wife's similarly colored, striped blouse.

Throughout our visit, the wife sits in a chair by a desk, speaking into the phone. At first I think she's contacting someone for us, recalling that Shmuel had called ahead to arrange for a candlelit ceremony at the massacre site in honor of my visit. But when nothing happens, when she doesn't even offer us water, I think she's gossiping or conducting some kind of business.

"What did the Jewish people here do for a living?" I ask.

Through Dov, Shmuel says, "They were shoemakers, dressmakers, bakers, mechanics, iron workers. My family," Dov points to himself, "had a hardware store. There were no cars, no buses, just horses and carts. It was about a 10-kilometer horse ride to the station, where you boarded the train for Brest."

I nod, taking notes.

"You must speak to Hanna Kremer in New York," Dov says. "She knows everything. She went to Russia, to prison. She suffered too." In Israel, Dov adds, there are about 25 people with ties to Volchin. Shmuel is the leader of this group.

We wait for what seems like an hour. The rain is not abating. Even Esther no longer says I must be an optimist. With a polite good-bye to the police officer, we get back into our cars and pass a few simple houses, a wishing well, and a large barnlike building with red and gray stones. Drora thinks the stones are from the old synagogue. At their last visit, they had found similar stones with Jewish lettering in the Catholic cemetery. We pass a different Christian cemetery, a stone-fenced mansion, more simple wooden houses. Suddenly we stop. We're at the beginning of the Jewish section.

"This is Hanna Kremer's house," Esther whispers, motioning to a green wooden A-frame building. She remembers from their visit the other day. "And here, here," she points right in front of me, "is your house."

My house, my family's house. Oh my God.

There's a wooden fence, with a symbol outside, one that I saw elsewhere. It looks like a V with wings. Behind the fence is a white-brick house, number 55. A boy peeks out from behind lace curtains. I wave. No response. Three stone steps lead to an enclosed porch area, with a green wood door and blue window trim. I walk around the property. The house is larger than I thought it would be. Rosebushes and some sort of orange flowers border the left side. I move closer to identify them.

"Forget it," Shmuel calls through Dov. "No, this is not the original house. I'll show you."

He guides me to the other side, facing a well and a water pump. Then I see, perpendicular to the front of number 55, another house, smaller and more primitive. It's also white brick, with the same corrugated metal roof. A double row of cinder blocks tops a green barn door. On the side, there's a closed, shuttered window and a blue-paned one. The house seems deserted. As if it's used as a barn, it has tools propped up against the walls, and a long wooden bench hugs the side.

"This is it!" Shmuel says. "Yes, it was very nice, clean and neat always."

"Can we go inside?" I ask.

Shmuel vigorously shakes his head no, making it clear I can't press the matter. I want to go behind the house, beyond the trees, what was once the orchard, to see the water. My aunt Ray said it was a swamp. But the rain comes down in thick sheets. Shmuel indicates that we can't go farther into the woods. Silently, I hand my camera to Dov. Without plans, Shmuel and I inch closer, arms around each other, and by the front of the house—my family house—we pose for a photo.

I circle and recircle the property, taking pictures. I no longer care if my camera gets wet. I'm in a trance. I listen for voices. I'm surprised that my grandmother doesn't speak. I strain to hear Iser. I squeeze my eyes shut, hoping for the chatter of the girls, my cousins, the clatter of my aunt Ziba speaking and cooking loudly, like the other women in my family. I cringe, waiting for their shouts, wails, screams to penetrate my consciousness. There's nothing. Even the ghosts are dead.

Gently, Dov says we should go. My legs won't move. I don't want to leave. With his arm in mine, he guides me back to the car. We drive down the puddled street, following a strange truck-shaped tractor. Large linden trees fan outward, forming a green, bushy archway, leading us down the death march. Past an old stone ruin, there's a very long one-story, bunker-like building, probably some storage area for grain. In front is a driveway or road, and in front of the road is a large, sloping field. By the car, the land is higher, a sort of wide hill.

I get out of the car and see, to the side of the bunker, down the slope, a green fence enclosing a tall triangular stone, topped with a red star. It's not a Jewish star, but it clearly marks the memorial site. Roosters and ducks waddle outside the fence, poking their necks inside.

With my two cameras slung over my shoulders, holding my umbrella, I stand on the hill, ready to descend. My sneakers step onto the wet earth but can't seem to find a firm spot. Suddenly, I'm sliding down, down, my raincoat acting like a sled. With a gigantic thud, I land on my back. I'm not sure if that last sound is the smack of twigs or cracks in my vertebrae. I know I must be paralyzed. Strangely, my cameras lie on my stomach, undisturbed.

"Oh my God!" Esther shrieks.

Everyone rushes toward me. Dov lifts me. "Are you okay?"

Esther screams, "My God, you fell all this way."

I take a deep breath. I feel a sharpness in the small of my back, but I can stand. Any minute, I expect, I'll collapse, crippled, but now I'm determined not to show my pain. I owe it to Shmuel, I owe it to Iser, I owe it to them all. As my consciousness returns, I look around to see where I fell. I am about 20 feet from the massacre site. *Bashert, bashert, bashert.*

"This is the memorial, erected by Hanna's uncle," Dov explains. "We think someone else came here—we heard, an American after the war." He points to a small stone, inscribed in Hebrew, resting against the memorial. "I had that made in Israel."

Shmuel climbs over the fence and wraps himself in his *tallis* (prayer shawl). We join him. Drora holds the umbrella over me. We stand, heads bowed, while Shmuel says Kaddish.

As we drive from Volchin, there's silence in the car. Images and thoughts swirl around my head as quickly as the rain falls. I have one nagging, overriding question. If Iser, Ziba, and the younger girl were killed here, what happened to Nahoma? And then, I hear my grand-mother's voice, silent for so long. "You must keep looking," she says.

Determination. During my grandmother's quest to come to this country, she overcame seemingly insurmountable obstacles. Learning about a law allowing American entrance for rabbi's families, including children only up to 12 years old, Masha convinced the American consul to make an exception for her older stepchildren. Since she was much younger than her husband, she argued, she needed the older ones to help supplement the family income and to baby-sit so she'd be available to earn a living. After more official rigmarole, all of the children were granted permission. What followed were more hassles, including waiting for money sent by her husband, who was by then living in Brooklyn, where he earned a meager living reciting graveside prayers. Eventually, she purchased tickets for everyone.

Finally, in 1923, 30-year-old Masha, her four stepchildren, and her five children boarded the RMS *Berengaria*. A Cunard ship with a passenger capacity of 2,800, it was bound for New York City. Masha's memories: "We had to stay downstairs, all the way down. . . . The kids had to be checked all over by the doctors. . . . They cut their hair through with the electric shavers—nothing was left, not a drop."

They landed in America on Columbus Day, October 12, 1923.

On one of my taped conversations with my grandmother, she gives an account of her arrival at Ellis Island:

> At the time, [the immigration officials] had to check us out over the windows so they wouldn't [admit] strangers. They asked my husband, "Are these your children?" He was so excited. His money was just stolen from his pocket. So they asked him, "How old is your youngest?" The little window was open and he looked at me and said, "How old is my youngest?" So I said, "Eleven months." Then he asked, "What is her name?" I got nervous too. I said, "Sara, Sara, Sara."
>
> Then they asked, "How old is your oldest?" Go and figure out how old is his children, *nu!* So I had to holler to him—I knew everything—"So much and so much." And for each kid, they asked. Like this, we came out.

I know from talking to my grandmother, from listening to her stories, from knowing her as I did, that nothing, no bureaucratic red tape, no official naysayer, nothing, and no one would have stopped her from coming to America. In my search, I can only try to follow her example.

On the bus to Brona Gora, the next day, June 24, those of us who took personal excursions share our stories. When Sara was in Poland, she visited a suburb of Lodz, the birthplace of her father. She found his home, still standing as it had been for the past hundred years, and she miraculously found her father's birth certificate. *Bashert.*

In Brest, where she lived until 1958, Sara located the fruit trees her father had planted around the house where she was born. Sara, her mother, and her uncle visited the elders' wartime hiding place. That day, they met a group of young deaf people signing. Thrilled to find someone he could communicate with, Sara's uncle discovered that he knew the father of one youngster. They made a date and spent the entire day celebrating. *Bashert.*

Sara's mother, Lily, comes up to the microphone to speak. A short, bubbly woman with impeccably coiffed blond hair and elfin features, she begins her story, at first hesitantly and then in a rush. With the German invasion of Brest, bombs fell. Lily's house was burned, and her father and sister were seriously wounded. A former employee of her father's named Peter offered them temporary refuge.

Months later, the Gestapo rounded up the Jews into a ghetto. Conditions were harsh; starvation, rapes, shootings were common. Lily's family moved to Peter's attic, where they helped him work by night and hid by day for 22 months.

Rosanne, fast becoming my friend, is percolating with excitement. In Kobrin, her grandfather's birthplace, she met a 94-year-old man who unearthed his treasure: a thick wad of papers telling the history of Kobrin's Jews from 1941 to 1945. Another find. *Bashert.*

Then it's my turn. I take the microphone and rotely tell my story. Feeling inconsequential, I quickly mumble my words. I want to sit down and hide my head. Something compels me and I complete my story, with increasing animation, ending with my falling into the ravine. I rush to my seat, upset that I mentioned myself at all.

Shortly after the last person speaks, the forests thicken, and I see piles of cut timber, railroad cars, and the tracks. Always those tracks.

Is this where they met, the 300 local peasants who had dug eight holes in the ground—each 40 to 60 meters long, six meters wide, and four meters deep? Is this where they untangled the balls of barbed wire to fence in the sector, to contain anyone with the will to struggle?

The bus stops, and we walk toward the forest entrance. This time the sun shines, casting slanted beams through the trees. At the clearing, a group gathers around a memorial, fenced in like the one at Volchin. Standing there, among the people, is my family from Volchin. Quietly, we embrace. Dov and Shmuel circle the memorial as I do, taking almost as many photos. Drora aims her video camera way beyond, up a series of hills. And then I follow a small clot of color, under a billowing cloud, undulating down those hills. As this enlarging blob nears, in balletic slow motion, it separates into stick figures and re-forms into bodies. Slowly, slowly, golden heads bounce, and I realize this mirage is a group of children, happily skipping down the hills, a classroom of blond, blue-eyed Belarusian innocents, joining their parents by the fence, joining them at the ceremony for the Jews.

Do these beautiful children know the truth? The truth that other children, 55 years ago, stood here, that those other children had no chance?

To the sides of the clearing, the forest is dense, but the tree limbs are distinct. Tall white birches, black-spotted like dalmatians and as graceful as giraffes, are interspersed with equally tall, straight, and branchless pines whose needle bouquets begin at the very tops. In the strange peekaboo highlights, I can almost see thousands of emaciated bodies, slinking and shivering behind the tree limbs, their white skin blending into the birches, sticking out behind the pines. I can hear the crescendo of wails. Superimposed on this Felliniesque image emerge the healthy faces of the blond-haired children of today. The children disappear again; the naked Jews come forward. They have no chance.

On that day, according to local eyewitnesses, the Jews were ordered to undress. Then, through the use of human brutality and growling dogs, the victims were forced to descend ladders into the holes and lie down, facing the ground, where they were machine-gunned. The next line of people lay atop the dead and wailing wounded and were shot. This went on until the hole was filled. The bodies were covered with dirt. They had no chance. Though the Nazis kept the lists, they exhumed the bones to get rid of the evidence.

On that day, they came to the forest. From Brest, from Kobrin, from Bereza, from Pinsk, from Bielsk-Podlaski. Today, they come to the forest.

From America, from Israel. They come to the forest, the forest primeval, the forest of evil.

Around the memorial, various people speak. The sun and clouds interchange. Leaves swish collective sighs, punctuating the most poignant moments. I try to listen, but my concentration seems weak at best. Whenever I turn from the speaker, a Volchin family member appears, watching me, taking my photo.

"How's your back?" Esther asks during a quiet moment, contorting her face as if she can't utter what she's really thinking. "I was up all night. My back was sore just from thinking about your fall."

I'm so touched, I can't speak. I smile. "It's okay," I whisper. She looks at me unbelievingly. "Well, it's a little achy," I admit. She nods.

Someone introduces a distinguished-looking man in his 70s. I think I hear something. "Who is he?" I ask Esther.

"From Brest, now lives in Israel," she says.

"His name, his name," I stammer.

"Lev, Gershon."

"That can't be. Don't leave this spot," I beg. "I must speak to him."

"Excuse me," I say, tugging at his sleeve. "Your name. I mean, my uncle's name is Gerson Lev, though he calls himself Lew."

The man, with a slight paunch, familiar thin lips, and aristocratic nose, says that yes, Lev is often called Leff and Lew, as he also calls himself. Then he mentions other relatives, including Abraham Lew. That was the name of my mother's brother, the one I was named after. Though he died during World War II, and I know it's not the same Abraham, I'm nonetheless shocked. I write out my relatives' names, including Isaac Lev, my grandmother's first husband and my grandfather, and Gershon says he'll look them up in his family book. Since the Levs were from a prestigious rabbinical family, he says that ultimately all of them are related.

Who would have thought I would meet someone from both my grandmother's *and* grandfather's sides of the family—and we would both be here in Brona Gora. *Bashert.* It's all too much for me.

In yet another case of *bashert,* Louis Pozez shows Gershon Lev a Tarbut (high school) class photo taken in Brest. In the last row, next to Louis, separated by only three boys, is Gershon Lev.

There are other speeches. Then the cantor begins to sing, and the sky darkens. Will it rain here too, as it did in Auschwitz and Volchin? The cantor leads "Hatikva," the Israeli national anthem, and the wetness I feel all over my face is not the rain.

Miles and miles of forests, banks of wild, purple lupine. We have one more stop on our way to Minsk. As the tour guide describes Mir, an original shtetl that was not destroyed, of course now without Jews, I feel my body lose some of its stiffness.

"Mir," the guide says, means "peace or world." I'm entranced by its history—the long and close ties between the Polish noble Radziwill family and the Jews who settled in the town. Once a flourishing religious and trading center, Mir was occupied by the Germans on June 27, 1941. At the time, Mir had a Jewish population of 3,000. What followed was a too-familiar story of murder, resistance, starvation. Today, one Jewish person lives in Mir.

At least there's something of that time left. It feels good to walk around a town that has not been destroyed. It feels good to take photos of people again, people working and people living. In the square, I face a white stucco orthodox church. Blue, triangular, bubble spires reach up in graduated sizes, much like a Disneyland skyline. There are vendors selling crafts, children on bicycles, women with shopping bags. I take pictures of them all. The people seem unconcerned; they must be used to gawkers.

Across the road, I notice a group of young men sitting on steps, huddling and smoking. I walk toward them. They wave. I wave back. I'm energized, exaggeratedly in love with humanity, certainly an overcompensation from my experience at Brona Gora. I snap the men's photo. One stands. Another shifts. I want to be sure that it's okay. I wave again. One man returns my wave. My arm extends in response. His reaches outward in a salute. I grin.

The man says something I can't hear. Then, repeating his arm gesture, he shouts, "Heil Hitler."

On the drive to Minsk, I think about the native people we saw—Polish actors mimicking Yiddish, Belarusian boy singers wearing yarmulkes, and these young men sitting on the steps that used to belong to Jews. And I understand again that those naked souls cringing in the forest had no chance. Eastern Europe is empty. The Holocaust is one big empty hole.

At our hotel, as bland and 1950-ish as the one in Brest, we have our final dinner with the Israeli contingent and enjoy wonderful choir music. At a long table, I sit with my Volchin family and the talk never ceases. There are faceless shushes, pleas to be quiet. I try to keep my mouth closed, but both Drora on one side and Esther on the other whisper to me in not-so-hushed tones—as only my family can.

"You know," Drora says to me during a program break, "we have spoken to many on this trip, but no one that we feel so comfortable with as you." Her chestnut eyes sparkle with good cheer. "And I can't tell you," she adds, "what meeting you means to Shmuel. He is so excited."

As if Shmuel suddenly understands her English, he hands my friend, Miriam, his camera and asks her to take a photo of us all, and then Dov asks the same thing. Everyone watches. I hope the redness in my cheeks doesn't show in the picture.

I dread the final song, the serving of dessert. I know it's time. The last of my group is out the door. "If you come to Israel," Dov says, translating for Shmuel, "I will show you the best time."

I hug everyone, saving Shmuel for last. His embrace is tight and long. He says something in Yiddish. I mumble, "*Besser den mein futter.*" I hope I say it right: "Better than my father."

During the rest of our trip, there are more incredible stories, more cases of *bashert*. In Minsk, in a pit called YAMA, we stand on the bones of 5,000 murdered Jews as our guide recites an original Yiddish poem with the refrain, "I can't forget, I won't forget."

We meet with the outgoing American ambassador, who describes the country's lack of response to economic reform and human rights. A weak national identity and the stubborn view of Jews as a separate nationality—there they are again, breeding grounds for anti-Semitism.

In Russia's St. Petersburg, our delegation separates into smaller groups for home visits. Four members and I walk down a residential street on our way to an elderly couple's apartment. Nearing the corner, there is a woman selling flowers from an open crate. Her companion is a large woman with a flimsy rayon work jacket covering a turtleneck sweater. On her head, she wears a golden scarf, busy with brown-and-black paisley designs, pulled over her forehead, hiding her eyebrows, and tied at the back of her head. Her hair sticks out of the sides, shaved off like a man's sideburns. As she talks to her friend, she smiles, showing the ubiquitous gold-capped teeth. Overseeing the flower vendor, she leans against the wall, which is painted with big, black numbers: 3.20/1.601.

This pose is so like a mug shot that I raise my camera and look again through my viewfinder, delighted that it's even more striking than I imagined. I snap one photo surreptitiously, but, as usual, I can't resist covering other angles. I pace about, snapping away, while my companions are engrossed in the flowers. Activating my flash for more light, I come closer to the woman. Suddenly aware that I'm focusing on her, she pounces on me and tugs my camera. Shocked, I pull back, but she's at least 80 pounds heavier than I am, and she yanks my flash off its mount. Then she goes after my pocketbook, ripping its strap and flailing at my head and shoulders.

I shout at her, "Photos, okay. No police, no newspapers," but it's useless.

Finally, our tour guide arrives, summoned by a delegate, and screams at the woman in Russian. The guide retrieves my torn bag and broken flash, and grabs my arm. "We must go," she says, pulling me down the street, explaining: "She is an ignorant Ukrainian peasant. Some of them think you will use the photo for some bad purpose. Some believe a photo takes away the soul."

All I can think of is the absolute hatred in this woman's facial expressions. There is no doubt that she would have killed me if she hadn't been stopped by our guide.

I'm shaking so violently that I need to sit down. "This is so terrible," Lily says, putting her arm around me as we slip into an apartment building and follow a dark hallway leading to a kitchen. "I have never seen such a thing."

Her words bring on my tears, and I think about her ordeal in the Brest ghetto. So much more.

A large basement area, with exposed pipes, two stoves, two high cabinets, and counters strewn with mismatched pots and utensils, the kitchen is one of nine rooms shared by six families. We enter a small dining area, where an elderly Jewish couple sit, the man, handsome though he is 97 years old, dressed in his best gray sports jacket, leaning on the table from his wheelchair. The woman is spry and unembarrassed by her misshapen face, one side of which is swollen, as if encasing a large tumor. They are delighted to see us and thrilled with the gifts we brought from America. Though I'm still shaken by the Ukrainian woman and embarrassed by our riches in front of these humble people, I'm happy that the translator can at least help us exchange our life stories.

Only last night, when we arrived in St. Petersburg at the luxurious Grand Hotel Europe, Rosanne and I were so excited to be released from the constraints of Belarus that we shouted, "We're free, we're free." How naive were we?

When we land in Frankfurt to change planes for America, a member of my group says, "I can't believe I'm happy to be on German soil."

Before I transfer to my plane, I am approached by the videographer hired by the Jewish Federation to record our mission. The Federation, he explains, also wants him to do a documentary on several personal stories from our trip, culminating in the Brona Gora massacre. He adds, "You would be the perfect person to write the script."

Honored, I accept, sorry that I didn't have this assignment before so that I could have paid more attention to certain details. Perhaps this was for the best, as I was able to devote my energies where they were needed—to my own story.

I say good-bye to the delegates, with new friends and a new work goal. From that moment on, I had another mission: Brona Gora.

My body is back, home in New York City. My body is back. I know it because I see my reflection in the mirror, but I have lost something, something.

I'm eager to tell my relatives about our new family. Through tears, my mother says, "I'm so touched, so overwhelmed, really, that you went there. But you should have gone inside the Volchin house."

I'd asked to go in, hadn't I?

Following my silence, she says, "Well, I would have insisted."

I tell the story to my 20-year-old daughter. "Will you help me find Nahoma?" I ask.

"Of course," she says, "of course." And then her phone rings, and she's off.

I call my great-aunt Ray, Iser's sister, who says, "I already knew what happened to him. Your grandmother went back, after the war. A neighbor told her. They had to dig their own graves." Veering into an argument she had with her cousin, she then recalls that she may have a photo of Iser's oldest girl.

"Please, Ray, you must look," I say.

I describe events to my husband, my friends. Everyone is genuinely interested, impressed, moved to tears. Yet the next day, and the next, they want to talk about other things.

Nagging at my brain is something Aunt Ray said. "Your grandmother went back, after the war . . . to see also about the property, but there was some stupid law." And then it clicks. Dov said there was an American who returned after the war. Could this have been my grandmother?

I call my mother, her brother. "Did Grandma go to Volchin after the war?" I ask, remembering that was the time when Masha's second husband died and she began to travel.

"Absolutely not," Uncle Gerson says.

"I would remember something about it," my mother insists.

But maybe, just maybe, they didn't remember. Maybe they had other things on their minds.

I feel lost. Alone. I need to reconnect to someone. I hear Dov's voice urging me to call Hanna Kremer in New York. "She knows everything," he said. "She'll be so happy to talk to you, even meet with you." I wait another day, to make sure I'm alert.

"Yes," Hanna says after my introduction. "Shmuel faxed us about you."

I tell her my family name.

"I knew the whole family," she says.

My heart stops. There is still more to this story.

"They lived pretty well until the war started. I was 15, 16 years old."

"You knew them well?"

"Yes. There was the wife, Bashka."

"But Shmuel called her Ziba."

"No, it was Bashka. I should know. I was in the house maybe three, four times a week. There were three daughters."

"Three? Shmuel said two." Then I remembered my aunt Ray, who had insisted that there were three.

"Ita was the oldest. Born around 1922. She went to school in Brest to study Hebrew. A private school. She came home for the holidays. She got money from America. Sala or Sara was the middle one. We were best friends. And Ester was the youngest."

"But?" I say, "Was it Ita or Ida?"

"Yes, Ida."

"Are you sure?" I don't know what to think. The name of Iser's sister was Ida. My mother's sisters were Esther and Sara. Again, I think about the Jewish custom of not naming children after living relatives. Maybe Iser's wife thought they were too far away or maybe they spelled them or pronounced them differently. Or maybe . . .

"I know it must be hard for you, but can you tell me what their house was like?"

"It was a nice house. With a garden next to a pasture. Apple orchards. In back, a swamp, with geese. Oh, I remember, they were the only ones with a gramophone. They had records and used to play them for us—out of this world."

"Have you ever gone back?"

"Yes, in 1946."

When she got to Visoke, she was stunned, speechless. There were no people: it was as if an atom bomb had detonated. Hanna knocked on the door of a friend's house, and a Russian soldier opened it. She started to cry, "My friend lived here." He found someone to take her to Volchin, where she learned of her family's fate, some of them shot before the massacre in their homes, in their gardens, on the street; some taken elsewhere, probably to Treblinka; and many killed on that same day in 1942.

I speak to Hanna's husband, who, like his wife, suffered other wartime horrors. "One thing I will never understand," he says. "Nobody lifted a finger to help. 'Don't help us,' I say, 'but don't betray us.' "

So many stories. Of course, I had my own. The members of my group called it *bashert*. How it sprung from nowhere, how it continued to grow, how it wove circuitously, almost makes me believe there is something stronger watching over me. When you look toward your past with an open heart, something zeroes in and fills it up.

Now, I write to Shmuel and to Dov with more questions. "Was it my grandmother who came to Volchin?" "Was the oldest daughter Nahoma or Ida?" "What happened to her?" Was that her behind the birches, her long legs entwined?

I've been a writer long enough to know that the more people I question, the more versions I will get. It's up to me to pick the best ones. But can I do it? Can I?

"Yes," my grandmother says gently, but with the kind of tone that lets me know there's no choice. "Write my story," she repeats. "Without our stories, we are nothing."

Chapter 2

Protest

I always loved getting mail. When I visited my grand-mother Masha in her apartment in Brooklyn, I often sifted through the opened correspondence she collected in a large black ashtray. There I found thin blue, airmail envelopes and those fold-up air letters that are impossible to open without destroying some essential last-minute message. The letters had smudged hand-writing; addresses with slashes through the sevens and number ones that looked like sevens; postmarks from Tel Aviv, Paris, Berlin, and Riga; and signatures from Luba, Shoshana, Michel, Boris, and Frau Schwanke. Each letter elicited a different emotion; each offered a different invitation; each told a different story. They were my grandmother's lifeline to a different world, the one she lived in her travels, the one she lived when she was away from us. More than anything, I wanted to have such a life, to have *my* mailbox jammed with letters as blue and tissue-thin as my grandmother's vein-colored hands.

It's 1954 again, and I watch my grandmother's eyes mist as she reads plaintive love letters from her third husband, Michel, writing all the way from West Berlin. I take the letter from my grandmother's hand, continuing from where her voice choked off. "Mashaleh, it's time to come," I read.

"What can I do?" she asks. "He wants me."

I know that for a while at least, I will lose my grand-mother again. Though I'm only nine years old, I know the power of words on paper.

At 51, I am nearing Masha's age at her letter-writing prime, and my friends and relatives—scattered in numerous states and countries—are poor correspondents. Interspersed among the catalogs, bills, and printed rejection notices, I occasionally find a postcard or note. Yet I haven't lost that almost primitive thrill when I hold a thick wad of unopened mail in my hand.

This is how I feel in July 1997 when I receive an envelope from the United States Holocaust Memorial Museum in Washington, D.C. Someone has responded to my search for Cousin Ida from Volchin. I can barely contain my excitement in the elevator. I hope nobody asks me to hold the door; I need the boxlike space to myself as I press the white envelope to my chest. I enter my apartment, close the door to my study, take the phone off the hook, sit on my blue swivel chair, take a long suck of air, and slit through the flap. There, on the front page of photocopied and stapled documents, in strange writing I interpret as Russian, I decipher a date and recognize the year: 1942. With pulsating heart and trembling fingers, I turn the page.

There are six columns; someone has translated the categories into English: Number, Name, Names of Parents, Year of Birth, Date of Issue, and Signature. Organized alphabetically by last name, this is the section I requested from the Brest ghetto list, those assumed to have been massacred at Brona Gora. My eyes begin at the top of the first page and slowly travel down. Toward the bottom, beside number 8444, is Midler, Mineza, followed by Midler, Helena. The parents' names are not familiar. I find Midler, Brocha, on the next page; Midler, Cypora, on the one after that; and Midler, David-Benjamin, on the fourth page. By the time I get to the last page and find the final three Midlers, I understand that unless Ida Midler went by another name, she's not on this list. I'm both profoundly disappointed and unexpectedly relieved. Though Jews certainly were killed at Brona Gora without their names appearing on the ghetto list, there's a good chance that my cousin escaped this unthinkable end. Was it better for her to have died of starvation, gassed at a camp, raped, or tortured? When you are trading such fates, mercy is nonexistent.

My disappointment grows daily, niggling, as I try to adjust my thoughts to other things. But, I want—need—to find a resting place for Ida. Why didn't I question my grandmother and aunt more vigorously about these lost relatives? Why now, suddenly, more than 50 years after their deaths, does the resolution seem urgent, as if time—maybe the time of anyone who knew them, maybe my own time—is running out? Why do I persist? It becomes more and more clear: if not me, then who?

Slowly, answers to my queries trickle in among my junk mail. With each missive, I hurry to my private spot and rip open the envelope. The International Tracing Service asks me to be patient; the Jewish Genealogical Society apologizes for its lack of resources; Brest-Intourist requests $350 for translating, photocopying, and mailing seven pages on Volchin from a recently published book and then agrees to $50 for the work untranslated; the archives in Grodno also wants $50; the Embassy of the Republic of Belarus has no information about towns in Belarus; the U.S. Embassy's Consular Section does not deal with searches for ancestors; Robinson Books in Israel regrets that it doesn't have the memorial book mentioning Volchin; the Central Archives for the History of the Jewish People has no relevant material; the Polish archives in Warsaw is also regretful. This feels more and more like my usual literary rejections, and I think that only a masochist would still be excited by mail.

When I get the package from Jerusalem's Yad Vashem, the world's largest and most comprehensive Holocaust archive, I can tell immediately by its bulk that I am to receive something other than a one-page apology. On the first page, I notice an exclamation point following my name. Even this venerable institution, with tons of requests, is excited for me.

In response to my query, Yad Vashem's search yields: "The page of testimony for Mydler Iser from Bielsk-Podlaski." The name is close enough. But Bielsk-Podlaski, the Polish town south of Bialystok where my Israeli aunt, Dina, spent her childhood? Not that far from Volchin, but far enough. . . . Yet when I turn the page, I make out enough words to answer my doubts: Treblinka; deceased children, Yafa and Shoshana. This was not my uncle, my Iser.

The envelope contains several empty pages on which testimony can be written. I place them aside. Hopefully, I will someday be able to fill out these blanks for Ida. I will be able to fill in the space for "Death place" and "Circumstances of death."

Then, in my mailbox, comes a total surprise. Inside a small white, cardboard envelope is a note from my cousin Barbara, Aunt Ray's daughter. "Hope these help toward closure," she writes. I see a smaller envelope within; written across it in large, shaky letters are the words, "My brother Issak Midler." I pull out six sepia-toned, black-and-white photographs. These are the best things I've ever gotten in the mail—far better than the letters my grandmother got from abroad. Here is my lost family. I've found them at last.

I never knew that Aunt Ray had such a treasure trove. This is the aunt who said all along that Iser had three girls, that the family was massacred, and that her sister—my grandmother—visited Volchin after the war. And this is the aunt who was surprised that I went halfway around the world to discover what she already knew.

The first photo shows a stout and short woman in a trilayered dress with scalloped edges. Her mannish, medium-brown hair is parted to the side, and her pert features appear incongruously serious. She seems the type of woman who could be pretty if she lost 25 pounds and did something with her hair. She holds a chubby toddler with dark hair and the same grave expression. They stand in front of open-shuttered windows revealing a diamond-pattern curtain and a small vase with flowers. On the back of the photo, there is Yiddish writing, which I later learn says, "For my dearest mother and grandmother Midler." This photo must have been sent to my great-grandmother and great-great-grandmother, older women who had seen enough of Eastern Europe to follow their other children to the promised land.

The second photo is the most heartbreaking—two girls against a dark background that, on close scrutiny, discloses vague outlines of trees. The older girl, about seven, stands with her right arm partly raised, her hand lost in a cluster of branches. She wears a sleeveless, V-necked, polka-dot dress with a low waist and flaring skirt. Her matching anklets fold neatly into her Mary Janes. Her hair, cut in a Buster Brown style with bangs, has the same straight, thin texture as mine, and her almond-shaped eyes and petite nose are more like mine than my sister's are. Mostly, I'm struck by her expression, a knowing smirk, as if she's not at all upset by having to pose for long stretches, instead finding the whole experience somewhat amusing.

Her younger sister, about five, sits in a child's wicker chair with her legs crossed and her arm cradling a long-haired rag doll. She wears a dark dress and sports a very large white bow on top of her head. Though she appears relaxed, she bites her lower lip and her eyes slant to the side, not in the direct, almost defiant manner of her older sister.

What surprises me most is that both girls are well dressed and modern for their time, not at all like the poor immigrant children I expected. Unlike my sister and me at similar ages, posing uncomfortably and with considerable irritation, these girls are poised and proud. And they are so beautiful.

I turn the photo over and read the names, Sala and Esta, below which is a purple oval stamp with the photographer's name, J. Bonder. Underneath it says "Wysokie-Litewskie." They went to the nearby town of Wysokie to get their pictures taken. Wysokie—or Visoke, as I knew the name. We stopped there after leaving Volchin and waited for Shmuel, who was looking for someone he knew. Wysokie. I was there.

The third photo presents an adorable girl of around three or four, slyly looking at herself in a full-length mirror. She wears a large white bow in her hair and a flouncy white dress, with eyelet trim. On the back, it says Ester Midlerovna. Here *Ester* is spelled differently, and her last name is longer—I suspect the custom for a female derivative. The handwriting is the same black-inked script. Judging from his models' poses, J. Bonder was a more sophisticated and artistic photographer than I would have imagined.

Now I have three photos, two marked with the names *Sala* and *Ester*. Where is Ida? Could she be the unidentified baby held by her mother? Again, Ida remains elusive.

The rest of the photos show groups. The clearest has four of the Midlers: Iser; his wife, Bashka; and two of the girls. Though the photo is not marked on the back, the girls are Ester and Sala. I recognize Sala's direct gaze and Ester's clinging to a prop, this time a stuffed animal.

While Bashka sits stiffly with her hands folded, Iser rests his palm gently on Ester's shoulder. Everyone is dressed fashionably; Iser wears a suit and tie. His hair is full, the top thick with ridges—the same hair as all the men in my family. And his face is strong and gentle, with the distinct handsomeness of a movie star. He looks so much like my uncle Gerson, I'm taken aback.

The next group photo displays a tier of three; in the foreground are two children, who look again like Ester and Sala. The top tier contains Iser and two men, all of whom are striking in their ties and suits. When I look at the girls a second time, I become unsure of the one on the right. Her hair, skin, and eyes are darker; her stare and frown hint at a fierceness, an element new and arresting. This girl could definitely be me, though I'm not quite sure she is Sala after all. Could this be another girl altogether—Ida? Are my eyes playing tricks, transposing and morphing, directed by wishful thinking?

The final photo is less formal—though Iser wears a tie, he's in his shirtsleeves. The five standing adults link their arms. Two boys sprawl on the grass, flanking a little girl. With an arm on the girl, an older female—probably still in her teens—kneels. Again, I'm struck by these people's good looks and smart clothes. This could be a comfortable and healthy group anywhere in the United States, probably in the late 1930s.

When I visited Volchin, I was impressed by its beauty, and now these photos present another serious challenge to my erroneous conceptions of poor and ignorant shtetl Jews. My grandmother always argued with those who called her hometown a shtetl. "No, it was a beautiful village," she would say angrily. I thought she meant that there were different people living together. When I found out that Volchin itself had contained primarily Jews, I thought her defensiveness had an element of shame. She was a proud woman. Now I realize she was merely trying to set the record straight; hers was, in fact, a village like any, a beautiful village.

I haven't heard my grandmother's voice in a long time, but now she smiles at me through the lips of her brother, Iser, the same lips of her other brothers and her sons—the uncles I knew. I haven't seen my grandmother since her death more than 15 years ago, but now she watches me through the eyes of these girls, the same eyes of my aunts, the eyes of my mother, the eyes of my own reflected in the mirror.

So many questions circle around my brain. If Ray received these photos, what else did she know about Iser and his family? I had questioned her before but obtained only sketchy information. Clearly, there must be more to her childhood experiences. How do her memories compare with those of my uncle Gerson and my mother, also at Volchin during those years? All three will be together in August at a party for my mother's 80th birthday. Perhaps then I will find some answers.

On the day of the party, with the three family elders sitting on the deck of my country house in Connecticut, I circulate the photos. My mother, Norma, in a fire-engine red silk dress that only her mother would have had the nerve to wear, stares long at the one with Iser in his shirtsleeves. "His face, he . . ." She can't continue, but she's clearly looking at someone she knows. The three pass around the photos, unusually silent. Soon, the talk resumes, and as always, gets around to my grandmother.

"She was liked by everybody," Uncle Gerson says. At 85 and well over six feet tall, Gerson still has the slim, erect physique and thick wavy hair of a man in his 50s. He clears his throat and bellows, "Masha was a ditzy dame, a little bit her own worst enemy."

My mother's back stiffens. "She was not such a ditzy dame. She was a very hardworking woman. She picked herself up like the phoenix, from the ashes, and supported us and took care of her children. No matter what kind of floozy she had been, she had courage—she had terrific courage. And she had terrific perseverance. She had responsibilities. If she had affection from men, I don't blame her. That's all she had."

"No one's blaming her," I protest, knowing that my family either blamed—or defended—my grandmother for everything. "But what I'd like to know is," I say, trying to steer the conversation away from controversy and looking at Ray, "you had said that Masha visited Volchin after the war—something about getting back the property or money for it."

"That's right," Aunt Ray says. "She told us all at my brother Bernard's house in Brooklyn. We said, 'You expected money for nothing?' She said, 'No, I didn't. At least I went to my father's, sister's, and brother's graves.' "

I watch Ray carefully to judge if this is closer to an embellishment than a fact. Her face is a smoother, more delicate version of her sister Masha's, and like her nephew Gerson, nearly the same age, she looks younger than her years. While she led a more religious and sheltered life than my mother and uncle, she is as stubborn as they are.

Yet doubt asserts itself about Masha visiting old graves in Volchin as I recall the photo that Dov, from my new Volchin family in Israel, sent me of a large boulder, one of the eight remaining tombstones in Volchin's Jewish cemetery. He wrote about his tour with the police officer when he was in Volchin before our visit together, "He showed us the place (not voluntarily). The cemetery is an empty place. With an area of about 2–3 acres."

The police officer told him that the tombstones were taken after the war as building material. There is a building on Volchin's main street that was constructed with broken rocks, similar, Dov suspected, to those of the tombstones from the Jewish cemetery.

"But Aunt Ray, Masha must have gone to see about her brother, Iser." Here I am, carrying the family tradition, defending my dead grandmother.

"Of course," Ray says.

Though my mother and uncle reiterate their misgivings, my mother begins to weaken. While Masha certainly wanted to find out about the fate of her brother's family, it was also like her to inquire about lost material possessions. Besides, Ray's access to these photos increases her stature as a repository of family lore.

As if to capitalize on her newfound credibility, Ray announces: "As it says in the Bible, all the Jews are sisters and brothers. When you turn around, there's a cousin."

Silence. I hope my mother and uncle won't challenge her on the accuracy or relevance of this saying. Fortunately, they turn their attention to an episode they do remember, also after World War II but before Masha's supposed trip to Volchin. Her second husband, one of Masha's early legitimate patients after she became a practical nurse, was murdered by a disgruntled tenant. His relatives fought with my grandmother over the inheritance.

"She won her award and decided she would see Israel for the first time," my mother says. "So she took a plane from Paris. She sat near this famous actor whose name I forget. He was interviewing Americans about their opinion of the Marshall Plan, giving aid to the Third World and European countries. So my mother gave her opinion."

"What did she say?" I ask.

"She sent us a cable to turn on the radio and listen to her speech. We were mortified. She sounded like, 'Yes, I tink, I tink is very nice, ve Americans, ve tink, ve help everybody.' I was so humiliated and embarrassed by her voice, her mispronunciation, her accent. I had never imagined that she spoke that way. Because for us, it was a natural thing for her to speak, but on the radio, it was something else."

"So do you think she traveled to Volchin?" I sense capitulation in the air.

"Who knows?" my mother says. "She was always traveling someplace. Don't forget, she also went to Russia many times. Maybe she tried and couldn't get in. Maybe she did go, and maybe she told me and I was too preoccupied by my own troubles, but I think it would have stuck in my—" She stops, undoubtedly realizing that it's more wishful thinking than fact that she would have remembered such an important visit. But it's so like my family to be sidetracked by my grandmother's shenanigans that I realize I will learn little more on that subject.

Although sharing my discoveries has been disappointing—or maybe because of it—I feel the need for feedback on my writings. But I'm cautious. I can't yet share the 34-page account I wrote about my Eastern European trip to my mother, aunt, or uncle for fear that they will have their own agendas and ask me to change certain facts. I fear that if I show it to others, the subject matter will overpower the personal story.

Instead, I present the piece to a select group of friends, fellow writers, and relatives. The responses vary, ranging from unadulterated praise to questions about Christian guilt and Jewish passivity. Though these issues are hardly new, they reawaken my own uncertainty about what I would do in such a situation. I remember my two experiences with violent crime. Both incidents happened in such surprising circumstances that I had no time to think, much less scream, yell, kick, or do anything to defend myself. Shock and fear enveloped me, and only when my consciousness returned did I react as a spectator to my own pain. Normal reactions do not occur in abnormal situations.

The most disturbing response comes from my husband. Though he expresses his approval, I notice yellow Post-it notes sticking out of the pages—typos, he says.

"How can there be?" I cry. "I mean, my writers' group read it and so did a very experienced editor."

My husband, born and educated in non-English-speaking countries, shrugs. Sure enough, he's right—or should I say, correct. This is a physician and scientist who doesn't let details pass unnoticed. But there's more.

"Can I tell you something?" he asks meekly.

"What?" I yell.

"I question the fact that there were only two Nazis leading the Jews from Volchin to their slaughter. It doesn't make sense."

"That's how it was," I say tiredly, ignoring my instinct that says to be an author, sometimes you have to refashion the truth in favor of believability.

"But," I continue my protest, "I asked several people and they claim this was more than one eyewitness report."

"I've read a lot about World War II," my husband says, trying to sound patient. "It's hard to believe that logistically, two men were able to contain 395 people. Even if they had to stop and reload their rifles, there was plenty of time for some to escape."

"You don't understand," I say. "When you read about the Holocaust, there are so many cases like this."

"But you don't want others like myself to stop and question it. I don't want anyone sidetracked from the poignancy of your story. You owe it to your lost family to get it right."

My husband may not be Jewish, but he knows how to drive the guilt straight to my heart. Is he right? Can the number of Nazis be a distortion? How will I ever know the truth? The eyewitness reports were recorded years ago. Probably no one is alive to verify anything.

"Leave out the number of Nazis," my husband suggests, seeing my distress. "The number isn't important."

"But I also have a responsibility to tell the truth or even this version of the truth." I can't admit to him—or to myself—that I harbor a smidgen of embarrassment that my people could have been led to their death by only two men. But who am I to judge? Who is anyone?

During this time, my grandmother's spirit begins to hover over me again. I wonder what she would have done with this information. If she went to Volchin after the war, did she hear the same story of the two

Nazis? To help get to the truth, I delve deeper into Masha's past, looking for clues in her character. I replay the tapes she made and stop where I last left off—after her arrival in New York. Managing to get her sick, headshaved children out of Ellis Island without being detained in the infirmary, she was approached by a man yelling her name. Masha says, "I never saw a dark-colored man. I was scared stiff, and the kids hid themselves."

I don't know what happened to her husband, who earlier had been at Ellis Island being quizzed about his children's names. Perhaps, with all the waiting, he had to leave the island. Or perhaps Masha's memory had distorted these incidents. Anyway, loaded with children and bundles, Masha followed this strange black man to the ferry, and, when they embarked, her husband, Isaac, was waiting to take them to Brooklyn. There were taxis, but he didn't want to waste the money. Then, he said, "You know, we're coming now to a place where we'll travel on the top of houses."

When Masha heard that, she thought, "A taxi, we had in Warsaw, but to go on the top—good!"

Trudging up the stairs of the elevated train, Masha says, "I had a baby here and a child there, and they were all crying, and the sick ones were boiling like fire. Sara had the measles. The people on the train said, 'This is a *greeneh* [greenhorn] ! This is a *greeneh!* Let's give them a place!' And my husband said, 'Look out the window. You see down there are people living in the houses, and we are on top of them.' I tell you—the kids, for them it was something to be on the top to travel!"

This was a woman who made a subway ride with her exhausted and sick family sound like the adventure of a lifetime. This was a woman who called all sexy women on soap operas *kurvehs* (prostitutes), ignoring the fact that she had lived openly with a married man when she ran a boardinghouse in the Catskill Mountains. This was a woman who, after divorcing her third husband, Michel, because of State Department problems, told her family that they had remarried, though no such certificate was discovered among her personal effects. This was a woman, I remind myself, who increased her age when she wanted to collect Social Security and reduced it when she wanted to marry a much younger man. This was a woman who never looked back, who had no trouble changing the facts. This was a woman who knew the difference between the facts and the truth.

Yes, Masha would not have hesitated for a moment. She would have exaggerated the number of Nazis to enhance the dramatic narrative, and then she would have convinced herself that her changes were the truth.

The facts; the truth. This is the dilemma I take to Arizona in September, to the reunion of our delegation. Maybe, just maybe, my fellow travelers will be the ones to settle these questions.

Rosanne, with whom I talked often on the phone, insists that I be her houseguest. A cancer survivor, an attorney, and incredibly generous, Rosanne is impossible to refuse. Within an hour after my arrival, I am the guest of honor at a dinner party.

We sit down for Shabbat dinner, with a moonlit view of Rosanne's saguaro-flanked garden. The candles are lit, prayers are uttered, and I, as usual with my new friends, shift uncomfortably with my mouth closed and my cheeks pink.

After exchanging delegate gossip and family news, we revert to our trip, our subsequent discoveries, and the account I wrote.

"Andrea has an interesting dilemma," Rosanne announces. "In her research, she found out from eyewitness reports that two Nazis led the Jews from Volchin to their death—one Nazi in the back of the group and one in the front. This is what she wrote in her article. But her husband thought it sounded unbelievable."

"Not that he thought I was making it up," I quickly interrupt, ready to correct any bad impressions. "He just thought that two Nazis were not enough to contain such a crowd, that there was time for many to run away, to protest. He's worried that people will get hung up on that issue and not give the rest of the story its full credence. He wants me to change *two* to just the word *Nazis*, but I don't know. I hate to tamper with the truth. Not that two is necessarily the truth. There could be more versions."

"I don't think that two sounds unbelievable," Ruth, a loyal member of a Bialystok memorial organization, says. "I have heard enough Holocaust stories that sound similar. People had experienced so much grief, there was no will."

"I agree," says a third woman.

"Aha, let's ask another man," Ruth says as Rosanne's husband, David, walks into the room.

After listening to the dilemma, David says that he's not the right person to ask. He isn't religious and isn't that knowledgeable about Holocaust literature.

"Neither is my husband," I say. "Besides, he's not even Jewish."

What you learn as the truth is the truth, David implies, surprised that we are making this such an issue.

Maybe he's right, I think. Let it go. What I learn is what I write. Yet I'm still dissatisfied. My need to be correct gnaws at me. David seems to realize what I can't admit. I will never really know the "right" answer. And unlike other times in my life, getting a consensus will not assuage my doubts. I hope that eventually this, like some of my other obsessions, will lose its intensity through the sheer force of time's attrition.

Though I had a paltry religious education, I nonetheless retain a broad interest in Eastern European history and culture and in the Yiddish language. This basically stems from my living on the East Coast—growing up in Jewish Flatbush and the Jewish Catskills and being exposed to all the Jewish cultural influences in New York. Maybe it's also because I have always been interested in Holocaust memoirs, in stories about human endurance. I have followed the people more than the events. Though as a professional, I have researched and written on numerous subjects, from refractory metals to sushi, I have approached my assignments as a creative rearranger rather than an explicator. With my proclivities leading me further into fiction, and as a photographer drawing me more and more toward visual encapsulation, I am perhaps too intrinsically undisciplined for the task before me.

Maybe I should just face this fact: I am, as I had suspected, an unlikely candidate for a historian.

The next night, we attend the reunion at the home of mission organizer Louis Pozez. Rosanne drags me around his sprawling, art-filled home, and it becomes real to me that this unassuming man could be the founder of Payless Shoes. At the dinner table, Rosanne again brings up my "dilemma." Louis offers another perspective. Not really questioning the veracity of the number of Nazis, he's more concerned in explaining the so-called issue of passivity. He says that many of the Jews who remained in Europe were deeply religious, and many of them were fatalistic. If it was their time, it was their time.

Though this was the case for some, and, historically, the religious response to oppression often encouraged identification with the persecuted, as far as I knew, many of the Volchin Jews who were killed were not extremely religious. I heard the theory that the more educated and adventurous had already left for safer places, yet it's still hard to believe that being trusting and loyal to your town equates with total submission. This is, of course, a complicated issue with a myriad of extenuating circumstances and interpretations, and it certainly has no pat or even definitive answer. It is, and will be, like many other Holocaust issues, unanswered, unimaginable, and unprecedented.

Most of the talk around the dinner tables at the reunion is less serious. We exchange memories, retell anecdotes, and later, pass around photo albums and view videos. As I was on the trip, I'm with them, but also different. I'm not part of this Federation; I don't live in Arizona; and for me, the trip—and all its attendant baggage—is not over.

When I get back to New York, I receive a letter from Israel. Dov again urges me to meet Hanna Kremer. After my initial phone conversation with her, she didn't return my call. Basically a shy person myself, I sense that she is reluctant to meet me, and I hate to push anyone. Yet Dov's admonition and the steady uncertainty, not ebbing with time, surrounding the village massacre draws me back to the telephone.

"I'm sorry to bother you," I say.

As if a preliminary to my real request, I ask Hanna if she ever heard of a female American going back after the war.

"My uncle went back, the one who erected that monument," she says. She knows nothing of an American woman, though she admits that there's always a possibility.

Again I begin to doubt that my grandmother returned to Volchin. Given her flamboyant demeanor and dominant personality, someone would have remembered her. I'm still uncertain, though, a feeling to which I'm becoming more and more accustomed.

In a fit of courage, or lack of it, I blurt out my question about the number of Nazis.

"Yes, there were two Nazis," she says. "You have to understand," she adds, "the Jews didn't know where they were going."

Why, I think, do we all have to feel the need for justification?

"They were without food, without water. They were near starvation. They were on their last legs."

"I know," I say. "But my husband was wondering about the Jews, why they didn't run, why they didn't protest."

"Who knows what really happened?" Hanna explains that when she went to Volchin in 1946, she heard a story from a man who witnessed the massacre.

"You know," Hanna says, her breath almost wheezing, "you know, it was your cousin. The more I think about it."

"What?" I say, my lips drying as I hear the amazement grow in her voice.

"Yes, yes, that's it. I remember now. Your cousin Ida, the oldest, she was there, in Volchin."

"But I thought she went to school in Brest, or maybe she went to work for the Germans."

"No, no. I remember specifically it was about her. Now it comes back to me what I heard. She was there. She was not in Brest at the time. She didn't go to a work camp. It was her. She didn't want to get undressed. She protested, and she was shot."

"Are you sure?" I ask, wondering why I hadn't heard this before.

As if she were reading my mind, Hanna says, "Yes, I heard it then, but not until I knew about you did I make the connection. That's it. Your cousin Ida. That's how she died."

So finally, I have an answer. Not the answer to the number of Nazis. But the answer to the bigger, more important question, "Did anyone protest?" And the answer to *my* question: "What happened to my cousin? What happened to Ida?"

I close my eyes and picture Ida's father, Iser, huddling naked, trying to reach out to contain his firstborn. I see someone holding his arms, pulling him back. I hear Ida's mother, Bashka, shrieking, in an animal cry, "NO!" There are Sala and Ester shivering and stunned, unconsciously peeling off the rest of their clothes, with one uniting hope, that they can join their sister as soon as possible.

I can picture my mother, Norma, in walled West Berlin, questioning a German judge about his role in the war and the disappearance of the city's Jews. I see her anger as I did then in 1964, when the judge claimed innocence and ignorance.

I can see my grandmother gathering her children and stepchildren—not far removed from childhood herself, still in her 20s—and hiding with them in the woods, going from town to town, back and forth, to escape the persecuting soldiers.

It's not surprising that a woman from my family would have been the one to say, "No, No."

And though I probably will never know certain facts about the massacre, I know one thing. If my grandmother hadn't left Europe, if she had been there in Volchin, she would have slapped the Nazi with one hand and with the other gripped Ida's, and they would have stood there—the two Midler women—tall and beautiful in defiance of death.

Chapter 3

Connection

October 1997

It's time to meet Hanna Kremer. On a bright, crisp fall day, on the train to Long Island, I consult my notes about the interview. I try to memorize my questions; I don't want to flip through my loose-leaf while we're talking. Doubts begin to cloud my comprehension. I read the questions over and over. I recognize the letters, but I can't form them into words. Maybe Hanna won't want me poking into her carefully compartmentalized memories. Maybe she won't welcome my camera, my tape recorder—or me. After all, she mentioned that twice she had refused to record her testimony with the Shoah Foundation.[1] "I can't talk about it," she said, "I can't talk completely to people who don't even know where the town is."

By the time I switch trains in Jamaica, I wonder if I will even find the Kremers. "Take the train to Hewlett; you'll probably have to change," Mike Kremer, Hanna's husband, told me on the phone.

"But do I need the name of the train or anything?" I asked.

When he assured me that I had all the necessary information, I refrained from asking more. Though Mike was retired, he had commuted to Manhattan for many years; he certainly knew the way.

As the conductor punches my ticket, I ask him if I'm on the right train. "Yes," he says, but I'm not sure he hears me over the noise of the engine's hissing. I close my binder and transfer my attention to a folder with the Midler photos and typed transcriptions from my grandmother's and other relatives' interviews. Perhaps I will need something in here to verify information with Hanna. I'm unable to concentrate. Instead, I watch the landscape change from apartment complexes to rows of modest houses; and, as happens when I travel, my thoughts weave into fragmented patterns, old patches crudely basted, their short, uneven threads begging me to pull them together.

I tighten one and envision Masha on one of her journeys as she must have felt in 1923 when she got off that elevated subway train in Borough Park, Brooklyn. Her husband, Isaac, had rented a large apartment.

My mother, Norma, barely old enough for the first grade, was impressed. I open the folder and consult a page from one of her taped interviews: "I was amazed at the immensity of the rooms—all for us, only one family. In Warsaw, there were five families in one place."

Shortly afterward, the family moved to 18th Avenue, across the street from a public school. They lived upstairs, above a storefront. Although the house was one in a row of similar ones, it was, my mother says, "so tremendous, I was appalled."

Not far away was the busy shopping district. "Thirteenth Avenue," Norma recalls, "was the Lexington Avenue of the Jewish neighborhood. All the stores were there, including the delicatessen and the butcher for kosher meat."

Masha was thrilled to be in this country, thrilled with her accommodations. I locate this story in her interview transcriptions. Despite her excitement, "America was not beautiful," she says. "My mother's house and Volchin, my village, were beautiful. But we run away from killings, and here we could eat everything."

Life in America was still hard. The family had to make a living. They set out to establish a Hebrew school and *shul* (synagogue) downstairs in the storefront. After Isaac earned money chanting prayers at cemeteries, he would go with Masha to junkyards and garbage lots and collect discarded chairs and tables. Using his wife and his eldest children, Rose and Jack, as teachers, Isaac now had the rudiments for his school.

According to Masha, she taught in two other places, often carrying her youngest children with her. "For me, the students had respect," she says with characteristic immodesty, "but for my husband, they didn't like him. They liked only me, the *rebbitsin* [rabbi's wife]. Then I had to come home and make supper for 11 people. I used to go at night to wash the floors, and go down the stairs to wash the steps, and after to come upstairs and wash out the laundry from all the kids. Such a life I had!"

"Next stop Hewlett," the conductor announces, nodding at me. The only passenger to disembark, I look up and down the platform. There's no one. I could be standing at the wrong end. Perhaps there's a station house and Hanna will be inside. Is it possible I had gotten the day or the time wrong? Or maybe I'm not supposed to come to Hewlett, and Hanna is sitting in the lobby of my apartment building waiting for me. I berate myself for not getting more specific instructions. Again, I think of my grandmother, fearless in the middle of a strange country, and I wonder what happened in my life to make me so different.

Then, in the distant parking lot, a woman steps out of a car and tentatively waves in my direction. I clutch the rubber band around a bouquet of flowers, lifting them to show her, like a Native American offering a peace trinket, that I'm not the intrusive, opportunistic Manhattanite she may have expected. My eyes take in her red-blond hair, her crinkling eyes, her open, cherubic face, and I immediately know that this woman has already incorporated the facts of my introduction: the reports from my new Volchin family, the conversations about my lost cousins. This woman will give me what I haven't yet earned—her trust.

Hanna introduces her husband, Mike, a distinguished white-haired man with a surprisingly sophisticated lilt to his speech, as if a British accent were trying to eradicate Yiddish, Russian, and Polish undertones. We take the short drive to their house, the three of us talking at once. The train schedule, the weather, the news from Israel, the time it took me to get to the station, the flowers, the streets of Hewlett—all these comments become intermingled, and I can hardly answer one question before I'm asking another.

We arrive at their house. Mike hangs up the coats and motions me to sit. Hanna's kitchen is modern, open, and friendly, a reflection of my hostess, and I admire the layout.

"I could fit all the kitchens I ever had in this space," I say.

As women usually do when complimented, Hanna indicates some unseen defect. Before long, at the kitchen table with a spread of bagels, lox, and accompaniments enough for 20 people, we nibble, sip tea, and talk as if we've known each other our entire lives. Soon, I feel comfortable enough to ask questions and, with Hanna's permission, turn on my tape recorder.

"You said that your uncle was partners with my uncle Iser," I repeat for benefit of the tape recorder. I hope my voice can adequately capture my profound surprise at this revelation.

"Yes," Hanna says. This time, with the recorder on, she doesn't elaborate. A few minutes before, she expressed her astonishment at our common bond.

"What was your uncle's name?" I ask, hoping to prod her memories with factual clues.

"Shuster. Hershel."

"They had a bike repair shop?" Again I repeat what she told me earlier. I will finally find out about my uncle's business. My family had heard so many stories—Iser continued his father's tile business; he sold Singer sewing machines; he sold fruit from his orchards.

Now Hanna responds, "I don't know." She must sense my disappointment and then says, "Maybe they had someplace a corner, an extra place. Maybe a shack outside, near the house. I was in their house maybe twice a week at least. Exactly, I know the layout of the house. There was a bedroom, a living room, and a dining room—a big room, you know—and then there was a hallway you walked in, and straight was the kitchen. And from the kitchen, you went out to the garden."

"Was there an attic?" I ask, recalling my mother's stories. I am tempted to open my transcriptions and look for some verification. But I decide to leave the folder where it is; this is not the time or place for fact checking.

"No. When you walked in the hall to the right was another apartment—a kitchen and a room. There probably, he had the shop. But later, probably they rented it to a Polish couple, I think. Two people were living there. That was a big place for a family."

I am struck by how many times Hanna says the words "maybe," "probably," and "I think." Yet her language changes over certain details—she is "exact" about the layout of the house and seems sure of the way out-doors. Some things are easier than others to reconstruct.

"We used to go behind the house," she says, resuming her visual path. "I can still picture it. There was a garden with vegetables and flowers. We used to pick the wildflowers."

Suddenly Hanna's voice loses its dreamy nostalgic tone. Memory is intruding; I can feel its tug. I let the conversation lag. Mike asks me if I went inside my uncle's house when I was in Volchin. I explain that I walked around it, but Shmuel had indicated that we couldn't go inside, and I, regretfully, didn't pursue the issue.

Without prompting, Hanna speaks, "In '46, I wanted to see the town. I told my uncle, and he said, 'Don't go.' He knew. I said, 'I have to see for my own eyes. If I wouldn't go, I'll never forgive myself.' And I schlepped—believe me, it wasn't easy."

Hanna then describes her arduous, lonely journey, stopping at towns, maneuvering through postwar travel confusion and destruction. From Brest, she took a train to Visoke, where she knocked on the door of a school friend. A soldier answered, and, through Hanna's hysterics, he learned of her destination. He arranged for a horse and wagon to take her home. Finally, she was back in Volchin, wandering the streets like a ghost.

"I was in shock. I couldn't talk."

I nod. Although I had heard some of this before on the telephone, it seems even more traumatic in person.

Hanna continues, "I went through the whole town, but I was so in hysteria. A lot of the houses were empty completely. It was like Hiroshima. The houses were still standing, but the people were gone. Nothing. It was so quiet. I started opening doors, and here used to be my aunt and here used to be someone else. It was a terrible experience."

Hanna doesn't have to say this. I can only imagine what it must have been like for her, a young woman coming back to her hometown, knowing what had happened to everyone, and finding a deserted village.

"Somebody—Russians—were living in our house. The chief of the village asked if I want to stay here. I said, 'Are you kidding? I'm going to stay here when every step reminds me of my family, of my grandfather, my grandmother, my sisters, my brother, my mother, my girlfriends, my aunts, my uncles. Impossible!' I stayed maybe three or four days, and I run away."

At that time, Hanna and Mike had just married. I ask Mike about his war years, expecting that he must have met Hanna somewhere during her journey through Russia, expecting that, although he probably also had a painful tale, he must have escaped the worst circumstances.

"I was in Auschwitz," he says matter-of-factly.

"I didn't know that." I feel inadequate.

"After the war, I took a train back to Grodno, where I'm from. I had some kind of a feeling that I'll find at least—I had four brothers and a sister. I figured I may find somebody. But unfortunately not."

In a hurried voice, Mike summarizes his war years, "Until 1943, I was in the ghetto. Then from '43, they shipped us first to Stutthof, which is on the Baltic Sea, a concentration camp, from there to Auschwitz. In January 1945, they shipped us to Buchenwald, and there was a death march from there. They didn't know what to do with us. We were walking in the direction of Munich, and they were shooting everybody right and left, and I escaped. I was freed on March 13, 1945. Germany surrendered on May 7."

As if embarrassed that he took up my time, he suddenly stops and says, "You continue with Hanna. I already recorded my testimony two times."

I want to ask him more. This seems too hasty. But I must leave the afternoon as open as possible. I need to return to our uncles, their shop, the town. In many ways, I'm going on a journey with Hanna and Mike. Though I'm here to have my questions answered, I must follow their lead. I must go the way that memories go—meandering, associative, back and forth, and, mostly, from darkness to light.

There is a poem I discovered in my journal, written somewhere in Belarus. As my own memory has deteriorated, I think I wrote this, but I'm not sure. It's scribbled amid a mass of notes. It could be that another person recited it, and I merely copied it down. I no longer can tell what is mine and what, in my inimitable way of crossing over into other lives, is someone else's. Called "Reaching into Darkness," it begins:

> We reach into darkness and pull out bones;
> We reach into darkness and pull out ashes;
> We reach into darkness and pull out another hand,
> reaching for ours.

And sometimes, we're lucky.
We reach into darkness and . . .

In my journal, there is nothing more. The search is not over. Not yet.

"You know, you look like your mother's family," Hanna says.

I'm startled. First because Hanna changes so effortlessly from the subject of her husband's horror. Second, because I had always believed I looked like no one in my family. My dark, olive complexion is nothing like my mother's rosy one; my petite features are nothing like my mother's thin, aristocratic ones; my small frame is nothing like my mother's tall and big-boned one. My mother in her heyday was a fresh-faced Ingrid Bergman; I was a more earnest Sally Field. If I had to look like anyone, it would be from my father's side of the family; though I had neither their thick, oily hair nor brown-black eyes. The fact that my parents claimed that their camera broke and there are no photos of me as an infant added fuel to my adoption fantasies.

Then I remember that I recognized similarities between Sala and me when I saw her photo, so I expect that's what Hanna meant, and I tell her so.

But Hanna surprises me again, saying it is not this sister—her coloring was lighter. "I mean the older one, Ida," she says. "She was only two years older than me, but she looked a lot like you. Your eyes."

"Shmuel said her name was Nahoma," I say. "But he was wrong."

"Yes. It was Ida, and Sara was the middle one. We called her Sala, as you know. And Ester was the youngest."

"Shmuel also told me that Ida was not killed in the massacre, that she went to Brest to go to school, and he didn't know what happened to her. But you told me that she was in Volchin at the time of the massacre."

"Yes. I remember the story about her, specifically. She didn't want to get undressed. They shot her with clothes. This was the most tragic thing I heard." Hanna swallows, her voice falters.

This unbearable information comes to me again; again, it cinches a knot around my neck; my breath suddenly stops. And I see her, a dark girl with my eyes, running in a circle, flailing her arms and then gathering them around her, trying to paste the clothes to herself permanently. Ida, the girl with my eyes.

Hanna says that she heard some of these stories when she went back to Volchin. "There was another woman with a child. She started running away. They shot her, too." Hanna's narrative picks up speed, keeping pace with her memory. "And there was one guy there, not Jewish," she reports. "He was crying. He was not eating; he couldn't sleep because they told him that he should cover the bodies. For years he was going crazy."

More images come, and I'm not sure whether Hanna heard all this in 1946 or through other reports over the years. Suddenly, it doesn't matter. I must abandon my obsessive need for a chronological narrative, for factual verification. Whatever I learn, I learn.

"The whole thing was Ukrainians. There were only about two Nazis. They came with the trucks."

Hanna then explains about the massacre site, on the road to Visoke. There had been a tile workshop where people got sand. When I remind her that we went there from my uncle's house, Hanna says that it wasn't far from her public school, the school she went with her friend, my cousin Sala.

Another former classmate, Anna Gagarina, who now lives in Brest, still corresponds with Hanna. Hanna quotes a recent letter: "I still hear your sister Rochal, her beautiful voice singing. I used to pass your house and call on her to go to school together."

"Your whole family stayed behind?" I ask gently.

"Yes."

"How many were there?"

"I had three sisters and a brother."

Unlike her aunts, uncles, and cousins, who remained in Volchin and were killed in the massacre, Hanna's parents took their children to live in the Visoke ghetto, which was larger and offered more places to hide. As far as Hanna has been able to learn, those ghetto inhabitants were taken to Treblinka.

In May 1941, a month before the war, Hanna went to a small town near Bialystok, where she planned to stay until music school would begin in September. Suffering from pneumonia, Hanna summoned her mother to care for her. Two weeks later, now feeling better, Hanna took her mother to the Bialystok train station.

"This was the last time I saw my mother. The rest of the family I never saw again. I never went back to Volchin." Hanna's lower lip trembles. I fear she is going to cry. But after a few seconds, she bites her lip and resumes her story, recalling the Sunday morning when the Germans came: "I was in another town. . . . I was running because the shooting was terrible. . . . I was going, going until I came to Bialystok. There was no way back."

In bits and pieces, I learn the harrowing story of Hanna's war years. Though only 16 years old, she managed to make her way deeper into Russian territory. In Siberia, she worked in a steel mill. Conditions were harsh; she was devastatingly alone. One day, she heard that her uncle, a singer in the Belorussian ensemble, was in a certain Russian city. Without documents, she took the train, searching for her uncle. She was supposed to change trains in Moscow, but the police arrested her for leaving her job without permission and sent her to the infamous Butyrki Prison.

At her trial, an incensed female prosecutor who happened to be Jewish asked, "How come your passport is Ukrainian and you're Jewish? I am Jewish, and I'm not afraid to say it."

Hanna explained that she too was not trying to hide her heritage, that her papers merely reflected a bureaucratic mistake, that she was fleeing from extreme danger. But the prosecutor—supposedly unconvinced of the occupied Jews' condition—sentenced Hanna to five years in prison.

"I thought it was the end of my life," Hanna says, though she later realized that this sentence saved her.

Hanna was sent to a camp near Smolensk and lived in a cave with about 300 others. She worked cutting trees to build an airport. With mainly wheat for sustenance, she was swollen from hunger, contracted dysentery, and suffered from frozen toes. When she was too weak to go to work one day, she was put in isolation, subsisting only on water. Nearly dead, she was then taken to the hospital, where she spent about a year recuperating and later working with other patients.

With no knowledge of the concentration camps or massacres, one thing kept Hanna alive: "That I'll see my parents again, my family again, my town again."

When Brest was liberated in 1944, she sent a postcard to Volchin, expecting and hoping it would reach her parents. Somehow, her uncle received the card and began to search camps until he found Hanna.

"They stopped me where you go through the guards. I said, 'My God, what are you going to do now?' I walked in, and I see my uncle. I started screaming. He looked at me, and he didn't recognize me. I was skinny, my hair was shaved. 'This is me,' I said. He started crying, and I was crying. We fell on each other. And the guard was also crying. I started asking my uncle, 'Where is my mother? Where are they?' He said, 'The war is not finished yet. People are coming home. We don't know yet.' He knew everything. He didn't want to tell me nothing."

This is the uncle, I learn, who put up the monument in Volchin.

I mention that I'm working on a documentary, a project initiated by the Federation and the videographer who went on our mission. Though we would be focusing on Brona Gora, we thought that the Volchin story would also be a profound parallel—the small-town massacre occurring in much the same circumstances, around the same time, as the huge catastrophe in the forest. "You would be an important part of the Volchin story," I explain.

Hanna shrugs and, instead of expressing interest, seems to remember some inescapable facts. "Motikali, a small village near Brest—that's where they shot them. From Volchin, they took the young people for work and kept them in Brest, in the ghetto. Some ran away and were shot in that village." She doesn't really know who was shot and how many and who remained in Brest. All she knows is that Dov's uncle and Shmuel's sister were among those sent to the Brest ghetto.

We're silent for a moment. We all know what happened to the people in the Brest ghetto. They were taken to Brona Gora.

I think of my cousin Ida and wonder why she didn't go with these young people. Hanna doesn't remember if Ida remained in Brest after the Soviet invasion of 1939, when Jewish schools, synagogues, and businesses closed. I did look for Ida's name on the Brest ghetto list. Ida somehow made it back to Volchin, somehow remained with her family—joined in their fate.

I mention the storm on the day I went to Volchin. I'm not sure if I choose this topic as a relief in the unexpressed tension as we think of Brona Gora, or if I'm making excuses for the quality of my photos, which I plan to show.

Mike instantly smiles with recognition. "Yes," he says. "We knew about the storm. I read about it in the *Times*."

At first, I'm surprised that a storm system in Belarus would make the *New York Times*. When Mike tells me of its freak nature and its swath of destruction, and I remember the weather that day, I nod. I recall 1967, when I was on the Greek island of Mykonos, lazily thinking about my future, and, during the worst protracted storm in living memory, we had to evacuate with the entire island population. I think of another, more recent occasion when a blizzard hit Morocco and all I had with me was a light spring jacket and rolls of daylight film. A severe weather pattern covering the land of burnt corpses should be no surprise.

We move to the living room to be more comfortable. Before I take out the photos of the trip, I open the folder containing my aunt Ray's precious pictures of Iser and his family. Gently, Hanna lifts up a photo, the informally dressed group.

"Oh my," Hanna says, pointing to the short, blond woman in the striped dress with her arm looped through my uncle's. "Sure, that was his wife, sure. She looks very young."

I look closely at my aunt's face. Yes, Hanna is right. This Bashka looks fair and open and pure—an innocent country girl, not the mother of three daughters. "I don't know who the children are," I say, suddenly doubting that any could be the offspring of someone so young.

"This is Ida," Hanna says, smoothing her finger over the young woman kneeling in the center. This was the person I had studied many times, the one I could never place. Darker than the other girls, Sala and Ester, with long hair draping over her full bosom. It's hard to tell if she wears a flowered ribbon around her neck or whether it's part of her dress, but it gives her an exotic air. Her belt reveals a wide waist and her long bare arms point straight down, the fingers of one hand surreptitiously resting on the collar of a seated girl. This woman looks nothing like her mother; they could be schoolmates. Though she has the swarthy, sturdy looks of her father, her features are less delicate. But mostly, she stands out from all the others in the photo. She could be a settler in Palestine, a gypsy fortune-teller, certainly a person with her own style. Like me, she is different from her family.

The two children flanking the young girl on the grass appear to be boys dressed in the same feminine sunsuits. While the boys have dour expressions, the girl has a smile as open as Ida's.

"This is Sala," Hanna says, her voice dropping.

Of course, this is Sala, I think. I recognize her pretty face, twinkling eyes, and blunt hairstyle. But I'm confused. If Ida is so grown up—she could be anything from 14 to 21—how could Sala appear to be maybe 10 or 11? And how could Bashka appear to be even younger than she looked in photos taken much earlier? For the 10th time that day, I turn the photo over. I'd give anything for a date.

"Ida was born probably in 1922," Hanna says. "Sala was born in '24 like me. And Ester must have been born in '26, '27, or maybe even '28. My third sister was like her age."

I quickly compute the figures. If Ida is at least 14 in this photo, it would have been taken around 1936, which would make Sala around 11 or 12. Looking at Ida again, I decide she must be older than 14, which would make the picture closer to the late '30s. This would be the last pictorial record of my family before they were killed.

Again, I wonder about all these strangers in the photos. Could they be from Bashka's family? Although I'm certain that everyone else from my family came to America, I harbor a few second thoughts—maybe there are other people here that are mine.

"Was Bashka a native?" I ask.

"She was from Bocki, near Bialystok. A little town. Her father lived with her."

Bocki, this sounds familiar. My aunt Ray told me that contrary to family opinion, my mother was not born in Warsaw. Ray claims that my grandmother went into labor when she was in Volchin and delivered my mother in a small town called Botka, which could really be Bocki.

"You have nothing to do with Bashka," Hanna says. "You're related to Iser."

"Maybe my grandmother went there, to Bocki. Maybe they already knew Bashka's family."

"Ida looked like Iser, and Sara looked like her mother." Hanna seems to sense that I am grasping. Iser's wife, Bashka, the town Bocki, everything sounds the same.

"My mother," I say. "Her relatives. They all have the same face." I point to Iser.

"That's why I say when I looked at you, the eyes."

Mike opens a map and motions me to sit next to him on the couch.

"Bocki," he says.

"Is that the same as Botka?"

"Yeah."

I see that Bocki is near Bransk. I note that Bocki is between Volchin and Bialystok.

"It's actually near Bielsk-Podlaski," Mike says.

All these names. Names that only a few months ago, when I was researching the area, seemed so strange. Now, I recognize them all. Bransk, the town from Eva Hoffman's book, *Shtetl*, which I just finished reading. Bialystok, the city that Ruth from our delegation visited for a day, looking for her ancestors' birthplaces. And Bielsk-Podlaski, where my Israeli aunt Dina was from.

Hanna and I return to the photos. "These are the two girls," I say needlessly.

"This is Sala and this is Ester."

"Aren't they beautiful?"

"They *were* beautiful." Hanna corrects my tense. "Sala," she says dreamily, "we were going to school together."

In the same faraway tone, Hanna picks up another photo. "This is Bashka," she says. And, caressing the baby in Bashka's arms, she adds, "Maybe this is little Ester." Suddenly, Hanna's dreamy voice breaks, "God, this is the house. You see the windows. I still remember the curtains hanging there."

This photo has no resemblance to the Midler house I saw in Volchin. From what I can see in the photo, the side of the house on which Bashka leans is wooden, matching the faded trim on the windows. The house I stood next to was white brick. Though I was there, Hanna is the one who is really there, transported to the structure she knew, the lace curtains she saw, the little flowerpot on the chipped window sill she touched. This is the house that was, the house Hanna knew.

"I remember the records—they had a gramophone with a big tube."

This fact, like others, Hanna told me before. But I don't mind. The repetitions begin to take on the feeling of shared family tradition, stories of which I can never hear enough.

The photo with Iser in a suit and Bashka in a formal dress, sitting with two girls outdoors against the side of a house, elicits murmuring sounds from Hanna.

"It's amazing though in a little shtetl how they were dressed," Mike says.

"They were very sophisticated," I say.

"Yes," Hanna says. "They were very advanced people in that town. We were all educated, self-educated. I have cousins, they never went to the university, but they knew Shakespeare. They knew everything. My mother used to play in the amateur theater. My mother and my uncle Hershel played in *King Lear* in Yiddish. I remember I was so proud watching."

"Did my oldest cousin, Ida, go to a university?"

"She went to Brest to the Tarbut Hebrew gymnasium. It was before the Russians came in 1939. She used to live there. We couldn't go back and forth."

"My aunt remembers that the family sent money for her to go to school," I say, amazed that stories told long ago are finally being validated.

"Yeah, you needed money. I couldn't afford it. Our parents did everything in their power to educate us. They sent me to another town. I went to a school in Visoke. It was Yiddish, geography, and everything. I took a room and went home for the weekends."

On Hanna's coffee table is a pile of photos and papers. She picks up a postcard and asks me if I read Yiddish. When I tell her that I can understand some spoken words but not written, she explains that this is a New Year's card from the Volchin rabbi, who sent it to her aunt in America before the war, probably around 1938 or '39. The rabbi's wife, Hanna says, was in a relief society. "On the committee was Iser Midler," she adds.

"He was on the committee?" I repeat needlessly. I am amazed that when Hanna drops these little nuggets of information, she doesn't notice that they sear through my lap like burning coals.

"He was the one who had the money to help."

"The treasurer," Mike says.

"There was a whole society then for the sick people."

My uncle was the treasurer for the town relief society—the treasurer, a very responsible position.

I think of my mother, Norma, who graduated from Woodridge High School in 1935 with a commercial diploma, a fact she still bitterly blames on the principal, Mr. McKernan. "He sat me down," she once told me, "and said to take a commercial course because with my family, I couldn't go to college. He hated us Lews because we talked back at him. And he discouraged women from doing anything."

My mother was a voracious reader and entertained literary ambitions in high school, keeping a scrapbook filled with flowery poetry and clever quips that she cut out from magazines and newspapers. Psychologically unable to counteract the principal's lack of emotional and financial encouragement, however, she left Woodridge for a hopefully more exotic life as a single woman living alone in Manhattan, an unusual lifestyle for women of her time. As a "career" girl with a line of suitors, including my father, vying for her attention, she worked a series of office jobs, primarily as a bookkeeper, before her marriage and years later when my father went bankrupt.

Now the president of her senior citizens' center, Norma loves overseeing organizational functions—and telling people what to do. Just last week, my mother's friend Sophie told me that my mother had just given a wonderful funeral for a friend. This was a man my mother had played cards with every afternoon for 12 years. "She had the rabbi speak and even a piano player," Sophie bragged. "And she gave the eulogy, all about playing cards and how they had accused each other of cheating and how now he could no longer cheat death."

My mother had finally found an audience for her metaphoric aphorisms. "Your mother," Sophie continued, "she always does things well. But you know, nobody there really understands or appreciates what she does."

I wonder again about Iser. I wonder if the people in his society complained about his fund-raising abilities. Did a few of the most skeptical suspect him of overspending or dispersing favors? Or was he respected for the fine fiscal manager and fair-minded townsperson that he undoubtedly was?

Hanna places a few color photos on top of the pile, and the sudden switch from black and white confuses me.

"I was with Drora in Israel then," Hanna says, and I see a familiar face from my new Volchin family.

"Look at Drora."

"This was from her son's bar mitzvah in 1974."

Again, I feel jolted. I knew that Hanna had met my Volchin family. But to see her with them in Israel shifts their relationship to a new sphere.

"Dov gave me this copy of a postcard from his grandfather. It must have been sent in 1939 or 1940. His grandfather writes this to his daughter, Dov's mother."

"Does it say anything?" I prepare myself for some more information.

"He writes about the terrible conditions they had to live in, but he's telling it diplomatically because otherwise it wouldn't go through the censors."

Hanna shows me his perfect handwriting and all the information he crammed into such a small space.

"He was a very smart man. That's what I'm telling you. Here was a small town, with no colleges, no universities. Today you give them everything to learn. They don't want to learn, they blame this or that.

If you want to learn, you do it on your own."

"I guess that was shtetl life," I say.

"Shtetl life was what you made of yourself."

Mike hands me an enlarged photo of the Volchin memorial in an Israeli cemetery. On a black background is an engraving of the fence and the triangular, star-topped stone by the massacre site in Volchin, although the name on the inscription is spelled "Wolczyn." Underneath the village name, in English, it says, "In memory of our beloved martyrs murdered in the Holocaust." I notice that beloved is spelled with a *w*, but I keep silent.

Mike translates the Hebrew above the English, "A memorial to the people of the town of Volchin that were murdered by the Nazis and were buried in a mass grave and to those whose place of burial is unknown."

Below the black background engraving is a marble base saying, "Dedicated by Hanna Goldfarb-Kremer and friends from Wolczyn." On each side of the memorial is a Hebrew list of those families from Volchin.

Mike points to the last name on the right panel, "Family Midler," he says. "They got together over the phone and they started to remember the names according to the homes, the way you walked down the street."

"I was looking for this picture of the school," Hanna interrupts and pulls out a photo of about a hundred children, from preschool age to teens, surrounding six adult men, three of whom have beards. Hanna explains that this was the religious Hebrew school, outside the synagogue, in July 1936. She identifies one of tallest girls standing in the back as herself and a delicate, blond girl, almost popping out in relief among the darker-complexioned and heavier-dressed classmates, as her best friend, my cousin Sala. A group of healthy-looking, attractive children. All of them, except Hanna, killed.

My finger caresses Hanna's and then Sala's face. My heart feels stuck in tar; I think it will never regain its normal beat.

"How many synagogues were there?" If I ask a factual question, maybe I won't have to worry about breathing.

"One," Hanna says. "There used to be two."

"What did people do for a living then?"

"Shopkeepers, tailors, dressmakers. Most of the people were dealing with the peasants."

We discuss our ancestors' time, when there was an old *shul*. I mention my grandmother's stories of pogroms and the Cossacks.

"Yes, they were raping girls," Hanna says. "I remember the story. They used to talk about it. My mother was hiding in the attic someplace."

"The emigration from that area—ours was the same—started in 1905," Mike says. "The biggest pogroms were at the beginning of the century. After the Russians lost the war with the Japanese, the situation got so bad, they had to take it out on somebody, and naturally it was the Jews."

Mike then brings up the next big emigration wave, he thinks around 1917–22, and recounts the contentious history between Poland and Russia. He hands me some photos and explains that they were taken in Cuba, where he and Hanna immigrated after the war, waiting to get into the United States. Finally, he shows me recent photos. "This was from our 50th anniversary, two years ago, in Florida."

In a group family portrait, Hanna identifies her children and grandchildren. "It was very emotional," she says. "We had a *chuppa* [wedding canopy] because we never had a real wedding."

"It's quite an accomplishment considering where you began," I say.

"Yes," Hanna says, "We were blessed from the other side."

After we stretch our legs, I show Hanna photos of my trip to Volchin, including houses in the Jewish section. Unlike her reaction to the old photos of my family, she flips through them nonchalantly as if she's looking at pictures of someone's faraway vacation, uttering only a few phrases—"I don't know," "You have to know where you are." Am I doing a good thing by showing them to her? Maybe the changes in Volchin only bring back all her losses.

When I get to one of the churches and mention that Dov thinks some of the stones are from the cemetery, Hanna admits that Dov knows better.

"Fifty thousand Soviet citizens," Mike says. "They never mention Jews."

"In Brona Gora, I know," I say. "Isn't that something?"

Hanna joins in, "This is how they wrote, they wrote *citizens*. They didn't write *Jews*."

She seems to have a reference for the photo of Iser's house. With her eyes almost closed as if dismissing this new photo, this modern intrusion, she repeats the house layout, the part rented out, the place where our uncles' shop could have been.

I study the photo, the barnlike shack. I can't imagine all that activity going on there.

"This was not the way it was," she says noticing my dismay. "It wasn't brick. It was a wooden house. Everything was changed. Nothing is the same." Then Hanna taps the side of the house, "This is where the orchard was." Sweeping to the left, she adds, "And this is where the policeman, Kotera, used to live. And a littler further down was my grandmother's house, my aunt's house."

Mixed with the new photos is an old one. "Oh, here is the last of the photos my Aunt Ray sent me," I say. It's the formal group shot—three men standing, three women sitting, and two young girls standing in the foreground. Again we comment on Iser's good looks, his proud pose in his double-breasted suit and striped tie.

"Oh my God!" Hanna screams. "This is my uncle! Hershel." She points to the masculine trio, and her finger stops on the man at the right, only a face away from my uncle's.

A tall man with round-rimmed glasses. His haircut and three-buttoned suit make him look contemporary. "The right one?" I say stupidly.

"Yeah, he was the one in partnership with your uncle. Oh, I can't. Here I'll show you the pictures. I have my whole family." Hanna plunges into a pile of old photos on the desk and finds one with a large group. Sure enough, I recognize a tall man with glasses, Hanna's uncle Hershel.

"He also was a good-looking man," I say.

"I can't believe it! Here I'm looking. I say to myself, 'Who is this guy?' I see it's Hershel. They were friends, you know. This is the guy." Again Hanna focuses on her old photo. "This is my family. This uncle," Hanna pants, indicating an older man, "is my grandfather's brother. He came in 1938 to visit the family. That's when we made the picture."

"Are you in the photo?"

"This is me," Hanna says, still breathless. "This is my sister, my little sister, and my brother. My father and my mother. My grandfather, my grandmother. That's Hershel and that's his wife. And that one," she says, gazing past Hershel, "is my mother's brother, his wife. That's the brother who survived."

Then I remember Hanna's story of her war years. This is the uncle, the musician, who was touring when the war broke out. This is the man who found her wasted away in the Russian camp. This is the one who told her about the massacre. This was her only relative to survive.

"It's a beautiful family," I say.

Hanna is still in shock. "Oh my God!" she exclaims again, returning to my photo. "Yes, this is Iser. And these kids, I see right away who they are. This is Sala, and this is Ida. Ester wasn't born yet. This is Sala; she was blond. Short, cute—she wasn't tall. She was a beautiful girl. But this is my uncle. I can't believe it."

Yes, this is Hanna's uncle, and this is my uncle. And even more remarkable, I see that this girl, the older one, about six years old, is indeed Ida. Since she had been identified in the other photo as a teenager, I can recognize her determined face in this little girl. When I hold it up to the other photo, I notice that the pose, though years apart, is similar. This little Ida also stands with her arms hanging by her sides; and though her lips are turned down here in a scorn, probably annoyed at having to pose, she has the same dark-eyed fervor, the same respect for life that made her the one to disobey the order to undress—the clear, determined, baggy-worried eyes of a fighter to the last. So all along, although I didn't know it, I had two photos of Ida, the one I thought was lost to me.

Toward the end of the visit, after I admire more photos of the Kremers' children and grandchildren, Hanna says, "It's funny—the picture you had with my uncle. That's really something. They were close friends, I know."

I had an unexpected knot in my throat. I was afraid to respond. Hanna, who had been through so much, who had lost so much, is able to stay in control. What is the chance, I think, that here in 1997, two women, two nieces, would be sharing photos of their uncles from another world? The word comes back to me yet again. *Bashert.*

I pick up my final few photos. "This is Brona Gora," I explain. "You can see the forest where they were all killed." Though unplanned, the next photo shows the massacre site and memorial in Volchin.

"My uncle put down the stone. They didn't have a *Mogen David* [six-pointed Jewish star]. They had a [regular] star, and he put a few words in Hebrew and he wrote 'Jew.' At the time, Stalin was still there, but the town didn't object to nothing. He did it the way he wanted."

In my picture, the stone memorial is shiny and wet. Hanna squints, trying to read the faint words. "I don't know. Everything is gone." "It's clearer in person," I say.

Hanna nods but looks at me skeptically. She knows about tokens. She knows about the fragility of faded monuments. But she also knows, I console myself, about the miracle of discovery.

Before I leave, I say to her, "Please take this photo," handing her the one with our two uncles.

"No, no, it's yours," she says.

"This is a copy. I have the original. Please take it."

Though she still objects, I feel she is now merely reflexively refusing, protecting herself out of habit. There is a glint of crinkling light from her eyes, and her fingers massage her uncle's face. Realizing I am watching, she moves her fingers quickly over the entire photo. What she gave me this day is beyond expression. And now, I'm so happy to give something to her.

For the first time in my life, I'm beginning to understand why some people still believe that the Holocaust never happened. If history books, tourist guides, and government-sponsored investigative reports show scant or no reference to an entire race of people, then it's safe to deny their presence. It's like that age-old conundrum: How can I be an atheist, for to deny God is to recognize its existence? If one even rejects the slaughter of six million people, then there is some discussion about a group, fictional or not. The only solution is to erase mention of anything or anyone remotely connected to the word *Jew*.

Before I traveled to Eastern Europe, I did some homework about the countries I planned to visit. First I bought the *Insight Guides: Poland*. Revised in 1996, written by a team of experts with an introduction by Lech Walesa, the book appeared comprehensive and authentic.

Walesa welcomes the reader to Poland and praises his people for their tolerance of diverse opinions, liberal spirit, Christian-humanistic tradition, simple solidarity, and kind hearts. I felt something awry.

Then I turned to "A Brief Outline of Polish History," and I scanned the dates. Although my knowledge of Poland was sketchy, I knew something about the country's Jewish history and rechecked my reference books. For about 600 years, Poland was one of the world's most important centers of Jewish life. Before World War II, Poland had the largest Jewish community in Europe—about 3.3 million people, comprising about 13 percent of the country's population. There were cities and towns

Disappearance

that were primarily Jewish; in the capital of Warsaw in 1939, Jews made up a third of the city's population. Even today, half of the world's 15 million Jews have a Polish heritage.

The "Brief Outline" began in the year 375 and ended in 1995. My eyes stopped at the years I knew best. In 1921, when my grand-mother and her five children and four stepchildren were squashed in a dining room in Warsaw, sharing the rest of an apartment with other families and desperately trying to get tickets to America, the *Insight Guide* reports heavy fighting between Poles and Germans. In 1926, there is mention of Pilsudski's coup; the listing for 1939 announces the beginning of World War II and the annexation of Poland's eastern territories by the Soviet Union. The war is then skipped until 1944, when "the Warsaw rebellion is the culmination point of an embittered and protracted resistance by partisans and the Polish *Armia Krajowa.*"

I was stunned. There is no other mention of the war. There is no mention of the Warsaw ghetto, with a May 1941 census figure of 430,000 Jews, and therefore no mention of its 1943 uprising, when about 750 barely armed youngsters and 40,000 unarmed Jews fought against 2,000 well-equipped German troops for nearly a month.[1] There is no mention of Auschwitz-Birkenau, Belzec, Chelmno, Gross-Rosen, Majdanek, Sobibor, Stutthof, or Treblinka—major concentration camps in Poland. There is no mention of the Jews.

Okay, this is just a summary. The next section, "A Glorious Past," would certainly present facts about the Jews. Nothing. "Dependency and Division," nothing. "Rebirth: The Second Republic," nothing. Oh, wait, there is a list of the 27 million inhabitants of the Polish territory around 1921: among the Ukrainians, Belorussians, Germans, Ruthenians, Lithuanians, and Czechs, it says, "Jews." Aha, there is more. A few lines about the National Democracy Movement, its link with the Roman Catholic hierarchy, its call for racial purity. The prime target of its attack is naturally the Jews, comprising more than 8 percent of the population, especially the "intellectuals" who believe in the socialist ideas of Utopia.

Not surprisingly, the chapter on "World War II and its Consequences" talks about Hitler, the Nazis, and Poland's great suffering—the loss of more than six million citizens. Then it praises Poland as the only occupied country that *never* collaborated with the Nazis in any form! I guess that helping to destroy a people who lived beside them for centuries, either by active participation or knowing silence, was not considered collaboration.

There is something else, another factor limiting the capabilities of the Polish forces: "The chaotic flight of thousands of civilians, primarily Jews, desperately seeking to escape from persecution by fleeing to the east." And in discussing Hitler's theory of racial purity, the book does note that Poles were regarded as a "sub-human species" and that part of the aim of the National Socialist policy was, beside the destruction of the Polish people, the extermination of Jews and Gypsies. Always the Poles were the innocent victims, and always, when scapegoats were needed, there were those intellectual, flighty Jews.

The most outrageous thing I read is, "Of the more than 5 million Polish concentration camp inmates, more than 3.5 million were killed— three million of those as a consequence of the *Endlosüng* (Final Solution) as had also been planned for the Jews." While it is true that Poland lost about three million non-Jewish citizens during the war, it isn't true that they all died in the camps. The exact figures vary. The United States Holocaust Memorial Museum recognizes at least 960,000 Jews murdered at Auschwitz-Birkenau and, among the other victims, 74,000 Polish Catholics. Holocaust scholar Yehuda Bauer puts the total number of those killed at Auschwitz-Birkenau at about 1,350,000, 1,323,000 of them Jews.[2] Whatever the specific numbers, I remind myself that the war accounted for the murder of more than three million Polish Jews, 88 percent of the country's prewar Jewish population.

Another section of the *Insight Guide* reads, "In one year almost 2 million Polish citizens were deported in cattle wagons. A large percentage was taken to concentration camps for 're-education.' " One minor omission—the word *Jews*.

At last, there's a section on Treblinka. The truth will come out. Here is the description of the people killed: "They were not only Jews and Gypsies, not only those in opposition to the Nazis, but also simple folk who merely wanted to continue living as Poles in Poland, who made their way to the gas chambers in Treblinka, Auschwitz, Birkenau, Majdanek and the many other camps."

After extolling the virtues of its people, there is one admittance of culpability: "Amongst the aspects of their past that did not necessarily show the Poles in a good light, was the relationship of the majority of the population to Jewish citizens. For too long certain dark chapters in Polish history had been suppressed, and it had been taboo even to mention them. These included the pogroms during the first two years after the war, which culminated in the murder of 46 survivors of the concentration camps by a hysterical mob in Kielce, a town in central Poland, the anti-Semitic campaign of 1968, as a consequence of which thousands of Jewish intellectuals left the country: an irreplaceable loss for Polish science and art."

Finally, on page 103, there's a section called, "The Jews." One line in particular grabbed me: "In Poland there was simply no general hatred of the Jews." In discussing the Polish Catholic Church's ambivalence toward the Jews, the author states that while the Jews were regarded as "the chosen people," they were also "the murderers of Jesus." The word *regarded* is subtly left out of this accusation, and of course there is no correction to this misbelief.

This chapter lists many of the Jewish contributions to the world of culture and politics and eventually confronts the issue of the Polish relationship with the Jews. "There is no doubt," the text reads, "that the attitude of the vast majority of Poles was either one of passivity or indifference toward the fate of the Jews. The reasons for this lay in fear of reprisal . . . the anti-Semitic resentment of the prewar period, and also in fresh evidence of disloyalty on the part of the Jews, since one section of this community had greeted the Red Army's invasion of Poland in September in 1939 with enthusiasm." Finally someone was taking responsibility. But was it responsible to immediately dismiss negative attitudes by blaming the victim?

In his controversial book, *Hitler's Willing Executioners*, Daniel Jonah Goldhagen refutes explanations such as passivity and indifference, blind obedience, and even fear of reprisals for German complicity in the annihilation of the Jews. Instead, he argues, the Germans acted with "willing assent . . . from conviction, according to their inner beliefs." He stipulates that the Germans'—and by that word, he means average citizens—fundamental anti-Semitic beliefs were the main cause of the Holocaust. While the author acknowledges that other national groups undoubtedly helped the Germans, he maintains that the Holocaust was primarily a German event, a systematic and barbaric undertaking motivated and perpetuated by a long history of misdirected hatred against the Jews. As I read about Eastern Europe, I see more evidence that these malevolent feelings were also present in the Russian and Polish national characters.

There are certainly countless instances in which such non-Germanic groups perpetrated anti-Semitic acts before, during, and after the Holocaust. A *New Yorker* article, "Annals of War: Neighbors," reports on a fascinating "role reversal." Jan T. Gross, a professor of politics and a researcher on Polish history, describes events in the northeastern Polish town of Jedwabne on July 10, 1941. In one horrifying day, a majority of the Jewish population, which numbered 1,600 before the war, was wiped out in a particularly vicious and uncoordinated pogrom, with only general supervision from the mayor. Although several bestial and murderous acts had occurred previously, on this day, improvised implements of torture included axes, clubs with nails, and iron hooks. The scores of humiliating crimes included burning beards, forcing Jews to sing and dance, rape, drowning, decapitation, and the gouging out of eyes and tongues. For efficiency, about 1,200 remaining Jews were rounded up and imprisoned in a barn, which was then set on fire. Young Jewish children found outside were pitchforked and thrown on the flames. While the Germans had issued an order that morning for the destruction of all Jews, the actions were voluntarily perpetrated (or witnessed) by the townspeople: ordinary, everyday Poles—the farmer, shoemaker, mason, letter carrier; the son, the father, the grandfather. During the atrocities, the Germans looked on—and took photos.

Explanations for such extreme anti-Semitism vary. In *Ordinary Men: Reserve Police Battalion 101 and the Final Solution in Poland*, Christopher R. Browning examines the same perpetrator testimonies as Goldhagen but offers a less condemning (and, according to Goldhagen, a less critical) interpretation. Browning charges that the 500 men of Battalion 101, through mass shootings, "Jew hunts" (tracking down and killing after ghetto liquidation), and aiding death-camp deportations, were ultimately responsible for the murder of at least 83,000 Jews. With a multilayered portrayal of the men—from eager killers to nonshooters, with most onlookers rather than activists—Browning contends that the men were indeed "willing" but not necessarily because of anti-Semitism alone, and even those racial feelings spanned a wide spectrum. The reasons Browning gives include "conformity, peer pressure, and deference to authority, and . . . the legitimizing capacities of government."

Eva Hoffman speaks in her book, *Shtetl,* about "the pathology of silence," the common Polish postwar response caused by a number of factors, including guilt. This "amnesia" was "abetted by the falsifications of communist history," which encompassed Jewish victims of the Holocaust under national categories. Hoffman makes a convincing case for the complexity of circumstances and behavior. She urges the world, in its anger against the Poles, not to forget the country's history of "collective existence and coexistence," its intervals of peace as well as its episodes of violence.

Yes, sometimes in the anger over the enormity of the Holocaust, heroic acts are overlooked. During the war, Poland was the country with the most "righteous gentiles"—non-Jews who aided Jews. If the Jews are to embrace their complex Polish past—the bad and the good—then the Poles should not rewrite history, should not omit significant chunks. Jews cannot have coexisted if they didn't exist.

A very hopeful sign is the December 3, 1997, removal of eight large wooden Christian crosses and 11 Stars of David from a field in Birkenau, placed by Polish boy scouts in 1983 to commemorate the Poles killed in World War II. The removal of these symbols represented the culmination of successful negotiations among Jewish and Holocaust organizations, the Polish government, and the Roman Catholic Church of Poland. What emerged was an agreement by all parties to preserve and protect Auschwitz-Birkenau and the economic growth of the adjacent towns.

In my search through the Polish guide, I tried to forget history and turned from the featured articles to the heart of the book: "Places." Here I would find evidence of the Jews. In Warsaw, at the end of the chapter, there are a few paragraphs about a street in the ghetto, a monument, and

Masha's parents,
Anna Siegel Midler
and Abraham Isaac
Midler, 1890s.

Isaac Lew's school in Warsaw, around 1913. Isaac and Masha are seated in the center.

Official photo. stamped for American entry, 1923. *Left to right*: Isaih, Esther, Abraham (Pee Wee), Masha, Sara, Gerson, and Norma.

Family portrait, Brooklyn, around 1930. Standing, *left to right*: Norma, Isaih, Jack, Rachel, Rose, Dave Kron (Rose's husband), Gerson, Esther. Seated: Masha, Sara, Pee Wee, and Isaac.

Wayside Inn (Masha's boardinghouse), Woodridge, 1933.

Volchin Hebrew school, 1936. Hanna Goldfarb (Kremer) is the girl with bangs (standing, back row, *center*); Sala Midler, with light hair (first row, standing, *second from left*). Courtesy Hanna Kremer.

Brest Tarbut gymnasium, 1936. Louis Pozez (top row, *far right*); Gerson Lev (top, *third from left*). Ida Midler may be in this photo. Courtesy Louis Pozez.

Midler family in front of
Volchin house, around 1930.
Bashka, Iser, Sala, *left*, and
Ester. Courtesy Ray Brooks.

Volchin scene, late 1930s: standing,
right, Iser and Bashka; kneeling, *right*,
Ida; seated on grass, *center*, Sala.
Courtesy Ray Brooks.

Pee Wee and Norma,
early 1942.

Family dinner, early 1940s. Seated, *left to right*: Charlotte (Isaih's wife), Isaih, May (Gerson's wife), Bernard (Masha's brother), Masha, Dave Miller (Masha's second husband), Fanny (Masha's sister), Benny (Fanny's husband), and Norma. Among those identified standing are: Florence Miller (Bernard's daughter, *third from left*), her mother, Dora (Vevie), Esther Miller (Hymie's wife), and Hymie Miller (Mashia's oldest stepbrother).

Masha's sons, early 1940s. *Left to right*: Isaih, Gerson, and Pee Wee.

Author's parents, Norma and George Simon, mid-1940s.

Masha and Michel, around the time of their wedding in Israel, 1950.

Michel and Masha, 1962.

Michel and Ella Fitzgerald in front of Chez Nous, Michel's cabaret in West Berlin, early 1960s. Female impersonators stand in doorway.

Recording memories, Brooklyn, 1977. Four generations: author, Masha, Norma, Alexis (author's daughter). Courtesy Andreas Neophytides.

Ray Brooks, Masha's sister, around 1993. Courtesy Barbara Reich.

Alexis and Aunt Dina, New York City, 1997.

Last meeting of siblings, Woods Hole, Massachusetts, 1997. *Left to right*: Sara, Gerson, May (Gerson's wife), and Norma. Courtesy Mike Lew.

the Jewish cemetery; in a 20-page chapter on Cracow, home to 56,000 Jews on the eve of World War II, there are 19 lines referring to Jewish sites; and in a chapter on Upper Silesia, Auschwitz gets 16 lines. There must be more mention of Jews in this book, but I gave up looking.

Nagging, or more correctly, eating away at my insides, is the fact that this country of amnesiacs was the birthplace of so many of my relatives. This cosmopolitan city of Warsaw, in its nonexistent ghetto, was the home of so many invisible children, including my mother.

When she arrived in Brooklyn at six years old, my mother was put into kindergarten. She reminds me of this story when I call her after my meeting with the Kremers and tell her about Hanna going to school with Sala. "I was left back because I didn't speak English," my mother tells me for the hundredth time. "I was humiliated. The kids made fun of me. They called me Choma for Nahoma. 'Choma Lew, we hate you.' One of my teachers, Mrs. Bloom, starting calling me Norma, after the actresses Norma Shearer and Norma Talmadge. So my name became Norma."

Within a few years, she had learned English. She says, "I became a troublemaker. Me and my friend Ester Zist terrorized all the kindergarten kids. We went to all the bathrooms—we were the first graffiti artists—and we wrote on the walls, 'The Black Hand is gonna kidnap you, cut off your hands, and cut them into little pieces.' The Black Hand was like the Mafia in those days."

That anger came from a complicated source, no doubt from being taunted for being different in a new land and from the disruptions to her family life. I wonder how much of it—and a lifetime supply would follow—had to do with being a Jew in Poland.

My mother's Polish heritage never left her for long; it seems there are still many out there whose views of the Polish Jews remain distorted. Only three years ago, I took her to Cyprus to visit my husband's family. On a shopping trip in the southern seaside town of Limassol, my husband's hometown, we stopped in a jewelry store. The owner seemed more interested in where we were from than in our desire to spend money. Finally, to quiet his persistent questions, I said, "I'm Jewish."

Not giving up, he asked, "Where are your people from?"

"My mother was born in Poland," I said, careful to raise my voice on the word *born*.

"Why did so many Jews like to live in Poland?" he asked.

Flabbergasted, but still trying to appear calm, I answered, "They didn't like to; they often had no choice about where to live." I decided to leave out more elaborate historical explanations.

Undaunted, the man continued, "But Israel is very clean."

Maybe, maybe, I told myself when I was conducting my pretrip research, things would be different when I read about Belarus. I bought the only book I found with Belarus in the title, *Russia, Ukraine, and Belarus*. I was disappointed because Belarus is relegated to the last section, a mere 51 pages in a tome of 1,194. Also written by a team of experts and revised in 1996, this book should have had the latest and most comprehensive material, reflecting the relaxation of secrecy in post-Soviet times.

I skimmed through the history, noting the mention of Jews during czarist rule. Then the identification of the dead gets cloudy. Recently, enormous mass graves were found in the Kurapaty Forest, outside Minsk, containing the bodies of an estimated 900,000 "victims of Soviet executions carried out between 1937 and 1941." The book summarizes that between 1939 and 1945, at least one out of every four Belorussians died, "more than two million people—many of them, Jews and others, in 200-plus Nazi concentration camps, many more in Soviet deportations and executions before 1941."

So this was it. My research into modern travel sources. I was so disheartened, I bought more books that promised a different perspective— *The Golden Tradition, Image before My Eyes, The Shtetl Book, Jewish Roots in Poland*—and reread numerous personal Holocaust sagas and historical memoirs. Every time I saw the word *Jew*, I rejoiced; I took new comfort in the written word.

Now that my trip to Eastern Europe is behind me, the trail to the Jews is still clouded. Shortly after my visit to the Kremers', I receive a letter from the International Tracing Service, based in Germany. Possessing information on approximately 16 million people, including concentration camp inmates, Jewish deportees, and displaced persons, the organization sends me questionnaires to fill out on my missing family members and directs me to the federal archives in Koblenz, which might provide historical facts relating to the Brest region before the war. Regarding my queries into the Brona Gora massacre, the letter states, "The International Tracing Service could not locate a place by this name in the pertinent records of localization on hand here."

Months ago, I had called the United States Holocaust Memorial Museum in Washington, D.C. Louis Pozez had sent the Brest ghetto list to the museum, and he referred me to his contact, the acting director of the Museum's Wexner Learning Center, Sarah Ogilvie. I told her that I was looking for anything on the Brona Gora massacre. She wrote that her staff had reviewed the material related to Brona Gora in the museum's library and archives, and she had enclosed two sources: an article from the *Encyclopedia of the Holocaust*; and Russian documents, including a Russian-language section sent by Louis Pozez and summary English translation from the records of the "Extraordinary State Commission to Investigate Nazi Crimes Committed on the Territory of the Soviet Union,"[3] a body established by Stalin before the end of World War II. She also gave me the address of the Brest archives, to which I had already written for information. I was shocked, but not surprised, that this museum devoted to the Holocaust had so little on this important massacre, and part of what it had was donated by someone from our delegation.

The encyclopedia listing for Brest-Litovsk refers to Jews beginning in the 14th century, giving the city's various Jewish populations until 1931. There is information about the June 1941 German invasion, mentioning that the town fortress held out for another half year—not the monthlong siege described elsewhere.

The encyclopedia reports on the activities of the *Einsatzgruppen*—mobile killing battalions drawn from the SS, Gestapo, and police that moved behind German army units and were supported by uniformed German police and auxiliary volunteers, such as Ukrainians. During the war, these killing squads murdered at least a million Jews in territories conquered from the Soviet Union, executing many in mass graves using the "sardine" method, layer upon layer. On June 28–29, 1941, the encyclopedia states, *Sonderkommando* 7b, a subgroup of *Einsatzgruppe* B, executed 5,000 men in Brest.[4]

In November 1941, orders were issued for the creation of two Brest ghettos, which were sealed the following month. The establishment of the underground and thwarted attempts at a ghetto uprising preceded the ghetto liquidation on October 15, 1942.

The excerpt describes how the Jews were rounded up and put on trains for the Brona Gora station and killed upon arrival. Partisan activities of the later war years are then recorded. The final notation on Brest-Litovsk concerns the city's liberation on July 28, 1944, when about 10 Jews who had been hiding were discovered.

Not very extensive information, but at least there was something. I read over the last lines, smiling because of the 10 Jews who survived in the Brest ghetto, I knew two of them: Lily Guterman and her brother, Nechamia Manker, both on our trip. Smiling Nechamia, whose twinkling eyes and kindly demeanor cheered us on our long bus rides; tiny Lily, who put her arms around me in St. Petersburg when the Ukrainian woman attacked me for taking her photograph. Lily and Nechamia, real, living Jews.

Interestingly, neither the library's edition of the *Encyclopedia of the Holocaust* nor the *Encyclopedia Judaica* has a separate listing for Brona Gora.

The summary translation of the 1944 State Commission explains that the material is based primarily on eyewitness testimonies and a special investigation carried out by members of the commission on the site of the mass murders. It contains the following:

> 1. The Brona Gora massacre site is located 400 meters northwest of the Brona Gora railroad station. In May–June 1942, the Germans began procedures for mass executions of the civilian populations by preparing graves covering 16,800 square meters. They used between 600 and 800 local people a day, as well as explosive materials.
> 2. In mid-June 1942, the Germans began transporting people of different nationalities (Poles, Belorussians, Jews) to the Brona Gora area and executing them.
> 3. The trains, which arrived from different Belorussian areas, including Bereza, Brest, Drogichino, Yanovo, and Gorodets, were guarded by SD and SS units.
> 4. The trains arrived in special places close to the graves, and the cars were unloaded one by one. The people were ordered to undress and walk along a narrow path and step into a ditch. They were forced to lay facedown. As soon as the row was filled, the killings began. The

Germans shot them row by row. Following the executions, railroad cars with belongings were sent to an unknown destination.

5. To eliminate evidence, the Nazis executed witnesses from the local population.

6. There are eight mass graves in the Brona Gora area. From June to November 1942, more than 50,000 people were killed.

7. In March 1944, to hide the final traces of their crimes, the Nazis decided to exhume the bodies of the victims and burn them. A special group of 100 inmates engaged in this labor over a 15-day period; they were then killed. On top of the mass graves and places of mass burning, the Germans planted trees.[5]

Finally, some translations arrive. Louis Pozez sends me one section from the report, entitled "Act" and dated October 5, 1944. It's from the Brest Regional Assistance Committee attached to the Extraordinary State Commission. The first paragraph establishes the committee's intention: to investigate "the facts of the annihilation of the Soviet people on the territory of the city of Brest and the Brest region during the provisional occupation." It charges the German-fascist invaders with murdering these citizens, including "children, teenagers, women, and old people . . . and thousands of Red Army soldiers and officers taken prisoner."

The committee examined the exhumation and autopsies of corpses performed in three major locations, the largest of them Brona Gora.[6] This report provides a more detailed analysis than the summary translation provided by the Holocaust Museum. Many of the "facts" differ from the summary.

In Brona Gora, 117 kilometers from Brest, five pit graves were found, camouflaged with young, newly planted trees. Some of the graves were as long as 63 meters and as wide as 6.5 meters. Three of the graves were opened. At the depth of 2.5 meters, human bones and ashes were found; at 3.5 meters deep, there was a second layer of ashes and bones, inside of which were locks of hair, a handkerchief, and hair pins. Under the layer of ash was dark, red-brown liquid.

Near the pits, the committee found six areas for burning bodies. Around these areas, the committee located many fragments of small human bones, including a child's shoulder bone, and other items, such as watches and coins.

The committee concluded that the Germans used various methods of systematic extermination. War prisoners were kept in camps, where they were held in unsanitary conditions, subject to infectious diseases, forced to undergo backbreaking labor, and starved to death. Others were beaten and shot. The civilian population, which was sequestered in special districts plus ghettos for the Jews, was also killed off in the same ways.

The committee charged the German-fascist administration with the killing of "150,000 civilians and more than 50,000 prisoners of war in the city of Brest and in the territory of the Brest region." Holding Hitler's government responsible, the committee singled out specific individuals.[7] Although the committee had no trouble naming the guilty Germans, it rarely, and only inadvertently, identified the ethnicity of those killed. Always the victims were peaceful Soviet citizens, civilians, or prisoners of war. Conspicuous in its absence was the word *Jew*.

From its seven pages, this translation does not encompass all the original. I call Louis Pozez and ask him about the remaining report. His translators claim, he says, that the bulk is filled with repetitions or illegible entries. I count 34 pages in all: some are handwritten, some have official seals and names, and some pages have clearly listed findings with numbers I can recognize. There is much more to this report. A friend recommends a Belarusian Jew living in Brooklyn, and I send her the rest of the report, asking her to translate whatever she can decipher.

I'm also tempted to give this translator material I received about Volchin. Then I hear of another Belarusian Jew who would like to translate. This woman's husband is very sick; I know she needs the money. I decide to have two translators: one for Volchin, one for Brona Gora. Somehow, the two events, like the two translators, have different stories but are connected by profound bonds.

In late October, I get a visit from my aunt Dina Lew Bronitsky, who has lived in Israel for about 30 years. The former wife of my grandfather's oldest son, Jack, Dina was born in Bielsk-Podlaski, not far from Volchin. I newly appreciate the precious nature of her life story and take advantage of her willingness to sit with me and my tape recorder. More than anything, I long to reaffirm the Jewish hold on Eastern Europe.

At 93, Dina is remarkable, still evidencing the verve and spirit of a much younger woman. Fortunately, her memories are sharp, going all the way back. Her most vivid one was during World War I, when her family decided to hire a driver and wagon and go to another town, Orla, where they had relatives and where they thought they would be safer because it had no train station and no battlefront. In that town, about 1915, Dina described what happened: "We decided to go and stay in the synagogue. We slept there for maybe a day or two. All of a sudden there was an alarm, and a bomb was dropped in the town. Many people were killed. We left the synagogue, my brother and I. We started running along the town street. We ran back and forth to see if we could find shelter in a store, but we couldn't get in. The town was burning. People were falling. We walked through the night, from this little town, along the road to Bielsk. Recently, I spoke to my brother in Florida, and I asked him if he remembered this. He told me he experienced the same thing. This recurring fear, this seeing bodies, running without purpose."

Memories, the memories of the Jews, run far and deep.

But, not so for others.

During my search for information on Volchin and Brona Gora, I wrote to many institutions in Eastern Europe. Unlike the majority, which directed me elsewhere or neglected to answer, two sources responded. K. P. Batrakova, the director of the archives at Grodno, wrote me a note, dated May 27, 1997, informing me that answers to my questions would not be supplied free of charge. Batrakova enclosed a bill for $50 to be paid before the search could begin. In case of negative results, she added, the money would not be returned.

Months pass, and I write another note to the archives, reminding them of my $50 check. Shortly after Dina's visit, I receive a letter from Batrakova and M. N. Sachek, head of the department. The stationery says, "Committee of the Archives of the Republic of Belarus, National Historical Archives of the Republic of Belarus at Grodno."

The letter begins, "In response to your request for information about the village of Volchin, the Committee has found documents in the archives dating from the 19th to early 20th centuries." My heartbeat quickens, but I'm confused. This letter is only half a page. Perhaps this is just the announcement of the findings; the rest will follow. Certainly $50 will bring more.

The letter goes on to say that a geographical book from 1893 contains an article that reports, "The village of Volchin contains 102 houses (5 of them brick), 804 inhabitants (mainly Jews), 2 churches, a Jewish prayer house, a city hall, a Jewish school, a windmill, and 14 shops. Three fairs per year take place in the village: January 30, April 23, and July 23. Private citizens own 336.5 acres of land, and the church owns 98.5 acres."

Archival information apparently has different figures, although the source date is not included. According to the archive, the letter concludes, "The village of Volchin contained 341 Jewish women, 367 Jewish men, 11 Russian women, 8 Russian men, 1 Polish man, 2 Polish women, 5 members of the clergy, 3 VIPs, and 7 peasants. The village also had a trade school. In 1913, a woman named Elizaveta Aronovna Tolochinskaya of the city of Grodno opened a pharmacy in the village. The archive does not contain any photographs, maps, illustrations, etc."

This is all the information on Volchin. Nine typewritten lines for $50. Each line worth slightly more than $5.55. The going rate in Belarus. I turn to the material I collected at the beginning of my search, when I went to the YIVO Institute. Besides discrepancies accountable to different translators, the material is very similar. In all these months, I haven't come very far. Though I'm heartened by the inclusion of the Jewish identity in the Grodno listing, I'm also depressed that my search has come back like a boomerang and that this repository of historical findings has little more than nine lines on my almost forgotten village.

My second correspondent seems more promising. Anatoli Yaroshchuk, vice director general of State Tourist Enterprise, Brest-Intourist, first wrote on July 11, 1997, informing me that he could send photocopied materials about the history of Volchin from a just-published book called *Memory*. Translation, photocopying, and mailing would cost me $350; Yaroshchuk also provided complicated instructions on how and where to deposit the money.

I wrote back requesting the materials without translation; Yaroshchuk responded that yes, indeed, this was possible. I could have the seven pages on Volchin for a mere $50. There was that $50 charge again. I figured I'd probably get seven pages of the same paragraph. I sent my check anyhow, feeling a familiar duality: a huge dose of skepticism interspersed with trace elements of hope. Surely, surely, there must be some records out there.

Yaroshchuk is a man of his word, and he finally sends me the material from *Memory*. I'm excited by the bulk of the envelope. Inside are a cover page; two inside front pages; a copyright page with the date, 1997; six pages taken from an encyclopedia-type book with subheads, photographs with captions, and bibliographic references; and two typewritten pages that I can decipher with dates, ranging from 1586 to 1994. The history of Volchin through the ages! The history covering my great-grandparents' life spans, my grandmother's years until she left Europe, my Midler family's last, torturous months. All those missing blanks there beneath my fingers, only a translation away.

A week later, I meet my Volchin translator in front of her workplace and inspect the English version—six typewritten single-spaced pages. Six pages—not so much, I suppose, for the history of an entire town. But, for me, it represents a huge reference book. Unable to wait until I get home, I open the package on the subway. Before I read, I suddenly become aware that this may be the only historical reference to Volchin. How can I risk its loss here on the subways of New York? I look across from me, to my left, to my right. Normal-looking people; no one who appears ready to pounce on me and snatch my papers. But how can anyone tell in New York?

I remember an incident a few months earlier, when a man in a well-tailored suit stepped into my subway car and began to mutter incoherently. Then he let out several loud cries, followed by several "Fuck yous." A black man, he spun around and seemed to stare right at me, yelling about how whites hate blacks and how blacks have been "fucked over" time and time again. As always happens in New York during crazy outbursts, people seemed to ignore the perpetrator and then surreptitiously check out the expressions on their fellow passengers' faces, hoping to gain a smile of recognition.

"I have a gun in my pocket," the man shouted.

I locked into the eyes of the woman across from me and saw there what she must have seen in mine: terror.

I agonized: Should I get up and move to the other end of the car? If I do, will I only call attention to myself? But if I sit here, am I being a passive participant in my own death? Luckily, I didn't have to answer my own questions because the man got off at the next stop, ranting and raving as the door closed. I noticed a glimmer of relief in the woman across from me, but she quickly looked down at her newspaper and tried to pretend nothing had happened.

As I sit on another train with my Volchin papers, that fear returns. I skim the headline: "Troisky (Trinity) Church/Polish Roman Catholic Church (village of Volchin)." Oh, it's about a church, just a building. I can wait. I put the papers back in the envelope and place the envelope into my satchel. I think of those questions again. What if that man had stayed on the train? Would I have remained in my seat? For the second time, I don't answer my questions; my stop comes and I get off, rushing home to read about Volchin.

The baroque-style wooden Troisky Church, I read, was built in 1629 by the owner of the borough of Volchin, A. Gusevski. In 1733, a new stone building was erected, founded by Stanislaus Poniatowski, the treasurer of the great Lithuanian principality and the father of the last Polish king, Stanislaus August Poniatowski, who was born in Volchin in 1732. The church underwent various restorations over the years and was badly damaged during World War II.

Following the introduction is a detailed description of the church's unique architectural features—its cupola, pediments, window apertures, ornamental details. I almost call my translator and apologize for what must have been an arduous and tedious task.

The next section is entitled "The King's Last Asylum." It begins like a fairy tale: "In the borough of Volchin, in today's center of the collective farm, Kamensky District, 260 years ago, in the Poniatowski family, who were the past owners of Old Volchin, there was a boy born by the name of Stanislaus Anthony, who became king in 1764."

I notice that this name is Anthony, not August. I compare the originals and discover there are two different names and different authors for the sections. I consult my guidebook to Poland, which lists Stanislaw Poniatowski, no middle name and a different spelling for the first name. I'm about to phone my Polish-speaking friend when I realize that there's a danger she could give me yet another spelling. All this is unimportant, anyway, and, for the hundredth time since I began this project, I vow to relax my standards of perfectionism.

Although this king lived in Volchin only for the first three years of his life, his remains—originally buried in St. Petersburg—were moved to Volchin and reburied in the Troisky Church in 1938.

As if to anticipate the reader's boredom about the long-lost king, the author segues into present-day Volchin, which is located near the junction of the Pulva and Bug Rivers and is "not any different from any other modern village in the Brest region." Of course, according to this "history," the village was indeed different. Back in the 18th century, the farmstead of Volchin, owned by the famous Chartariski and Poniatowski families, was one of Poland's cultural and political centers. At that time, the village attracted renowned musicians, politicians, poets, artists, and ministers, many of whom debated the great issues of the day. In short, Volchin was a haven for the rich and famous.[8]

In 1792, when Stanislaus August Poniatowski was still king of Poland, "Volchin had 13 Christian and 37 Jewish fiscal houses for manufacturers." It's unclear if these were homes or places of business. In the center of town, there was a stone village hall and marketplace. The yeshiva was made of wood. There was also a cloth factory from 1792 to 1830.

In the 1820s, many buildings were renovated, including the palace. The palace park, a 42.6-hectare complex bisected by a canal with beautiful cascades and hydroelectric devices, included not only the 36-room palace and the church but a theater, greenhouse, hothouse, pavilions, workhouses, and an archives building. One of these buildings had been the birthplace of King Poniatowski.

The only mention of World War II in this "history" concerns the church collections, which had to be stopped at the beginning of the war. After the war, many of the region's Poles immigrated back to Poland.

The church's priest also left Volchin, and the church was later closed. Over the years, the book laments, this once-adored and beautiful church had been robbed, destroyed, and abandoned.

But the story of the church did not end there. In 1988, a prominent Polish group visited Volchin. In the ex-king's burial place, they found fabric with the Poniatowski family emblem. The Poles asked the Soviet authorities to intervene and help preserve the last king's burial place. Even Gorbachev was involved in the matter. As a result, a joint Belorussian-Polish expedition was created to investigate the burial place and find the king's remains. Archeologists identified remnants of the king's coffin, covering material, and other memorabilia. However, none of the king's bones were found. The theory is that after the church and coffin were rediscovered, someone reburied the king elsewhere. All artifacts were transferred to Warsaw.[9]

The two typewritten pages are entitled "The Historical Reference about the Village of Volchin, Kamensky District." It begins with a geographical note: "The village of Volchin is located 35 kilometers (about 22 miles) northwest of Brest in Kamensky District on the Pulva River." Although it was unknown when the village was established, the section continues, for many centuries Volchin was a private estate, with various owners, including, of course, the father of the last Polish king, who was chosen with the support of Catherine the Great and the Prussian King Frederick II. Abdicating the throne in 1795, Stanislaus August Poniatowski spent his last years in Russia, where he died in 1798.

The final item in the package from Brest-Intourist is a geographical dictionary entry from the end of the 19th century: "There are 102 houses and 804 residents. There is a public school, an orthodox church, a Catholic church, a temple, and a local government. There are 14 small market shops. They have three street fairs a year. There is a working water mill."

There is that listing again. The same 102 houses, the same 804 residents, the same two churches, one temple, 14 shops, three fairs. This time, there's no reference to the population. To the Jews.

The last entry says that in 1894, Volchin's owners, the Puslovskis, moved away, and the Narbuts became the new owners of the town and its surrounding farmsteads. But wait—when I first scanned the material, I thought the dates ended at 1994. I look again at the translation; it says 1894. I search the original. Sure enough, it's slightly smudged. It could have been 1894. I should have known not to have expectations.

It seems that Volchin's history revolves around the architecture of its churches, the transfer of ownership, and the story of the last king of Poland. All the names—Soltan, Gusevski, Poniatowski, Chartariski, Puslovski, Narbut—are not those of the families I knew from Volchin. Of course, Jews were not allowed to own such land; yet, in this book's entire history of Volchin, there are no names of a single Jew. A village that, even to the admission of the Grodno archives, had "mainly Jews."

The history of Volchin during World War II is reduced to the cessation of church collections. The major event—the massacre that took the lives of all remaining Jewish people, 395 Volchiners—receives no mention. The only commission noted was formed to investigate the remains of the last king of Poland. No commission to investigate the remains of those shopkeepers, those craftspeople, those members of the fire brigade, those students, those mothers, those fathers, those children.

I remember what Hanna Kremer said about her return to Volchin in 1946. It was as if an atomic bomb had gone off. The town was still there, but the people were gone. Not a trace, as if they never existed.

Since I had been approached to write the Federation-sponsored documentary script, I doubled my efforts at searching for information. Not only was I investigating facts about Volchin for my research, but I had an even larger mission: to find out whatever I could about the fates of the Jews in other Belorussian villages and towns, particularly those who wound up in Brona Gora.

Now that the information is coming on both fronts, I'm banging my head against two giant stone walls. It's as if that old iron curtain has been drawn around Belarus; and instead of pulling the cord to open the view, I'm smack against a fake diorama glued on the impenetrable metal. The title of the diorama is, of course, in Russian, but I know it has something to do with the history of villages and cities. There are faces and buildings cut and pasted in a varnished collage. On closer look, the buildings include an ornate stone church; the faces are those of priests and non-Jewish property owners and—wait, there he is—the profile of the last Polish king. On closer examination, underneath the Russian title, letters emerge. Faded like pentimento, is the line, "Where are the Jews?"

Feeling desperate and almost desolate, I return to one of the places I began—the YIVO Institute. I call Dina Abramowicz, the elderly woman who first helped me locate Volchin on the map. I tell her about the proposed documentary and the information I'm seeking on the Brona Gora massacre. If anyone can help, it will be this woman, who worked in the Vilna ghetto library from 1941 to 1943 and who is one of the world's foremost authorities on the Jews of Eastern Europe.

I explain the nature of my mission. She asks me to send her a letter from the documentary maker assuring that we will give YIVO credit for research. She also tells me that she's extremely busy and can only do so much. When I tell her about our trip, she asks me to spell Brona Gora. Then she wants to know where it's located. She will make time, she tells me, to look in some of her reference materials. There is a book about Brest, she says, published in Israel, and other documents. If she finds something, she won't have time to translate, but she'd be happy to give me the gist if I come in person. I quickly fax her a letter, signed by the videographer, and, as always, I hope for the best.

Yet, yet, yet, if Dina Abramowicz hasn't heard of Brona Gora, then what chance do I have that there will be more materials chronicling this tragedy? How can it be, how can it be, that 50,000 people—no, not peaceful Soviet citizens, but peaceful Jewish citizens—how can it be that these 50,000 human beings disappeared off the face of the earth? Did anyone ask, "Where are the Jews?" We have no evidence of them—rumors maybe, but nothing substantial. Therefore, these figments of myth, this so-called race of people never existed.

I think again of the repression and bureaucratic red tape that my grandmother overcame to arrive in America and how she managed to make *her* existence known despite a language barrier. On one of the tapes, responding to my question about how she learned English, Masha says, "I don't know. Just by picking it up, from the kids." In Brooklyn, she couldn't go to school because "it wasn't until midnight that I finished from the kitchen."

Masha gets more melodramatic: "I cannot tell you how I lived out. It's only God, God was with me. That's why, now in my old age, I believe in God."

According to Masha, her husband, Isaac, was no help: "I hated him like poison because he made me to be a slave for the whole family. For him, he had fun. If he wanted to pick himself up and go to Coney Island, he did. He told me that I'd live like a princess. And when we came to this country, I had to work like a dog."

Even if Masha was self-aggrandizing, it was true that life in America had its toll. First, after Norma eventually mastered English and skipped ahead several times through the years, she came down with the dreaded diphtheria. The entire family had to leave the house—even the furniture was moved out—and Norma was quarantined with Masha.

"My mother wouldn't leave my side for a minute," Norma interjects on this tape. "I remember I was dead. I suddenly revived, and my mother was crying bitter tears." As Norma speaks, her voice lowers with emotion. This was probably the only time in her life that she had her mother to herself.

After months of recuperation, Norma was ready to attend high school. But then Masha became seriously ill, and a major life change was in the cards.

Before I continue with this tape, I pick up another, recorded during one of my last interviews with Masha, because I vaguely remember something else she had said about this time. By then, my grandmother had an illness of another kind, and I'm again amazed at how fragmented her responses had become. My questions yield little information other than, "I don't know."

"Do you remember in Brooklyn, being sick?"

"I got sick," Masha states, and that is all she says on the subject.

I thought there would be more on this tape, but I also seem to have a faulty memory.

After a series of questions, followed again by, "I don't know" or "I don't remember," I ask her about her daily life.

"How could I know?" she says. "Just like a baby. Very little, very little I know. Oy *vay!* Nothing. I don't know a goddamn thing. Like this happened yesterday, but I don't know what it is."

I stop the tape, riveted by a sudden insight—that's what happened to the Jews. They are victims of disappearing memory. All of Eastern Europe has collective Alzheimer's disease. They are just like babies. They know very little. Nothing. Not a goddamn thing.

The closest I ever came to shtetl life was my exposure to Woodridge, New York, in the Catskill Mountains. During the Depression, my grandmother Masha suffered from respiratory problems. Her doctor said she was literally choking to death in Brooklyn and prescribed "country air." The Catskills were already a popular destination for those with tuberculosis, a vacation retreat, and one of the few American rural regions with a concentrated Jewish population. The plan was to find a house big enough to accommodate Masha's family, as well as provide business opportunities.

In Woodridge, Masha's family found a three-story house that was, according to my mother, "big and ugly." The top floor was reserved for the children and was dubbed "the penthouse." The children, undoubtedly instigated by the older teens, decorated the space with garish colored lights, thus ensuring that few adults would trudge up the stairs. Masha converted the second floor into apartments for the farming families who came to town during the winter so their children could attend school. On the first floor, they created a *shul* and Hebrew school for my grandfather Isaac.

While Isaac struggled to attract a congregation, Masha assumed most of the cooking and cleaning responsibilities for the tenants, who were becoming more frequent year-round. It didn't help that Isaac, already in his 50s, would dissolve into jealous rages over his young and beautiful wife's flirtations with the "customers."

Longing

According to Masha's tape-recorded recollections, "I had a couple of people who came for the whole summer. First a man whose brother had a barbershop in town, then another from the butcher shop. My husband hollered from the street that all the men were coming to me to stay because I'm in love with them."

My grandmother hotly denied this accusation, insisting that she had no time for such a frivolous thing as love. As the family later learned, she eventually made the time for at least one special person.

The children became well-entrenched in the village's school and social life, but Masha and Isaac separated and later divorced. The *shul* became a dining room and my grandmother's bedroom; to make ends meet, Masha turned her home into a full-fledged, strictly kosher boardinghouse named the "Wayside Inn." Especially in the summer, her children worked at local businesses and contributed their earnings to the family pool. Credit, trades, and goodwill often took them through the long, cold winters.

Although I knew Woodridge when I spent my summers there (until my late teen years in the early '60s), I was always fascinated by what village life must have been like year-round, what it must have been like to live in a town that was primarily Jewish. In my experience in Brooklyn's Flatbush, Jews were parents, relatives, teachers, businesspeople, professionals. I couldn't believe that here was a village where truck drivers, street sweepers, and milk deliverers were Jewish. I couldn't believe that here was a village where being Jewish was taken for granted, a way of life, a common experience. Here was a village like another one far away—even the first two letters were the same—Woodridge and Wolczyn, or Volchin.

Of course, the Jews of Volchin, like those throughout Eastern Europe, were forced to live in close proximity by government-backed anti-Semitism, especially after Hitler took power; whereas the Catskill Jews lived together by choice. But in daily customs, social hierarchy, and even in environmental details, there were many similarities. One main street, a nearby river, a church and a synagogue, public school and religious instruction, a mill; the climate, the ambience—a provincial life whose primary access to the outside world was the railroad.

I play back my tape of Hanna and that of my mother, recorded during her 80th birthday party, and list both villages' qualities. The parallels are eerie. Hanna says, "Volchin was 90 percent Jewish. The gentiles were the Polish farmers." My mother says of Woodridge, "Almost everyone was Jewish. There were some gentiles, but not in the town itself. They lived in neighboring farms."

As in Volchin, the non-Jewish children around Woodridge attended school but normally didn't socialize with the Jews. When my mother mentions that her high school principal was an Irish import who took charge of the school like a tyrant, I remember Hanna saying that the police and teachers were non-Jews coming from different towns.

My mother tries to reconstruct the village of Woodridge by visualizing the main business street, curving up a hill, and describing the various shopkeepers. This is the same thing that the surviving Jews of Volchin did when trying to list the names of the dead families.

On my mother's tape, she states, "Smith's Drugstore."

I hear my voice saying, "Smith—a non-Jew?"

My mother, who sounds surprised at my comment, says, "Nobody questioned these things. Nobody thought of anti-Semitism in those days." Of course, she means, nobody in her immediate world.

Even for Hanna, who went to school with Russians and Poles, childhood was a protection of sorts. In her immediate world, she too felt safe. "I heard about anti-Semitism," Hanna says, "but I didn't feel it."

Most noticeable and poignant to me is the longing I hear in both women's voices. For a moment, Hanna Kremer puts aside her later associations and conjures earlier, cherished memories: "We went by foot, by bicycle. We had a lake, which fell into the Bug River. . . . We went swimming in the water; we had a *mikva* [ritual bath] too. . . . The scenery was so beautiful, I mean the way I remember it. . . . There was a place we used to go for walks Saturdays. The beautiful blossom trees and the flowers were unbelievable, and the smell of the narcissus, and the peonies were so big. . . . Volchin was very picturesque. I miss it many times. I miss the people—and the town." What she didn't say was, "as it was."

In reminiscing about Woodridge, my mother says: "In the winter, we went ice skating on Silver Lake and we had marvelous sleighing parties. In the summer, we went swimming in the river. We were a group of tightly knit friends. We had a wonderful life, with hindsight now. At the time, I thought it was terrible. We all wanted to get out of town and see the world." What teenaged Norma and Hanna, seven years younger, didn't know was that in the 1930s, the world was becoming more and more ominous for the Jews.

Hanna Kremer told me about another Hannah, spelled with an *h* at the end, who lives in England. This Hannah, Hannah Williams, is Shmuel Englender's cousin. According to Hanna Kremer, Hannah Williams, her mother and father, and her six siblings "were lucky people," leaving Volchin for Israel, where Hannah met and later married an Englishman.

Although she left Volchin as a young girl, Hannah Williams had visited the village three times since 1993 and gathered information. Not expecting much, I write to Hannah.

"I have heard from my cousin Shmuel about your visit to Volchin," Hannah answers. Then she apologizes for not being able to remember my family because she was only eight years old when she left Volchin. But, she proudly adds, "I was the first Jewish person to visit Volchin since the war." By that I know she means recently, because Hanna Kremer and her uncle had visited shortly after the war.

When Hannah Williams went the first time, she taped villagers speaking about the Jewish people during the war. She would be happy to send this tape to me, along with material about her visit, if I am interested. If I am interested? Could there be any question?

She ends her letter with, "I was delighted to hear from you."

I feel I have just connected with another lost relative, and the thought of receiving more information about Volchin leaves me almost breathless. Hannah's envelope also contains two photocopies: a Yiddish letter and a photo of Jewish children before the war. It is the same photo I saw at Hanna Kremer's, of the religious Hebrew school in July 1936, the picture with my cousin Sala.

I give the Yiddish letter to a translator. She says it's very difficult to understand, and though she can make out "November 27," she can't decipher the year. The letter begins, "Dear children," and is signed, "Your father, Yerachmiel." After preliminaries, Yerachmiel writes, "I have milk and honey. Right now I do not have milk because the cow is expected to give birth soon . . . otherwise I have everything to eat. It should only continue this way that I will not miss anything until I will be called."

I don't know if this is a literal description or a veiled message. If it's written right before the war or during its early years, perhaps he's assuring his children that life is okay for the time being. Then, Yerachmiel speaks about Berel, who is a bookkeeper in Visoke, earning 300 rubles a month and paying 10 rubles a month for board. Finally, he mentions "the old man who still travels to Brisk [Brest] for merchandise and keeps the store open for him." Afterward, there's a paragraph of greetings from Mineh, who also mentions Berel and describes making a dress with an apron and being ill in Visoke for eight days.

This is a letter of family news, with possible forebodings. Certain words and images make me think it was written years earlier than I had assumed, perhaps even during my grandmother's time. I wish I knew more. I wish I knew who Yerachmiel, who Berel, who Mineh were.

Another letter—this one thick—from Hannah Williams in November tells me more. Before she left Volchin for Palestine in October 1936, Hannah went to a Polish school for two years with Jewish, Polish, and Russian children. Each Friday, the children had religious instruction. Her mother, who was Shmuel's sister, told her there were 100 to 110 Jewish families at that time; she thinks there are now about 500 people in Volchin, mostly Russians.

In the massacre, she writes, Hannah lost most of her aunts, uncles, and cousins. Her father's brother and his family were massacred in another village. In a bit of historical gossip, she relates that there is a shrine in Volchin marking the place Napoleon stayed on his way back from Russia. Yet, I'm confused. With all the "history" I received about the last Polish king, I saw nothing about Napoleon. I feel sure, as sure as I am that Jewish life is missing from the book *Memory,* that had such a noted figure as Napoleon visited Volchin, there would at least have been a special chapter.

In response to my query, Hannah says she has not heard about the only Volchin/Visoke *Yizkor* (Memorial) Book. Compilations of articles and other memorabilia on the Jewish community of one town, most of which were published after World War II, these books are unique records of a lost people. When I discovered that there was one printed in 1948 about Volchin/Visoke, I contacted many sources, including YIVO. No one had a copy. Hannah, however, promises to investigate her contacts and get back to me.

Best of all, Hannah sends me her special gift—the audiocassette she recorded when she first visited Volchin. The tape includes eyewitness accounts about Volchin during the German occupation. Although the Kremers tell me that their copy of this cassette is difficult to understand, I nevertheless send off my copy to the translator, hoping that something is decipherable.

Hannah Williams's package also includes some articles she wrote for her local Jewish magazine about her visit to Volchin. The first, entitled "A Journey to My Birthplace," begins: "I have fulfilled a lifetime ambition. I had a dream for many years of visiting my birthplace. . . . Until a few years ago, it was impossible to visit the little villages because the communists would not allow any tourism."

Then Hannah relates how she corresponded with a Volchin town hall employee named Svetlana, asking whether it was possible to visit the town. A series of letters ensued, and Hannah received an invitation. Her friends and family kept asking her why she wanted to go. Her answer: "This is something I have to do, and I want to do it before it's too late."

Hannah Williams and her husband began their journey on June 23, 1993. June 23 is another auspicious date, a day after the anniversary of the German invasion. They stopped first in Warsaw, then traveled to Brest, and from there drove to Volchin. They went to her correspondent's home, a small three-bedroom structure, complete with appliances, television, and VCR—a world away from the one Hannah remembered, a world with houses lacking electricity and indoor plumbing.

Svetlana, I recall, is the name of the police officer's wife, the woman whose house we visited when I was in Volchin. Hannah is now describing that same house. Unlike my cool reception, Hannah enjoyed a cup of tea and gave gifts to Svetlana's children. Afterward, Svetlana took Hannah and her husband on a tour of the village. They stopped at the property of Shmuel's parents, her aunt and uncle, who owned a bakery. The old house had burned down. Hannah cried when she saw the new one that stood on the same location and remembered the happy times. All her relatives who lived there, except for Shmuel, were killed.

During their tour, Hannah did see a few remaining old houses. Svetlana had explained that they were preserved so that the younger generation would know that it was once a Jewish community. Knowing what I do of Belarusian historical preservation, I wonder if this is true or if they're just abandoned houses that no one wants to bother rebuilding. My belief system has been seriously damaged.

Through Svetlana, Hannah met an old man and asked him if he remembered anything that happened during the war. He said, "Yes," and she invited him and an elderly woman to Svetlana's house to record their stories. Hannah explained to them that she needed some record of her family history, her reason for taping: "I have one cousin. . . . He is the only relation from Volchin I have left alive." She was speaking about Shmuel.

The man told Hannah how the Germans kept the Jews in the ghetto and held many in the church for a while. In her article, she writes what she learned: "Some of the old and young were murdered early on; some went to work for the Germans. And in 1942, they took the rest of the community outside of the village and shot them and left them in the fields. The people from the village, Polish and Russian, dug a big hole and put the bodies in one big grave—of my relations and many more, 395 of them—and buried them."

Probably the most emotional moment for Hannah was returning to the house where she once lived. She remembered that it was near the synagogue, which had become a factory. Opposite this site, she noticed a little house with a sunken roof. "I felt something inside me," she writes, "and I turned to my husband and said, 'I am sure this is the house where we lived.' We stood looking at it and I felt sad, remembering my childhood. They were happy days."

A woman passed and Hannah asked her who had lived there. The woman answered that it was the Berezowskis—Hannah's family. "I couldn't move. It was a terrible feeling. I had recognized my old home. She told me nobody lived in it because they do try and preserve these places."

Hannah then showed the women photos of her relatives and asked if anyone looked familiar. "Yes," the woman answered, pointing to a girl. "I know her. I went to school with her. She used to be my friend."

"I felt so happy," Hannah conveys, "that somebody did recognize and remember my relations." I know how Hannah felt.

Hannah met more people who corroborated the story of the Jews living in the church, how the Jews were tortured, the conditions and hunger in the ghetto, and the massacre.

The next day, Hannah and her husband went to find the cemetery, but there was nothing left except for some large stones. It was like a jungle, and Hannah crouched, searching in the overgrown grass for a stone, something with Yiddish writing. But there was nothing.

At the massacre site, Hannah walked in the open field, emotionally wrought. She describes her feelings: "I just laid by the grave and cried and cried. I had a little Bible with me and said Kaddish. . . . I kept thinking that if my dear father had not taken us out from that village in 1936, my mother, father, brothers, and sisters would have been here."

Hannah also visited the other villages, including Wolkovyst, where she noticed that as in Volchin, the people were well-dressed, there were many cars, and the shops showed expensive goods that no one could afford. Despite these outward signs of prosperity, there was only one small light in each large store because electricity was too expensive, and food was very scarce—mostly bread, potatoes, and borscht.

As I read this account, something clicks. The name *Wolkovysk*. I go to my files of family papers. There on the petition for naturalization for Masha Lew, I glance down at her husband's name, Isaac, and his place of birth, Wolkowisk, Poland, August 15, 1876. *Wolkovysk—Wolkowisk—* this must be the same town.[1] The town of my grandfather. I had looked at my maps endlessly to find this name but couldn't. Here it is on Hannah's itinerary. *Bashert*.

Every time I read another account, I see another spelling of a village, a different surname spelling, a different fact. For me, it has the effect of spilling ice water over my eyes. It keeps me alert; it gives me pain. I want so much to be accurate, to tell the story with dignity. If I let out these facts as I hear them, will I be barraged by those contradicting me, accusing me of inaccurate reporting, of being lazy, of being a worthless relater of the lost stories? I must relax. This is all negative thinking.

After all, I'm not a historian, I remind myself. As I repeat this internal dialogue and feel some of the tension leave my temples, I also ask myself if all these rationalizations are not just that—rationalizations for not delving deeper, for not doing more.

At the end of Hannah's letter, she writes, "I don't think that any of us will ever know the real truth of what happened in the Volchin massacre. As I have been told in my visits to Volchin, each time, I heard different stories of what happened there." Yes, Hannah, you are right. And I must go on.

By the time Masha moved from Woodridge back to Brooklyn, before the start of World War II, my mother was again attached to the small village she had tried to escape. While my mother was a single woman living in Manhattan, she met my father, whose family built a small house in Woodridge. My father's parents, Latvian immigrants, had dreamed of living in a village after years of operating a sweater business in New York. Perhaps they too needed to get back to those shtetl roots.

That house, designed by my grandfather, complete with a secret door to the attic and a multiroom cellar, became our summer retreat. For me, growing up in the 1950s, the brown-shingled cottage, fenced by towering pines, was a place filled with curious passageways and corners; a place jammed with rowdy children, screaming adults, and card-playing grandmothers; and, always, a place imbued with the sounds of Yiddish and the aromas of the Old Country.

But the most exciting part of my summers in the country were my trips to the village, especially on Saturdays, when all the fathers were there and the hotel guests were arriving and departing. The streets were thick with car fumes and steamy air, the sidewalks jammed with sweaty-faced children and squeaky-beaked birdlike tubes hanging from toy-store ropes. To escape the adults, we reveled in refreshing egg creams, created from spritzes of seltzer bottles aimed into paper-cone-top metal holders, and the click and clatter and bells of pinball machines verging on the precarious "tilt."

I loved going to the village because I loved the locals: the hardware store owner, Mr. Hecht, who tried to best me in my tongue clicking; my uncle Abe, owner of the toy store, who slipped me candy bars while I skimmed the latest comic books; the butcher, who allowed us to construct hills of sawdust on the floor; Lillie, my mother's high school friend, who owned the luncheonette where we ate BLTs and french fries away from the disapproving eyes of our grandmothers.

And there were the other village regulars—the non-Jews. My favorites were the nightclub owner, who was so huge he had to remove the back-seat of his car; and the black albino girl I called "Albie," not out of any disrespect but because I didn't know her real name. Albie lived in the first house on the main street, and I often saw her peeking from behind her curtains or sitting alone on the shaded area of her porch, shielded from the sun. I felt so sorry for Albie, figuring she must have felt lonely, resembling a black person but with the pinkest, whitest skin.

When I look back at those years, I realize that my summers there were the only times I truly felt at home. Woodridge represented a way of life, a life of a Jewish community, that is no more. Woodridge was my village, my shtetl.

Throughout her life, my aunt Ray, who spent her childhood in Volchin and her adolescent and subsequent vacations in Woodridge, used those two places as her frames of reference. When describing Volchin, which she remembered as a daughter of a wealthy man who traveled and managed property, she said, "It was nicer than Woodridge. Woodridge was a filthy town. In Volchin," she insisted, "you could eat off the floor."

Volchin takes on more reality to me as I read the translation of Hannah Williams's cassette. The title on the tape is "The Russian People of Volchin Telling Their Stories about How the Nazis Killed the Jewish People in 1942."

Side A begins with a man whose last name is Zaretski. He tells of his father: "He was a friend of your people, Jews. . . . They trusted him. When they needed to borrow money, they came to him. . . . They came to him to fill in mattresses with straw. . . . Our family, my father, was very close with Jews till the end."

My enthusiasm wanes as my doubt rises. I turn to the last page, page 10. I hope that I will not find 10 pages of how the locals loved the Jews. After all I've come across on this, my search through the past, I can't take any more distortions.

I read on. Zaretski says, "When the ghetto was organized, Volchin's Jews used to come to my father and buy things." Finally, reality must have set in, and he changes his thoughts. "Everybody was very afraid. It was horrible. . . . The same fate was expected by not only you but by us."

The next man to be interviewed is Dimitry Petrovich Takachuk, who knew Hannah's father and remembers when the Jews were forced into the ghetto: "They began to kill them. . . . They gathered the elders . . . and killed them. . . . The younger ones were driven away to work. Where, I don't know, and what happened to them, I also don't know. Nobody knows for sure who was taken where . . . because the Germans surrounded them and took them someplace. I don't know who dug the holes." At that time, he says, he lived in a nearby village.

Then in a series of quick questions and answers, Takachuk rattles off the names of the dead Jews and returns to the time before they were killed: "The ghetto was located behind the church, and it was surrounded with wires. In the right brick house, there was the police. There was the police chief and policemen who saw that no Russians would bring any food into the ghetto. . . . It was horrible, because if a policeman had caught them, they would have shot them immediately. That's why almost nobody knows who really was helping."

A watchman, Takachuk says, was killed because he inadvertently shot someone. Then the Germans placed an artillery station on a hill and began shooting people from there.

The next speaker is Yurchok Anatoly Dimitrevich, who recalls names—Scholnik, Nastigal—and professions. "There was a tailor, Dancha. I don't remember his last name. . . . The Nazis took him with them, and he sewed their uniforms." When Dancha returned to Volchin, he found that his family had been killed.

Dimitrevich insists that local people helped, although he isn't specific; instead, he veers toward how Jews tried to escape. One in particular, Muska, was shot by a policeman. Except for those isolated incidents, the Jews were locked in the ghetto. "They lived there very poorly. They were given only 150–200 grams of bread. However, that wasn't real bread, because half of it was sawdust." And he tells the rest:

Jews spent the whole winter of 1941–42 there. In the fall of 1942, Germans came and said they would transfer them to the Visoke ghetto, where living conditions were better.[2] Everybody gladly gathered together. There Germans brought in wagons. Big families received two wagons, while small families received only one. . . . At this time, workers were brought in from Kotechi to the place where sand and gravel were extracted, and they dug the hole where all the Jews were put after they were killed. About 400 Jews were killed from Volchin and Chernavchich. Among those, there were no young people or those who were capable of working. The ones who were capable of working were in Chernavchich, where they were building a road.

Children were killed when the Germans hit their heads on the ground. I myself did not witness it. At that time, I was delivering food to those Jews that worked on building the road.

When Dimitrevich returned, he learned what happened to the Jews at the massacre site: "They were immediately surrounded by the police. There were about 20 policemen and three Nazis. Nazis were killing them."

There they are again. Contradictory facts. This man says there were three Nazis and 20 policeman. I think back to the first account I heard from Shmuel, stating there had been two Nazis; and I recall my husband's skepticism regarding such a small number. Perhaps he wasn't so wrong after all.

Finally, Dimitrevich recounts that in 1944 when the Red Army came, he was working as a teacher. A prosecutor and other authority figures came to Volchin and collected information about the massacre. They opened the hole and removed a few passports from the people on the top, including the tailor. I doubt this part of the story. The naked Jews would have had no place to put their passports, and why would the Nazis have thrown in the passports?

Hannah questions a woman named Vera Vladimirovna Makarevich Shpagina, who speaks about a friend of her father's, Srulya Stach: "He was a joiner—he made tables. In the evenings, he used to climb under the wires and run to us . . . and my mother used to give him flour or potatoes . . . and something to drink. We walked him back to the ghetto along the river. Everybody was afraid that he would get caught and killed. . . . Everybody was starving in the ghetto."

As to the final hours, Shpagina says, "I don't know about those because I was in Brest." Another one who conveniently was away. But, later in the conversation, she seems to forget what she said, or perhaps she tells what she heard from others:

In the morning, the Jews were told to get together, and they did. Some walked by themselves; those who couldn't walk were given wagons. They were told they were being taken to Visoke. . . . Before that, they got together our people with shovels and made them dig a hole. Once the Jews came to that spot, the Germans started shooting at them.

When Germans were killing the Jews, some Russians fell in the hole because their hearts couldn't stand it. They knew those Jews very well. They used to go to school together and to the stores that the Jews kept. [The Jews] were tailors and shoemakers. Also, when some locals used to need money, they went to the Jews to borrow. Many of [the Jews] were very good people. They gave money because in their synagogue they had a fund for helping people in financial need. They brought in matzo to school, and all of us ate it.

They healed my father. They came and told me to take the money . . . and go, near Warsaw, to the tuberculosis sanatorium, where my father stayed for two months. . . . At first, to send my father there we planned to sell the cow. However, the Jews said that we couldn't do that because after my father would come back, he would need fresh milk. They gave my father 100 zlotys, which he used to go to the sanatorium. Not one local Russian gave any money.

One line in particular sticks in my throat like undigested oatmeal: "When the Germans were killing the Jews, some Russians fell into the hole because their hearts couldn't stand it." Maybe this is what Shpagina was told, or maybe this is what she needed to believe.

In other reminiscences, Shpagina talks about the blacksmith, the wallpaper hanger, the butcher who cut cattle, the Jewish woman who sold fabrics, the shoemaker. Suddenly, she breaks from these memories and a stronger one emerges:

I also remember how they drove the Jews to the execution. . . . All of them got together with the children and went until the hole where the Russians were standing with the shovels. The Jews started screaming. Their screams were heard as far as we were standing. . . . We could hear the scream-ing. Nazis were shooting, drinking schnapps when they got tired, and then went back to shooting. It was horrible.

The wife of one of the people who buried the Jews, his name was Alexei, said that after he came back he didn't eat anything for two days and he was sick. He was laying around like he was dead.

The Jews went to their death silently. They said that they have a book that says all of them should die. One of the killed was a miller. . . . He had a very beautiful wife and a daughter, Riva. . . . They were forced to strip down. Many men couldn't watch that and turned away. It was horrible.

I'm confused. First Shpagina says she could hear the screaming, then she says the Jews went to their deaths silently. And, unless the translator has mixed up the names of the speakers, this Shpagina had previously said, "I don't know about those [last hours] because I was in Brest." Now, she seems to remember seeing the Jews going to their death, hearing their screams.

I flip back in her testimony and see she has more memories that sound as if she was there: "They took with them some things. However, those things were taken away from them and then sold in the synagogue. The local residents who didn't have any conscience used to buy them. They bought pillows and comforters."

When questioned about certain Jewish classmates, Shpagina reverts to ignorance: "I don't know anything. They were either taken to Brest to work, or they were shot here. I don't know because they didn't let us close to them. When the Nazis were killing, they never let us watch. They only let through the people who were digging the hole." Shpagina does recall that one woman from Chernavchich survived by hiding.

Shpagina also tells about how Jewish homes were bombed or destroyed and new ones were built. Again I wonder how these people seem to know detailed history of the Jews' homes but are vague about what happened to the occupants—except, of course, the ones the local villagers supposedly helped.

While I realize that the original tape was disjointed, that the translator may have had trouble understanding who was speaking, and that most of the villagers must have been very old, I am still disturbed by these memories. Certainly, these villagers remembered the Jews, remembered them as people in their community, as people with professions, as people with children who were their schoolmates. Certainly, as I have heard over and over again in the testimonies of those whose histories were tainted by collaborator guilt, some villagers must have been sympathetic to the plight of their one-time neighbors. When pressed for details, many suddenly claim to have been absent either by chance or by orders from above. Yet someone must have been there. To have known the details, conflicting and sketchy though they may have been, means someone must have been there or, at best, stood by watching, stood by listening, stood by collecting the leftovers.

Yes, these were villagers, basically simple people, with work to do and children to feed. Unlike such people elsewhere in the world, they had disturbing memories. Not so simple after all.

I can't imagine such a thing happening in the village I knew, Woodridge. I can't imagine the non-Jewish farmer I used to visit as a child, the one who used to put me on his wagon for a surprise hayride, I can't imagine him locking the latch on his hayloft. I can't imagine the non-Jewish man who delivered the milk, the one who left the sliding door of his truck open so we children could easily climb aboard, I can't imagine him closing his steel door.

I close my eyes and try to see Woodridge as it was in my childhood. I remember Albie swinging on her gliding couch, pretending to be happy on her porch. And, I'm sorry, so sorry, I didn't stop and talk to her. I'm sorry I didn't tell Albie to move over and make room for me.

I visited Woodridge a few times after we sold the house and was deeply saddened by its neglected and deserted character. Many store-fronts were boarded up; some were missing altogether, like gaps in a once-gleaming smile. The majority of nearby hotels and bungalow colonies were abandoned or razed; the remaining, most dilapidated, were run by religious or spiritual groups.

The formerly well-manicured gardens surrounding my family's house were overgrown with weeds and strewn with building supplies. The bungalow that we stayed in each summer looked like a storage shack for unused junk, not unlike the house on the Midler property in Volchin.

I recently returned again, prepared for the sadness of my previous visits. This time, I brought my daughter, Alexis, now 21, who hadn't been there since she was a child. A small, family-run hotel remained on my road, remained so close to my childhood memories. Most of all, I was happily surprised by my family's old property, lovingly restored by a new owner. Yet judging from other places in the area, still dominated by disrepair, my former family compound was merely an exception, possibly and probably a last holdout.

We drove to the village and passed the post office, built in unimaginative redbrick. As a teenager, my mother was an active participant in a nightly ritual. At seven, after listening to their favorite radio news program, the villagers marched to the post office for mail call. If my mother was lucky enough to have received a letter, she would display it prominently sticking out of her pocket. In my family, mail has always been important.

On the main shopping street, we found a parking spot. I took in the general ambience. Though this section had retained its ghost-town image, I was heartened by a busy restaurant and wholesale meat businesses. We got out of the car and checked some of the perpendicular streets. I knew Masha's boardinghouse was on Bank Street, but the street closest to the one in my memory bore the name of Maurice Rose. Of course, the street name could have changed, or I could have been mistaken about the location since I never saw the house itself. The Wayside Inn had been razed before my time.

Even though I had the opportunity to visit Volchin, I, of course, would never be able to see its life as a Jewish village. For that, I had to rely on secondhand reports. Thankfully, some were coming to me, the only way I was becoming accustomed to receiving information, via my mailbox.

The mail once again doesn't let me down. I receive the English translations of Shmuel's impressions and of his taped interviews, originally conducted in Russian and translated into Hebrew. My translator, an Israeli woman, says the job was complicated as Shmuel often interspersed Russian and Yiddish words. When I sift through the work—109 handwritten pages—I notice caked blobs of white correction fluid, notes in parentheses, crossed-out words, neat printing, brisk script, assorted inks, formal stationery, loose-leaf pages. This material was labored at, taken to work, discussed, and consulted about. In short, the translator lived with the work and, as an Israeli, must have known its worth.

I couldn't wait to begin. Page 1, entitled "The Summary of My Trip to My Hometown, Volchin, in Belorussia," presents Shmuel's longing: "For me in person, the trip to my hometown, Volchin, was a dream come true, which I had since the day I left the village on April 15, 1941. For 56 years, I couldn't stop feeling the need to come, to see, and hear how an entire small community of Jews had been destroyed, that their only fault was being Jewish."

Even during the war when he was in the Red Army, and when he lay wounded in a small town near Gomel, all Shmuel's thoughts were of Volchin—walking the streets, visiting his home and family, praying in the synagogue, arguing politics with his friends. Despite rumors as early as 1943 of ghettoization, deportations, and killings, he still couldn't allow himself to believe that any harm could come to such peaceful people as the Jews of Volchin.

Collaboration

In 1944, when his army service was completed and he was in Siberia, Shmuel wrote a letter to his family at his home address as if nothing had changed. Every day, he expected an answer; when it finally came, it shattered all his hopes. Another person who lived in his home responded that all the Jews were taken in one day, shot, thrown into a pit at the edge of town, and covered with earth. One of Shmuel's brothers, the correspondent reported, came to Volchin a day after the massacre. Dirty, thin, and frightened, he darted around the house looking for his family. Without saying a word, he ran crying toward the pit. He was caught and shot.

On hearing this news, Shmuel was devastated: "It was so hard for me . . . to recover from that. . . . I was thinking and thinking . . . why do they deserve this? How can women, babies . . . they didn't commit any crime? How can humans do such a thing, without reason?"

And so, years later, Shmuel still felt compelled to go to Volchin, to visit the "grave" of his loved ones. For a long time, he couldn't fulfill his dream because of the Soviet regime. When he heard of the Israeli group being organized to visit Belarus, he enlisted. Although he was filled with trepidation about his emotional responses, he felt that at the age of 78, he had to take advantage of this rare opportunity. The group included two others with ties to Volchin—Dov and Drora, the children of Tama Birenboim and the grandchildren of Yerachmiel Stabesky. There he is, Yerachmiel, the man whose letter I had read, the man who was grateful for "milk and honey."

Shmuel begins the travelogue with his arrival in Minsk on June 18, 1997, and talks about his impressions of the former Jewish communities he passed the next day on the way to Brest. In the city, he visited the streets where he studied and shopped. There was nothing left of his past; new buildings replaced the old. He was "sad in my soul." That night, anticipating his upcoming trip to Volchin, he was unable to sleep.

The following day, the strong sense of loss continued as Shmuel, Dov, Esther, and Drora entered Volchin. They passed the ruins of a Jewish home, the former mill, the once-flowing river that was barely visible, on the way to their hosts, the Kuntz family. Later, they toured former homes of Jews—Shuster, Tarchenik, Zeltzer—until they arrived at the site of Shmuel's former home and his family's bakery.

There, on a hill in the center of town, stood another house. He says on the tape, "I didn't have the courage even to go in the house and to our yard."

By the church, the group passed two memorial statues for the Red Army soldiers and the partisans who died in the war and then some Jewish houses that were intact.

On the south side of the ghetto, the group photographed a stone wall, painted in white. Dov postulated that this wall was painted so that observers wouldn't notice that the stones had been taken from the Jewish graveyard.

As the group entered the ghetto area, they saw remains of burned houses within piles of garbage. The exterior of the synagogue survived. This was where Shmuel prayed and studied as a child and where he attended political meetings as a young man. This was where Shmuel's father, Itzhak (Isaac), had a regular seat next to Dov's grandfather Yerachmiel. The two became in-laws when Itzhak's daughter, Raisel, married Yerachmiel's son, Berel, who was apparently among what Dov said was about 6,000 Jews, some of them from Volchin, killed in July 1941 in the Brest Fortress. As was the custom, the memorial stone there indicates in Russian that those buried were civilians, not specifying that they were Jews.

The Israelis went inside Volchin's old synagogue, now a workhouse for the school. When Shmuel noticed the neglect and the machines, with no sign of the building's former use, his emotional reserves dissolved: "I couldn't hold myself. I remembered all the stages of my life, the connections to this place, and I broke into tears."

The group ended its first day in Volchin with a stop at the open field, 100 meters from the road to Visoke. At the gravesite of the massacred Jews, Shmuel stepped over a neglected wooden fence enclosing a pyramidal memorial stone topped with the star of the Red Army. The stone's plaque says in Russian, "Here in the year 1942, the German fascists shot 395 civilians from Volchin and Chernavchich." On top of the inscription, a Volchin resident named Polke, a soldier arriving with the Red Army, engraved a Star of David flanked by Hebrew letters saying, "Here buried," indicating that the dead were Jews. This is the only memorial to the town's Jews.

As Shmuel relates, "We stood by the grave, and with broken hearts, Dov and I said Kaddish and *Yizkor* [memorial service] for their memory. With great pain and tears, we left."

At the hotel in Brest, Shmuel learned about a village, Motikali, 25 kilometers from Volchin, where there is a six-meter-deep grave containing 500 Jews who had escaped from the Brest ghetto. They had been caught, killed, and buried in the village's Christian graveyard.

The next day, when Svetlana Kuntz and her husband, Gregory, Volchin's district police officer, picked up Shmuel for the drive back to Volchin, they detoured to Motikali and found the graveyard, where a stone says, "Here are buried 500 Jews who were murdered by the German fascists."

Shmuel and his hosts stopped nine kilometers from Volchin in Visoke, which once had a thriving and cultured Jewish population. Those Jews were either killed or transported to Treblinka, the probable fate of Hanna Kremer's immediate family. Shmuel visited the town's synagogue, now a clothing factory. There, he encountered women sewing. Explaining to them that this building had been a Jewish synagogue, most of them seemed impressed, though some looked at Shmuel as if he were from another planet.

In Volchin, Shmuel met the chairperson of the village council, Ivan Ivanovich.[1] After Shmuel explained his background, Ivanovich admitted he knew that there was a Jewish community in Volchin and was aware of the horror conducted by the German fascists, although he did not mention the locals' complicity. In school, Ivanovich said, this massacre is not studied; the young people are not aware of the atrocities.

To help remedy this omission, Shmuel asked Ivanovich to have the council continue to maintain the massacre site and erect a memorial for the Jews similar to the existing one for the soldiers and partisans. Shmuel feared that the village would extend the building (currently storing gas) over the massacre site and that the stone by the memorial would deteriorate further, resulting in no reminder of those who once populated the town, the Jews.

Ivanovich apologized for the stone's poor condition and pledged that if the Jews provided a new stone, he would build an extension leading from the main road to the site and erect a new fence around the memorial. Shmuel's second request, he said, was more difficult to grant because decisions such as erecting a memorial remained under the jurisdiction of the central government.

Before Shmuel left the meeting, he asked Ivanovich to procure documents relating to the massacre or lists of Volchin's Jews. The chairperson answered that there was no such material; although, in Shmuel's presence, he contacted other government officials who suggested searching the Brest archives. Ivanovich promised to do so in the near future.

After the meeting, Shmuel met an older woman on the street. He introduced himself and asked how the people felt about the village's Jews. With others around her nodding approval, she responded that when the villagers saw the hunger and suffering in the ghetto, when they heard the screaming and the shooting, when they learned about the terrible humiliation of undressing and how babies were lifted by their legs or arms, they thought that the Jews couldn't have had a god.

According to Shmuel, another female resident added, "It's a sure sign that not only don't you have a god, but you killed Jesus and this is why you got this terrible punishment."

Shmuel learned that the Jews were killed the day after Yom Kippur, when most of them had prayed to God asking for forgiveness. He too asks, "How did God see everything and not do a thing to stop it? How is it that he didn't turn the day to night, the light to dark?"

To the woman, all he could say was, "I really don't have an answer."

Shmuel signs off his introductory remarks, "Shmuel, the son of Isaac and Hinda Leah." The son of dead Jews of Volchin.

The first testimony Shmuel recorded was from Vera Vladimirovna Shpagina, the same woman Hannah Williams interviewed four years earlier. For the interview, Shmuel went to Shpagina's house, one of the few remaining buildings from the ghetto.

Shpagina was a resident of New Volchin (the Polish section) until 1939 and subsequently lived in Brest until the beginning of the war, when the bombings forced her family to flee. They returned to Volchin and moved into the home of Srulko, the Jewish carpenter and a friend of her father. This must be the same man called Srulya, who made tables, on Hannah Williams's tape.

As in her testimony with Hannah Williams, Shpagina repeats that she was in Brest on the day of the massacre. Also as in her previous testimony, she says she heard the screaming. How could she be inconsistent in two interviews unless she confused her own experience with what she heard from others—or unless her story was so rehearsed, because of guilt, repression, or fear of reprisals, that she repeated it rotely?

After Shmuel recorded Shpagina's testimony, he returned to the Kuntz house, where three elderly villagers gathered. The first to speak, Poltrok Ivan Pavlovich, who called himself Ivan, resided in the same house as before the war, not far from the Kuntzes. Before he began his testimony, he requested a glass of vodka "to make my memory sharper." As Pavlovich sipped his drink and his tongue loosened, two other villagers introduced themselves. One was Vivituk Pavel Ivanovich, 15 or 16 years old at the time of the invasion, and the other Kutshuk Genady Michaelovich, who speaks very little on the tape.

A methodological interviewer, Shmuel repeats many questions, trying to catch discrepancies and uncover details. From these three "witnesses" and the interview with Shpagina, he manages to cull a coherent and consistent picture of Jewish life in Volchin, from the German invasion to the village massacre. This is their story.

On the morning of June 22, 1941, after a strong bombardment and the retreat of the border watch, the Germans entered Volchin from the direction of the Bug River. After an hour or so of shelling, airplanes dropped bombs, one of which destroyed Shmuel's family house and bakery. German tanks moved down the main street, accompanied by soldiers on motorcycles and armed with machine guns. They continued toward Visoke, leaving behind a few German soldiers who assembled in front of the church.

A while later, more tanks and cars with soldiers arrived. Some of them entered the building of the Soviet Council, joined by two civilians who spoke German and Russian. These men then drove through the village and, with a microphone, ordered everyone to gather on the field by the church. When the people came, another German arrived, standing in his car, and shouted that Volchin had been released from the Soviets. From that point on, there would be a German government. Moreover, he warned, everyone must obey orders; anyone who resisted would be severely punished. In war, death is, he said, without trial.

"At first," Pavlovich reports, "they didn't make a difference between the Jewish and the Christian population. A few days later, an older German, maybe 50 years old, arrived. His name was Krauze and he brought a German female soldier and a few civilians who spoke Russian and German, and they started to organize a government."

They appointed a Polish resident, Korshneivsky, as head of the village. They also appointed an ex-prisoner, Rose, a Polish Catholic whose parents had a carpentry workshop and lived in New Volchin, as head of the police. Three or four men from neighboring villages, including opponents of the Soviet government and former criminals, became the police force. At first, the police wore stripes on their sleeves with the letter P for *Polizei,* and their job required them to follow orders from the Germans and Rose.

Shmuel remembers Rose as a fellow student. Even then, Rose was violent, anti-Semitic, and anti-Russian, and he excelled in the German language.

This line of discussion makes Shpagina defensive: "I want to tell you that the policemen were not saints, but they did what Chief of Police Rose and the Germans told them. There was the German Krauze and more than four Germans with him, who worked with a group of Catholic Poles that lived at the farms around Volchin."

Krauze lived with his wife and children in the former Soviet Council headquarters, and he had a big farm with animals tended by the villagers. According to Shpagina, Krauze was "kind of sympathetic, personally not involved, only gave orders." I guess to Shpagina, giving orders was not a culpable act.

For the governing of the Jews, the Germans also created a *Judenrat,* or Jewish Council. As each questioner lists the members, I cringe. Knowing that my uncle Iser was a respected member of the village, I keep expecting to hear his name. I'm so relieved that there is general agreement on the members: Shlomko Zufrik from the village mill, Avrum Kupershmidt, and Berenson from the mill of Kotera.

"Nobody wanted to be in the *Judenrat*," Pavlovich explains. "One day, the Germans called a few people and simply forced them to accept the job. . . . The Germans demanded that they collect all the Jews' gold—watches, necklaces, rings—and give everything to the Germans. Many times, they collected hidden belongings, which . . . the Germans and the police took for themselves. Besides this, the *Judenrat* organized people to clean the streets, German offices, and yards."

In the beginning of the occupation, before the young people were sent to Brest, the *Judenrat* formulated a list of those physically capable of cutting trees in the forest. These "workers" were then transported to the Bug River. Witness Michaelovich remembers his father doing this kind of work, which he says was very dangerous, with many injured and killed. Yet the job was popular because each worker received extra bread and occasional sugar.

Shmuel asks Shpagina where the police were located, and I'm not prepared for the answer: "Iser Midler's house. If you remember, they had such a nice house, with a lot of fruit trees in the yard. The chief of police was in his house, . . . the head of the village, and also the *Judenrat*, which didn't have a regular place."

I don't know why I'm so shocked. After all, it was a small village; everyone knew everyone else. I had been prepared for some identification, I thought. Still, to read Iser's name feels like a fresh wound. At least, I tell myself, he was not forced to administer unspeakable acts as a member of the *Judenrat*, an awful responsibility for a Jew. And then another question comes to me: If the Midler house was used for all these official purposes, what happened to the Midlers? Where did they go?

Shmuel presses Shpagina for more names of Jews, but she says she has forgotten. Again she mentions the carpenter, and again I'm unprepared for her answer: "I still remember Iser Midler. He was together with my father and another man, Moshko Zuberman, at the Fire Department."

This reminds me of a recent letter I received from Dov. Along with it was a faint photocopy of an old photograph, which I reexamine. It shows a group of 22 men, most of them in uniform. On the first row of seated men, underneath the man on the extreme left, Dov drew an arrow and wrote: "Isaak Midler." It's a photo of Volchin's Fire Brigade. Even though it's a poor reproduction, I can still see that Iser appears assured and comfortable, looks directly ahead, and is understatedly good-looking. If someone were to ask me to pick him out, without any indication of name, I would have no trouble. By now, I know him well.

When Shmuel was at Shpagina's, she asked her granddaughter to bring something from the closet. It was a photo. "This," she says in Shmuel's report, "is my father. This is Iser Midler. And on the other side, this is Moshko Zuberman in their uniforms." The same photo as Dov sent me.

Shpagina must have been about 19 in 1941, close to the age of Iser's oldest, Ida. They must have gone to school together; she must have known all the Midler girls. If only Shmuel had met me before he questioned Shpagina, perhaps he could have asked more. I will write to her, I decide. I will explain who I am; maybe she has more memories of the Midlers.

Shmuel must have been emotional when Shpagina said she remembers his sisters. And with prompting, she recalls seeing them a few times during the German occupation. I wonder if she saw the Midler girls too? Then again, as she did with Hannah Williams, Shpagina says that she really doesn't know much because the young were taken as workers to Brest, their fates unknown.

As his narrative continues, Shmuel tries to get his witnesses to tell their story chronologically. Shpagina relates that in the beginning, the Jews lived in their homes; after a few months, a ghetto was created. The police and the *Judenrat* went from house to house, telling the Jews where to go and to take only essentials.

Witness Vivituk Pavel Ivanovich says, "There was fighting and screaming among those who had to move. . . . Eventually there was no choice."

When the Volchin ghetto was organized, the Jews were transferred to already crowded houses and stores. The ghetto began east of the church; included the Midler house, the synagogue, and the home of Mendel Kaplan; and extended southward to the house Shpagina lives in now.

Jews were scattered wherever there was space, Shpagina says. "The sick and children lived in the synagogue; some people lived in storehouses, barns, and even cowsheds. If you remember, Mordeku had a grain barn, across from the Midlers' house. In that barn they put those who came from the town of Chernavchich." What she doesn't say is that they waited there until they too were massacred.

Chernavchich, about 32 kilometers from Volchin and 10 from Brest, is the same village, Michaelovich says, where some of Volchin's young people, who were sent to work in Brest, had been seen building a road.

Volchin's young adults were initially sent to Motikali, where they boarded the train to Brest. When Motikali is mentioned, Shmuel retells the story of his stopover there. Ivanovich fills in more of the story. His uncle was from that village, and everyone there knew about the Jewish massacre. Shortly after the Volchin Jews were killed, he says, a group of Jews escaped from the Brest ghetto. German soldiers, police, and villagers from all around chased after the fugitives. Many of the villagers were told that the escapees were partisans. Some Jews were caught near Kobrin, others near the town of Malorita. From this group, 500 were brought to Motikali because the German headquarters was near the graveyard and "help" in the killing process was thus readily available. One huge pit was dug and the Jews were shot there. Ivanovich thinks it's possible that some of these Jews could have been from Volchin or Visoke.

According to Shmuel's interviewees, the occupiers erected a fence around the Volchin ghetto that was about two meters high and patrolled by guards. Near the church, the fence was wooden; by the river, it was wire. "After they put the fence, it was impossible to get out of the ghetto without permission," Shpagina says. There were two entrances. One was for carts and horses and for removing the dead. It had a gate, locked with a chain. The other entrance, near the Midler house, was for pedestrians after they were checked by the police.

Shmuel asks Shpagina what happened to the things that the Jews left in their homes. "Policemen were the first, and after that all the rest of the people . . . took out what was good," she says. Some Jews hid things in their yards and had villagers dig out the treasures, which the Jews traded for a little food.

Ivanovich says, "People took from everything and emptied everything."

Life in the ghetto was very hard. Jews didn't work there, although those able were sometimes forced to do menial chores for the Germans.

"There was great hunger," Shpagina says. "The *Judenrat* gave everyone 200 grams of bread . . . and from time to time brought some milk for the children. . . . The Jews looked like skeletons, thin with big eyes. . . . A lot died from hunger and infection, but who, I don't know, because they were usually taken out at night and buried in the graveyard. . . . They ordered the village people to dig the pits and bury the dead. . . . I think one who died was Zelig . . . and another Meila Sendler, who was living across from [Shmuel's family's] bakery."

Ivanovich says that when his mother went to church on Sunday, she would see the Jews behind the fence. "They walked around like skeletons, thin with big eyes, reaching out, asking for a piece of bread or a potato. . . . When the guards weren't watching, some women would throw a few potatoes."

Strange, I think, that Ivanovich used the same words as Shpagina: "skeletons, thin with big eyes."

Shpagina also remembers that anyone caught transgressing in the ghetto was severely punished. They were assigned backbreaking work, "transferred," or shot—according to the German's mood. In one case, she recalls, Mendel Kaplan, the owner of a fabric store, climbed over the fence and crossed the frozen river toward another village, where he planned to exchange some material he had hidden for milk and cheese. On the way, he got caught and was arrested. He was brought to the police and beaten. The *Judenrat* intervened, and the police agreed not to turn Kaplan over to the Germans in exchange for fabric. Although Shpagina knows the name of the guard who informed on Kaplan, she withholds it to protect his family.

Michaelovich recalls the story of "the richest [Jew] in town," named Sobelman, who owned a big merchandise store and a factory that made roof tiles. This man was Shmuel's father's cousin. During the Soviet time, because of his wealth, Sobelman was declared "bourgeois"—a category of "undesirables" not allowed to live close to the border. Since Volchin was only about six kilometers from the Polish border, Sobelman was ordered to move to a town 50 kilometers away. His property was "nationalized" and confiscated. After the German invasion in 1941 and the subsequent creation of the ghetto, Sobelman and his family managed to return to Volchin.

Chief of Police Rose remembered the Sobelmans' former wealth and accused them of hiding goods. The Sobelmans claimed they had nothing and asked the *Judenrat* to find housing for the family and were relegated to living in Kaplan's windowless storage hut with hay-stuffed sacks for beds. Their two daughters were sent to work in Brest, joining the other young Volchiners.

One night, a distraught Mrs. Sobelman wandered outside her quarters, climbed the barbed-wire fence, and ran to the river and drowned herself. Pitying the grief-stricken husband, the *Judenrat* moved Sobelman to an unused corner of the synagogue. Unable to eat and ceasing to function, he eventually died of "a broken heart." Michaelovich says, "That was the end of Mr. Sobelman, the richest man in Volchin. This story you can't forget."

When Shmuel comments on the humiliating circumstances the Jews faced on a daily basis, Michaelovich says, "They had a very hard time. . . . Perhaps a few were like Sobelman, but I think most of them still wanted to continue living."

This story of the Sobelmans haunts me. I wonder again why some people have the will to go on living and others don't. I think of my own family and go back to the time of Masha's young married years. Suffering certainly clouded the personality development of her children and stepchildren. Some turned deprivation into survival techniques; others never adjusted to the losses.

When the family settled in America, there were only a few good years before the Depression hit. Life was particularly difficult for Jack, the oldest son of my grandfather Isaac Lev and his first wife. Jack bore the brunt of his father's misdirected ambitions. Creative and idealistic, Jack probably would have been happy as an artist, giving little thought to material concerns. Instead, his conservatively religious father ridiculed his bohemian views, and the closest Jack came to a palette of paint was by applying coats to people's walls.

But this life was only temporary, because Jack had had a dream since his youth in Eastern Europe: he wanted to go to Palestine.

In the 1930s, Jack attended Zionist meetings and worked when he could. He soon met a woman, Dina, a native of Bielsk-Podlaski whose "most inspiring" teachers had included Isaac Lev. Jack and Dina married and moved to the Bronx. Jack taught Hebrew and worked sporadically as a housepainter and for the Works Progress Administration.

At the time, Masha was still living in Woodridge. Although she was now divorced from Isaac, and she often claimed she had no time for boyfriends, my family had their own versions of her social life. Even after they divorced, Isaac never got used to Masha's ways.

When I interviewed Dina (see chapter 4), she said that Jack heard both sides of the story. "His father," she says, "complained about Masha and her behavior. But his father didn't approve of Jack either. And that's how I got an introduction to the family."

But Dina was always kindhearted. To her, Masha was "good, giving us a honeymoon—two weeks—at her boardinghouse, the Wayside Inn."

Masha's children learned to accept her male "friends," including one in particular who regularly shared her bedroom.

In a tape-recorded interview, my mother recalls, "They lived openly in the house, like man and wife. He gave my mother money. He had an invalid wife and two boys. Masha only slept with him. And when she later left Woodridge and went to Brooklyn to live with my grandmother, he came there. Masha lived openly with him in Brooklyn, too. They didn't make a thing about it. He helped support her. He got me a job in the fur district, where I worked for four years, and I went out with his son."

My mother was also totally sympathetic to Jack. "Since he was the oldest, Jack was completely abused by my father. He took the burden of my father's vitriolic temper. My father expected high standards from Jack, expected him to earn a lot of money and bring it to [their father]. My father was a very greedy, self-centered man. But Jack was adorable. He was artistic and sensitive, a gentle person. I loved him, I really did."

My mother, like her own mother, was always extreme in her judgment of people. When she liked someone, that was it.

Early in their married life, Dina gave birth to a girl. With an extra mouth to feed and Dina no longer able to work, Jack faced severe financial pressures. He became increasingly depressed, but conventional medical care was inadequate. In those days, people had little experience, or vocabulary, to deal with mental illness.

My uncle Gerson was close to Jack and called him a poet and a writer forced to drive a delivery wagon and do other menial chores. "The future looked bleak to him," Gerson comments on my reunion tape. "He fell apart. He was sick."

Although he spent some time in health-care facilities, Jack failed to respond to treatment. In 1936, he ended his life. He was 31.

Sometimes survival is just not an option.

Years later, when Jack's daughter, Shoshana, was a young teen, she became enthralled with Zionism. Her mother, Dina, said, "I didn't encourage her at all. She just wanted to go to Israel. There was no other dream."

After Shoshana went to art school, she went to Israel and became a pioneer in the kibbutz movement. As an artist and art therapist Shoshana remains a resident of the same kibbutz—one of the few women to successfully interweave personal creativity with collective living. Dina eventually moved to Israel and now lives in Ramat-Gan, only blocks away from Shmuel Englender and the Bars, my "Volchin" family. *Bashert.*

Unlike Jack, Shmuel chose to live. And one of his compulsions has been to record the stories of those Jews who had no choice.

In his interviews, Shmuel eventually gets to the most difficult part, asking about the last day Volchin's Jews were alive. In the morning, Shpagina's mother said that the Jews were gathered, dressed in their *Shabbes* (Sabbath) clothing. Shpagina (the same woman who claimed to be in Brest at the time) rushed out of her house to watch.

Their friend Srulko approached the fence to say good-bye, since he thought the Jews were being transferred to the Visoke ghetto. Srulko began to cry, and Shpagina's father reassured him that the war would soon end, and they would be neighbors again. Srulko replied, "I don't believe that anymore."

Shpagina relates the next events: "We saw the policemen together with the *Judenrat*, walking from house to house with lists, and collecting people from the lists. We saw the old and children gathered near the synagogue, waiting, some carrying packages in preparation for leaving the ghetto. We too believed that they were being taken to make things better for them. At about noon, everybody started walking to the police station and to Metrone's house. There were carts with sick people who couldn't walk. . . . After some time, a few Germans came and stood behind and in front of them. Around them stood unknown people without uniforms who spoke Russian, Polish, and German, and they all started to walk."

Again, Shpagina reports that she heard screaming and shooting. And she remembers that the next day, when she learned what happened to the Jews, a lot of people, including her parents, were crying. Shmuel presses her for the names of more eyewitnesses, perhaps someone who saw the executions. Shpagina says that one of the men who knew something, Yurchok Anatoly Dimitrevich, died a few months earlier. This is the man Hannah Williams interviewed.

When Shmuel asks the other witnesses about that fateful day, his body shakes with trepidation, as he interjects in the testimony. Pavlovich, by now having finished the bottle of vodka, says, "I am the only person alive from those who saw the poor people on their last day, how they were humiliated in their final moments, how parents and children were separated, how babies were killed being held by their legs, how they were shot, and their bodies thrown into the pit—all that I saw with my own eyes, and until today sometimes I dream about it."

After reading Pavlovich's description of that last day, I can understand how he needed a bottle of vodka—and how he still was haunted by those memories. According to him, preparations were under way before the massacre: "Two or three days before, people came to town from somewhere; a lot of village people were called up. The guarding around the ghetto was stronger, especially from the side near the river, because there were only wire fences. Perhaps they wanted to make sure the Jews would not escape to the river and drown themselves, which would be an easy death. A day before, the head of the village arrived with two policemen with lists. They called up people with horses and carts. They didn't say for what, only that the next morning they should come to Metrone's house. There was an exit gate there; and by Iser Midler's house, there was the police headquarters. . . . When Korshneivsky or the police were asked for what reason [the people were being gathered], they said they didn't know."

According to Pavlovich, on the morning of September 22, a day after Yom Kippur, his father was called for work detail but was not feeling well and asked his son to cover for him. Only 16 years old, Pavlovich was tall and healthy and accustomed to helping his father with chores. Taking food and drink for the day, though he didn't know what he would be called upon to do, Pavlovich set out for Korshneivsky's house, where he met other people from the village. There were also people from the village of Metrona, standing with horses; and near the German head-quarters, he saw unfamiliar Germans, many without uniforms.

Even with all these unknown people assembled for an upcoming action, Pavlovich claims no one, except perhaps the Germans and the head of police, anticipated the purpose of the gathering. After a few hours of waiting, members of the *Judenrat* and a few policemen entered the house of the head of the village. A half hour later, they all left for the ghetto. At about that time, someone informed Pavlovich that the Jews were going to be transferred to a larger ghetto.

Then a German and two translators told Pavlovich and five other Volchin "coworkers," including Dimitrevich (who was also present at the reopening of the grave), to follow the carts. They passed Metrone's house, where the Jews were still standing, and continued past the Catholic church to the edge of New Volchin, on the way to Visoke. There they turned right and waited in Denisko's barn.

At this moment in Pavlovich's narrative, Ivanovich interrupts. Although he was not an eyewitness to these events, he feels compelled to verify Pavlovich's testimony. The entire village, he says, knew well the story of the last day of the ghetto. That morning, the German Krauze; Rose, the head of the police; Korshneivsky, the head of the village; and the *Judenrat* walked from house to house and demanded that everyone congregate at the synagogue. There, the German read an announcement, translated into Yiddish by a member of the *Judenrat*, stating that within an hour everyone should collect their belongings, dress in their best clothing, and reappear to be moved to a bigger, more comfortable ghetto in Visoke. Carts would be provided for those unable to walk and for their belongings.

Before the hour was up, the *Judenrat* and the police returned to the homes and made sure no one was there. Then the Jews were ordered to walk toward the edge of the village, joined by more Germans and a few of the other unknown "guards." The sick were put on the carts, and the rest of the Jews started to walk toward Visoke. Two Germans led the convoy, along with the *Judenrat*; the unknown "police" and the "guards" from the other villages patrolled the sides of the convoy; and a few more Germans brought up the rear. "Like that," Ivanovich says, "they walked their last walk to death."

Ivanovich also thinks that only a few of the Germans and their helpers knew the true destination. The convoy walked until it reached the edge of the village, where the guards ordered the Jews to stop. After a while, they were told to turn right toward a pit, about 60 meters wide by 30 meters long, the same place from which Sobelman had taken sand to make roof tiles at his factory during the Polish regime.

Here, Pavlovich resumes his story. Still waiting in the barn, he heard a car arrive. A large German entered the barn and began to shout orders:

He wanted us to take our tools and go with him. We went outside, and two more people without uniforms were waiting. One of them took us about 100 meters from the house. There were two pits, one larger, the other smaller. The man spoke Russian and told us to get into the large pit. Inside were dirt and a lot of grass, trees, and debris. We were told to clear the grass, uproot the trees. . . . Like that we worked for a couple of hours until this man, together with another German, told us to stop, take our tools, and go to the other side of Denisko's house and to sit, rest, and eat something and wait until we will be called—for what, they didn't say. And so we did. We learned that with the Germans, the fewer questions we ask, the better.

We sat and talked among us, and all of a sudden one of us saw far away on the main road a lot of people standing, and all at once they turned in our direction. At first, we didn't know who these people were, . . . but when they came closer, one of us said, "Those are the Jews who were left in Volchin." We noticed they were walking very slowly, and around them were the Germans with guns in their hands, policemen, and more people with sticks, as if they were forcing [the Jews] to walk. The Jews were dragging, very miserable. Some of them were holding children, some were carrying sick people, some holding hands, until they stopped only 100 meters from us.

Their escorts ran around them, screaming. Everybody was screaming. The Germans were screaming, and the escorts in Russian and Polish ordered [the Jews] to take off their clothes. . . . All at once, everybody began to scream and cry. Only then did they probably understand what was going to happen.

As if unable to go on, Pavlovich breaks from his narrative to reflect on the strength of the screaming. Where, he muses, did such emaciated and weak people find the energy to cry and scream so loudly? Strange. How can Pavlovich question this behavior? He's probably really recalling the shock of hearing that cacophony of horror. With this memory out of the way, Pavlovich continues: "Without mercy, the Germans and their helpers forced the Jews to take off their clothes. Whoever resisted was shot on the spot, and the bodies were thrown into the pit. Naked in the cold of September, they stuck to one another, crying. At the end they apparently didn't have the energy to cry. Some came closer to the pit; and then in the corner of the pit, a German was standing with a machine gun and shot them. Every time there were four or five bodies at the edge of the pit, a few people came and pushed them into the pit. Some [Jews] didn't want to approach the pit and lay on the ground. A second German shot them from afar. And there were those who screamed and cursed and had to be carried far to the pit."

When Shmuel asks if any Jews resisted, I feel my body tense. Remembering the story Hanna Kremer told me about my cousin Ida, I wait to hear her name. Pavlovich says, yes, there was a Jewish woman from Russia whose husband was a Christian. She refused to take off her clothes; after much shouting, a German shot her. She was thrown into the pit fully dressed.

I read over that statement. A Russian woman married to a Christian. This was not my cousin Ida. I skim the next line. Shmuel asks if there were any other protesters. Pavlovich replies that these people, when they stripped, were like skeletons, too weak to protest.

There is no mention of another protester. Could it be that Pavlovich doesn't remember or doesn't want to admit that he watched others running away? Could it be that Pavlovich just didn't see the entire scene? After all, there were hundreds of people, screaming, crying, falling, being dragged. He couldn't possibly have seen it all. Yet wouldn't someone have told him about another woman refusing to undress? I thought I had a resting place for Ida, but now I'm becoming doubtful. And how about Sala? She was old enough to have been sent to Brest for work purposes. The Midler girls, where were they?

The more I learn, the less I know.

Disheartened, I read on. Maybe I will find something to clear up these mysteries.

Pavlovich reports that after a section of the pit was filled with Jews, the *Judenrat* was ordered to get inside and carry bodies to the other side. The members of the *Judenrat* were killed at the end of the massacre; however, they were allowed to wear army coats.

Pavlovich remembers one story of the wife of *Judenrat* member Zufrik and their daughter. A German ordered the naked mother to approach the pit. The daughter clung to her mother, so the German shot them where they were and "with his legs pushed them into the pit, like that, holding each other."

Though I'm moved by this story, I'm becoming more and more perplexed. Yet another young person is still in Volchin, not sent to Brest for "work." Of course, she could have been too young. As I read further, I see that Shmuel is thinking along the same lines. He asks, "How come Zufrik's daughter—as far as I remember, her name was Riva, and she must have already been 18—remained in the ghetto?"

Pavlovich answers, "I think she was the only one who stayed in Volchin and was not sent to work, and that's because, first, she had connections because her father was in the *Judenrat,* and second, she worked at the German office."

My heart sinks again.

Pavlovich recounts the end:

They killed all of them. The killing took place in about four hours. When they finished, it started to get dark. . . . A few of the helpers organized the bodies in the pit; and then the German who was in the pit with his machine gun climbed outside the pit. In one hand, he held his gun, and in the other an almost empty bottle of vodka. He stood on the edge of the pit, drinking the rest of the vodka, threw the bottle on the bodies in the pit, and with big steps, walked in our direction. We thought now it's our end. . . .

He came to the barn, lay on the straw, and fell asleep. . . . One of the helpers came and ordered us to take our tools and go to the pit, cover it with sand. . . . As we worked . . . it was possible to see the Germans, the police, and their helpers in a circle near Denisko's house, quietly talking as if all that happened during the last few hours was not their concern. Some of them collected the dead's clothes. . . . On the other side, a few more people came with horses and carts and collected the clothes, wrapped them with sheets and stuffed some in bags; and, with the escort of a German, a policeman, and a few more people, returned to the village. More people helped us with the work, and it was dark when we finished. A few Germans remained. One of them shouted that when we return home, not to tell anyone anything we saw.

We left the place, tired and sweating. Suddenly everything was quiet. We didn't dare talk among ourselves. We walked to the main road, and there were two more carts with clothes. We walked home as fast as we could. . . . When we got home, it wasn't necessary to tell. The whole village knew already. Everybody heard the screaming and crying.

Shmuel questions the concepts of conscience, justice, and mercy. He questions how the universe didn't turn over; how something so horrific could occur in daylight; how the ground didn't open and swallow the murderers; how "human beings" could lift babies by their legs, shoot them, and, like balls, throw them into the pit. How could this happen, he implores, to a people whose only sin was that they were Jews?

Like one of the village women he questioned earlier, Shmuel wonders, during all this torture, where was the god of the Jews?

The aftermath of the massacre is predictable. Ivanovich says that the Jews' clothes were brought to a storage area behind the German head-quarters; the best items were divided among the Germans and their helpers. After a day or two, people came in the evening to the Jewish homes and searched for hidden valuables.

Following the Liberation, the Soviet government arrested the head of the village, Korshneivsky, and the policemen. A long investigation followed. Korshneivsky was tried not for the massacre, but for cooperating with the Germans. He was sentenced to about six months in prison. The policemen were granted the same lenient sentence.

Ivanovich thinks that Chief of Police Rose and those outsiders who backed up the Germans were the only locals who knew the exact nature of the operation in advance. Rose and his family, he says, were among the first to escape with the Germans. Their fate remains unknown.

Shmuel seeks specific figures. As to the exact number of Germans taking part in the massacre, Ivanovich responds: "I don't think there were more than five or six Germans in uniforms, but there were other Germans who arrived without uniforms." There were also a few Poznantzkim (Polish from the Poznan area who settled nearby) policemen and about 40 locals.

It's time for Shmuel to ask the most sensitive questions, those that involve personal culpability. "What was the reaction of the people?" he begins.

Ivanovich answers, "Most of the village residents didn't like the Germans, but the truth is also that the Jews were not liked. [The villagers] said the Jews are cheaters, don't like to work, and get rich on the backs of non-Jews. Yet [the villagers] didn't expect such an end. Yes, there were those, especially very religious people, who claimed that the Jews deserved it because they were anti-Christians, they killed Christ. But almost everybody had reservations about the behavior of the Germans toward the Jews. They had reservations about [the Jews'] suffering in the ghetto, the humiliation, the hunger, and especially the cruel killing . . . about the way [the Germans] killed the children."

Shmuel does not let Ivanovich off the hook. Even if the villagers did not approve of the German tactics, he asks, "Were they truly sorry about the killing of the Jews?"

"They may not all have been sorry that the town remained without Jews," Ivanovich says, "but they were surely sorry for the tragic death and the cruelty."

Still unbelieving, Shmuel recalls his youth in Volchin. Always, he says, there were problems between the Jews and the Christians. On Sundays, Christians came to town to attend church. After services, the Russian Orthodox and the Polish Catholics would get drunk and start fights with each other. When they'd meet Jews, they'd hit them.

Furthermore, some village non-Jews had worked with and lived near the Jews for generations. But none of these people hid a Jew.

Shmuel thinks again of his terrified little brother, returning to Volchin after the killings. Why, he wants to know, didn't someone from the village or from the church do something to save his brother? There were such cases of bravery in other villages and cities, but none in Volchin.

Pavlovich responds with the all-too-familiar litany of rationalization: "You ignore the situation that was there, the fear of the Germans, you know, [of the punishment] even for giving a piece of bread to the partisans who were in the woods in our area. [The Germans] would burn the houses and shoot people, especially for holding a Jew. Whoever would be caught, for sure, without any trial, they would kill the whole family."

Ivanovich turns the questions around. What would Shmuel do, he asks, if he were ever in a similar situation? Would he risk the lives of his family and his property to hide someone else?

Shmuel admits that there is no certain answer to such a hypothetical question.

Svetlana Kuntz, silent throughout the discussion, says perhaps the situation was God's wish. Pavlovich adamantly disagrees, blaming the Germans and denying that God exists.

Not wanting to digress into an ontological discussion, Shmuel uses the remaining time to extract further information, first about the memorial. Pavlovich says that a few days after the Liberation, an official from Brest arrived, and, together with the chairman of the Soviet Council and a few of Volchin's residents, including Dimitrevich, they opened the pit, re-covered it with earth, and erected a wooden plaque that said there were dead lying there. Afterward, a survivor from Polke's family came and worked with the village officials to erect a memorial stone.

The Soviets suspected anyone who had cooperated with the Germans. One day, a Jewish officer from the Red Cross arrived in town and asked questions about collaborators. Many people were arrested, and the majority of them were transferred to Brest. Some were convicted and returned after a few years in prison. According to these elderly witnesses, one suspect, an invalid, was, because of his Jewish identity, "worse" than those who cooperated or joined in the killings.

Pavlovich himself was arrested, detained, and questioned about his participation in covering the pit. Eventually, the investigator was convinced Pavlovich was not guilty and sent him home.

Why, after all these years, Shmuel wants to know, are the remains of the ghetto, particularly the Midler and Tanteshe houses, still visible?

Pavlovich says that people from the village removed everything from these houses. During the Soviet era, some houses were moved to other villages. People removed the windows and doors from the remaining dwellings and destroyed anything of value. Part of the Midler house stands, and there's a brick storage area the priest built on the field. Some of the houses were nationalized. Most of the other houses in the ghetto were totally destroyed.

Shmuel explains that he's not looking to reclaim any land, only to find precious memorabilia, including valuable Jewish religious books.

He concludes his meeting with the town's elders by thanking them on behalf of all the relatives and descendants of Volchin's dead Jews, with the hope that such atrocities would never happen again.

Following this visit to Volchin, Shmuel and the other Israelis met in Brest with Hanna Kremer's former classmate, Anna Gagarina, who lived in Volchin before and after the war.

In his report, Shmuel picks up the narrative. Gagarina says that before the war, she went to school and befriended Jewish girls. She knew the other witnesses well. Shpagina lived near the ghetto's fence, and her father had connections with the town's Jews. The other witnesses were her neighbors; Pavlovich, in particular, had been called upon to "help."

Could Pavlovich have been more of an active collaborator than he admitted? Gagarina says that Pavlovich's story must be true because after the trial, only Pavlovich and another person were released back home. The rest were sent to work camps in Siberia.

It is ironic, Shmuel muses in his account, that he too was sent to Siberia. Perhaps he was working and living side by side with the murderers of his family. Characteristically, Shmuel doesn't allow himself the luxury of rumination. Instead, he uses his time well, asking the same questions about the ghetto and the massacre.

On the day of the invasion and bombing of Volchin, Gagarina remembers, she ran to the graveyard and lay on the ground until late at night. From there, she could see the tanks, motorcycles, and cars with soldiers moving through town on the way to Visoke. The next day, German soldiers arrived and were joined by townspeople who, Gagarina assumes, hated the Soviets and were eagerly awaiting the moment they would be granted guns of their own.

Most of Gagarina's subsequent recollections jibe with those of the other witnesses, from the arrival of more Germans, to the announcements of ghetto rules, to the organization of the local police and the *Judenrat*, and to the arduous work details.

Gagarina remembers a demand that the *Judenrat* provide a list of all the Jews above 16 years old who were capable of working. All these

Jews were told to wear warm clothes since they would be building a new road from Chernavchich to Brest. They would work during the week; on Sundays, they could return to Volchin.

"Was this true?" Shmuel asks.

"Once or twice they really came back on Sunday and brought food to their families. Afterward, they stopped coming. They were transferred to the Brest ghetto."

Though Gagarina explains that at first the Germans didn't take all the young people, a later order required everyone physically able to move to Brest. "Like that," she says, "all the young were taken out."

So here is yet another voice that seems to tell me that Sala and Ida were probably not in Volchin. I await a response to my letter to Gagarina. Maybe, just maybe, she knows more about the Midler girls.

On Shmuel's tape, Gagarina also remembers the last days of the occupation: "The Soviets came from Visoke, with a lot of arms. But the Germans kept resisting. The shooting and the bombing were from all sides. . . . The partisans brought down parachutists behind the German lines. Only then did the Germans run away to the Bug. . . . A lot of Germans were killed, and their bodies were taken to the Christian cemetery, where they remain. . . . In the center of Volchin is a memorial to the Soviet soldiers who fell during the battle of Volchin."

In general, Gagarina and the others agree on certain massacre statistics: five Germans; 8–10 policemen; about 10 helpers, probably German without uniforms—a total of 23–25 perpetrators/collaborators.

Lastly, Shmuel asks the question that I heard so long ago in my search. "Mrs. Gagarina," he begins politely, "if there were only 20 [Germans and associates] and 400 Jews, why didn't anybody run away? Even if they killed more than half, a few could still have run away and survived."

Gagarina's answer is predictable. Of course, it is better to die running and not standing, she says. Yet many of the Jews were old or were women with children. They were all weak. She again tells the story of Riva Zufrik, who protested.

Finally, she says what must be to her, and many others, a rationalization that allows them to sleep at night: "Many of them perhaps wanted to die because of all the troubles: hunger, illness, humiliation. Death was a solution to them."

In another excerpt from the tapes, Shmuel discusses the next day, which he spent in Brest. As he introduces his stop at the Fortress, when the Israeli mission encounters the Americans, I feel strangely uneasy. This is the time of our introduction. What will Shmuel report? Will this meeting be as important to him as it was to me? He says:

> The four of us who came from Volchin hear a message on the microphone in Hebrew, asking if there are people from Volchin in the Israeli group. At first, we are shocked by this announcement, knowing that the only [American] people [originally from Volchin] supposed to come on this trip were the Kremers, and they had canceled their plans. We went to the woman who made the announcement, an Israeli who immigrated to America and the organizer of the American group, and next to her was standing a young woman, very good-looking, speaking only English. Of course, Dov, Esther, and Drora, knowing the English language, got into the action and learned her name is Andrea and she lives and was born in the United States, but she had family in Volchin. Her mother, uncles, aunts, and also her grandmother lived in Volchin, and they are the family Midler, Iser Midler. . . . Of course, who didn't know Iser Midler?
>
> For us, and also for her, this was a big surprise, and so she joined us as a fifth person from Volchin. She is a very nice and kind woman. She told us she came specially to visit Volchin; she was very interested and asked that we tell her about the village, her family, and the way the Jews were killed.

As I read this, my heart swells and tears stream. My connection rekindles; my loneliness in doing this research subsides, at least temporarily. I did matter to Shmuel as he mattered to me. I am the "fifth person from Volchin."

I begin to read about our day together. I relive the wretched weather and hear how one local told Shmuel that for some time before, the weather had been dry. I relive how Shmuel said Kaddish amid driving rain, black clouds, and strong winds. I relive how, without really visiting the village the way we had planned because of the weather, we didn't say a proper good-bye to all the past sites. "It was a very hard and emotional parting," Shmuel says. "The skies cried with us. And like this we left Volchin, with the feeling that this was the last visit."

After the trip, Shmuel reflects on his impressions. Like me, he regrets missing many things—not going to the remains of some of the Jewish homes or inside the synagogue's attic. Perhaps, he thinks, there was something hidden in these places, something precious of the dead. And he regrets that he didn't pose enough questions—about the stones that disappeared from the graveyard, for example.

Although he asked some of the older residents if they knew any of the collaborators and if any were still living, he got unsatisfactory answers such as, "I don't know," "I don't remember," "It was so long ago." He is sorry that he didn't push the issue.

His impressions of the locals' current attitudes were particularly vivid: "They are not sorry at all that there are no Jews. It's not only in our village, but in every city and town, because a lot of Jewish houses and properties remained at their disposal."

Shmuel is just as disheartened by the young people. They too are not sorry about the absence of Jews. "First," Shmuel says, "they don't know Jews, never met them. . . . They heard from the older people that Jews . . . always cheated the non-Jews."

Perhaps some of the locals felt sorry for the Jewish suffering. As one person tells him, "It was possible to clean the cities and towns from the Jews without killing them; for example, they could have been transferred to Palestine or somewhere else."

He remarks on the selective memory of those he interviewed. They seemed to agree on certain facts—sometimes the details were so similar they seemed rehearsed—about the German invasion, the transfer to the ghetto, the description of the Jews, the allotted bread, the time and date of the massacre. They knew the names of the *Judenrat* and clearly described their responsibilities and actions, as if to imply that the Jews also did things without choice. In this way, the regular duties of the villagers (though only vaguely mentioned), such as guarding the ghetto or procuring food for the Germans, seemed no different from those of the *Judenrat*.

Yet when the questions concerned the property of the dead Jews and the names of those policemen and helpers who cooperated, the witnesses' recollections were poor. Often, they said, it was not worth remembering after 50 years. People were already dead, and there was no point in harming their children with old accusations.

One of the biggest discrepancies involves the villagers who helped the Nazis. They were strangers. They were from the village of Kotechi, the village of Metrona. They were outside Poles. There were few, if any, like Pavlovich, from Volchin itself. And, even Pavlovich had no idea what he would be doing and was later officially exonerated.

As has become the norm during my search, I receive more information that clears up some of these questions but clouds up others. Dov sends me a package with a letter explaining that he and Shmuel are planning to go to Yad Vashem, which has some information on Volchin. As a follow-up to Shmuel's request to the Volchin Village Council, Svetlana Kuntz, the secretary, received massacre confirmation, dated September 29, 1944, from the archives in Brest and sent this information to Shmuel.

According to Kuntz's letter: "On September 22, 1942, nine Germans, with the help of about 20 local policemen, carried out a mass shooting of 497 Jews from Volchin and Chernavchich." She then explains how the Jews marched to the massacre site, undressed, and were executed. Particularly gruesome was hearing again how the small children were held by their hands and legs. She concludes, "The bodies of the murdered Jews were buried in a common grave and were covered by earth where they were killed."

Kuntz also reports that the list of the ghetto Jews was not found in the Brest archives.

Dov tells me that Kuntz had also sent the copy of the Fire Brigade photo. This is the same woman who seemed so remote and disinterested when I sat in her living room. Little did I know she would send such gifts.

As for the information on the massacre, I am again jolted. Now the number of German executors rises to nine and the number of police increases to 20. This is the official Brest archival account. It must be correct. My husband, a non-Jew, knew all along that the Jews of Volchin must have been smart enough to gauge the odds. And, for them, their fate was never a matter of chance. They had no chance.

Dov, it appears, is also disconcerted. In a booklet he prepared, entitled "The Journey to Volchin," he not only describes his pilgrimage, bringing a memorial stone to the Volchin gravesite with the names of his massacred relatives, but discusses his search for information. The Volchin memorial stone included the figure of 395 people from Volchin and Chernavchich killed, but Kuntz's letter puts the total number at 497. Dov writes that it's possible that Volchin's Jews numbered 395 and that the additional 102 are from Chernavchich. This number matches eyewitnesses' guesses about the number of Chernavchich Jews crowded inside the ghetto barn.

The "official"—but as I know by now, not definitive—word comes to me shortly before Thanksgiving, a few weeks after I receive Dov's booklet. He sends me the document he and Shmuel obtained from Yad Vashem on Volchin's massacre. It's a photocopy with seals and signatures. Dov attaches his English translation:

Although this document contains much of the same information provided by Kuntz, I read it over and over to digest some new "facts":

Document Number 8

Volchin, September 29, 1944. The committee for the investigation and prosecution of the murderers for their crimes in Volchin territory and the surrounding area, during the German-fascist occupation in the years 1941–1944,[2] . . . witnessed the writing of this document.

On September 22, 1942, a group of nine Germans with the help of 20 [local] police, organized a mass killing by shooting of Volchin's Jews and some of Chernavchich's Jews. [They were brought to the Volchin ghetto.] The total killed by shooting on that day was 497 people.

When we opened the big pit, we found many bodies. Most were naked and were thrown on top of each other. Bodies of men, women, children, and babies. We took a photo of the bodies and covered the pit again.

According to witnesses, documents, and articles that were brought to us, the committee came to the conclusion that on the same day, September 22, 1942, an order was given to the ghetto Jews to take their valuable belongings and be ready for transportation to the Visoke-Litovsk ghetto. To avoid delays, all the belongings were put on the nearby wagons, where they also put the disabled people. The convoy, including the Germans and the local police, went slowly in the direction of Visoke-Litovsk. Two hundred meters from the end of Volchin, they were led to a former sand quarry, to a pit where it was intended to throw the bodies after they were shot. Prior to the killings, the victims, including men, women, and children, were ordered to remove their clothes and remain naked.

The killings, by shooting, were conducted in groups of three to five people. They were led to the edge of the pit, were shot, and thrown into the pit. People were shouting, crying, and begging for mercy—nothing helped. The fascists ignored all and continued with the shootings. Those who refused to go to the pit were shot in place, and, sometimes when they were still alive, dragged into the pit. Some of the babies were lifted from the ground into the air, shot, and thrown into the pit.

In this way, the German fascists and their helpers killed everyone. All were thrown into the pit. After the killings, the Germans and their helpers took the Jews' belongings on the carts for themselves.

In addition, the Germans killed, near Volchin, [non-Jewish] people from the villages: Machulishche, Blochin, Stefan, and Nikotin Gerasim. Fifteen people were killed in Zelesie, six in Ozuky. Altogether, 551 people were killed [including the 497 Jews]. Another 78 people from the surrounding areas of Volchin were deported to Germany.

Along with this document, signed by the committee members, Dov sends other material, including a poor-quality copy of a photograph of the massacre. In it, I can barely discern about 20 standing figures overlooking a large mass of black-and-white shapes. I can't believe I am actually looking at the massacred bodies. I hold the photocopy under a magnifying glass, but it's impossible to decipher anything. I write to Dov asking him to find out where we can get a real photo. This seems as necessary to me as my next breath of air.

The last of Dov's papers are two eyewitness testimonies gathered from an investigation of the crimes committed by the German fascists, conducted by the general prosecutor in Visoke, on September 28, 1944. The first witness, Pavel Iosefovich Kovalev, on his way to the village of Kotera, was not far from the massacre site on that fateful day. He says that the massacre was conducted by the Germans, their helpers, and policemen from the village of Motikali, the same village where 500 Jews from the Brest ghetto were killed.

"After they were led to the pits, they were told to strip entirely," he testifies. "They formed a line by the pits and were shot at close range. Some were pushed down into the pits and shot there . . . others were shot and then thrown into the pits. Children were forced into the pits with whips. . . . When the executions first began, the people in the back of the line could see all that was happening and were begging for mercy, mothers kissing the policemen's hands and feet, asking them to spare the children. But they were pushed back with the butt ends of the guns." Instead, the murderers lifted the babies in the air by their hands and legs and shot them in front of their mothers' eyes.

Most heartbreaking is Kovalev's final image: "After the executions, the pits were covered with earth in a most haphazard fashion, so that arms and legs could be seen sticking out of the ground."

Kovalev estimates the number of Jews killed at 350; and his testimony that "all those who resisted were shot in place and thrown into the pit" implies that several Jews resisted. Perhaps, perhaps, he saw Ida.

The second witness, Mark Gerasimovich Vavriniuk, a Volchin resident, puts the Jewish death toll at between 350 and 360. He says that a Polish man commanded the Volchin police and verifies the participation of the Motikali policemen.

Dov says the people of Motikali were known to be anti-Semitic.

Around this time, I receive translations of the remaining Yad Vashem documents relating to Volchin: the account of Vasily Timofeyevich Semenyuk, a former mason, Polish army officer, and police officer under the Ukrainian Committee's auspices. Semenyuk was appointed commandant of the German *Gendarmerie*[3] in late 1942, supervising a force of 40.

I am prepared for the usual shifting of blame, the usual amnesia.

The first sentence of Semenyuk's testimony, recorded in 1945, sounds familiar: "I do not remember the exact date in the fall of 1942 that I was ordered to go to Volchin with my whole police force to execute Jews, but I got drunk and did not go to Volchin." Then he goes on to report the hearsay reports: "My assistant, a Polish man named Kesarov, later told me that they killed about 300 Jews near the church, including women, children, and the elderly. Their clothing was taken away and sold to the peasants." While he maintains that the executors were four Germans, including three from the Gestapo, he says, "I cannot recall their names."

So far, I am not surprised. Semenyuk reports that the German police executed 130 civilians in the village of Lishitsi, discusses his murderous role in the Brest ghetto after liquidation (see chapter 7), and just as routinely lists his other crimes: "Also, I killed six people in Motikali and one in Sukharevichi. Another one was killed in Sukharevichi by one of my policemen, a Pole named Felix Zhukovski. This man killed more Jews than anyone could count. He even wanted to kill his Jewish wife, but I did not let him. During transport, he killed those who were sick right on the road. According to my calculations, he killed about 120 people. I know that Jews worked on the Chernavchich highway; and when the work was done, they were all taken to Chernavchich and shot—more than 60 people. We were told to conceal the graves of the Jews so that there would be no traces."

The rest of Semenyuk's testimony is disjointed. I don't know if this is because the photocopy of the Russian document is difficult to decipher or if it's because once Semenyuk got started, his confessions rushed out. He states that the Germans, who worked for Commissar Pavle, came to Brest and grabbed the first people they saw, presumably Jews. These prisoners were taken to a Dr. Meneker, who examined them before sending them to concentration camps. Those who didn't report for examination were ordered to be executed, their homes burned by the doctor himself. In Semenyuk's area of jurisdiction, 700 of those "shirkers" were sent "as slaves" to Germany. Any POWs caught, of course, were also killed; two in particular were known to have been hanged in Rakow. This is the first time I have heard of this doctor.

Although he is vague about specifics, Semenyuk charges several people with the commission of such crimes, including Alexander Panasyuk, a willing murderer and confiscator of the victims' belongings, particularly in the Motikali and Volchin massacres.[4]

While I admire Semenyuk's accounting, I cannot understand this man's casual recitation of murder by his own hands. During my research, I have found those who were conveniently absent from the action, those who reluctantly admitted to "hearing about" atrocities, those who even confessed to digging trenches—for what, they couldn't be sure. Up until now, I have not come across one person who owned up to murder.

Wasn't Semenyuk afraid of retaliation or indictment? Wasn't he, like so many of his counterparts, mired in denial? Of course, there is the possibility he was honest, ready to assume responsibility for his actions. However, the mere listing of his crimes makes me think otherwise—that perhaps he felt invincible, a man merely following orders in wartime. Or perhaps he felt that Jews were subhuman and, as such, should be killed as a favor to humanity. Therefore, he committed no real crime.

Toward the end of Dov's personal booklet, he speaks about our meeting at the Brest Fortress and the subsequent time we spent together. As with Shmuel's description, I approach this part cautiously. He mentions my surprise and excitement when he introduced himself and Shmuel, my friend crying, and my gratitude at going to Volchin with them. Then he describes our day in Volchin, including my slipping down the ravine and our visit to the Midler house. He says that while we were there, the land-lord or tenant who lives in the main Midler house came outside and asked what we were doing. Shmuel explained, and the tenant allowed us to enter the yard and take photos. I have no memory of this exchange.

Best of all, Dov says, "A true friendship was made between us from Volchin and Andrea Simon, the American, also from Volchin."

The Holocaust became a reality to Dov because of his personal journey, a journey that continues to reverberate. He says, "I started to gather any piece of information on Volchin. . . . Shmuel and I are in the process of 'hunting' after documents. Helping us a lot is Andrea. Ever since we met her in the Fortress, we write each other and exchange information to memorialize the Volchin Jews."

As I read this, my smile becomes too wide for my face. I can't contain it; I am joyous with the knowledge that on the other side of the world are people who share my passion. I am grateful beyond words.

Dov, like Shmuel, doubts the veracity of the villagers' testimonies. He thinks that their information is "limited" and that some of it is suspect because there were too many identical patches. And he wonders, like Shmuel, why no villager in Volchin hid a Jew.

I remember the villagers said there was "no point" in remembering.

But there is a point. It's called responsibility; it's called truth. Words to live by.

I remember. The trip my mother and I took to West Berlin in the 1960s and our meeting with my grandmother's German friends. I remember cringing as my mother questioned their participation in the war and cringing even more as they denied knowledge of the Jews' fates.

I remember. I was in my 20s and a group of boys dragged me into the vestibule of a deserted Brooklyn tenement. Hearing my screams and watching my abduction, neighbors sat on their stoops, frozen in place.

Fortunately, one man burst into the building and interrupted my attackers, seconds away from committing gang rape.

I remember. A decade later, I was viciously attacked in a supermarket parking lot in suburban Maryland. Bleeding and bewildered, I stumbled into the store and nearly collapsed by the checkout counter. I prevailed upon the manager to call my husband. Shoppers watched, but no one even offered me a tissue to wipe the blood from my face. Days later, the police told me that many people witnessed the incident, though they didn't call for help. Even after the attackers left the scene, even after there was absolutely no danger, they did nothing.

I remember. More recently, on a ferry in the Aegean, I saw someone distributing pamphlets and learned they were anti-Semitic diatribes. My Greek guide blithely said she never reads them. Ignoring them, she thought, would diminish their importance; my anger, she felt, was wasted—an overreaction, she undoubtedly thought.

There are many ways to collaborate.

I remember what Hanna Kremer said in her interview, how she went to school with the Russians and Poles. I remember how desperate she was to get to Volchin after the war and how when she finally did, she felt as if she had visited Hiroshima.

I remember what she said about the massacre, in one of her most emotional moments: "I couldn't believe it. How could something like this happen? Innocent children, women, men. These were neighbors who lived with us for hundreds of years. I was angry. I questioned. Nobody did anything to save a soul. There was one little boy, the tailor's son, who ran away. The locals brought him to the Gestapo, and he was shot. Why couldn't anyone hide him? The honest truth: there were plenty of people who could have done something. Or even just not to point."

That, to me, sums up the entire collaborator controversy. Okay, you couldn't always expect the locals to protest, to hide a Jew, to close their eyes, to risk anything. But you could expect them, you could expect a former friend, neighbor, business associate, schoolmate, just plain human being, not to point.

Chapter 7

Isolation

Chances are that years after a flower is planted, a weed will sprout. The flower may have bloomed for a season, or even for many; but, sooner or later, a weed will overtake its spot—a reminder that beauty is transitory, that tampering with nature can backfire, that some roots are buried deep and their sheer power can impel them through any barrier.

And so I am learning.

Fifty thousand Jewish citizens can't be buried in a forest without a trace. As with Volchin, sooner or later, a bone pokes out from the spring thaw. Sooner or later, a voice croaks from the phlegm of repressed memory. Sooner or later, a strangulated wail hisses between the brain's synapses. Sooner or later, something emerges of the lives that were once lived.

When Arizona resident Rosanne Lapan, from our delegation, took her one-day detour to Kobrin, about a half-hour drive from Brest, she had an experience that she later characterized as "profound on an intellectual, emotional, physical, and spiritual level." In Kobrin, where she traces her lineage to her great-great-great-grandfather, Rosanne visited the Museum of History, displaying precious artifacts of Jewish life; and toured various sites, including the remains of some Jewish homes, the school, and the synagogue.

This town, whose first recordings of Jews reach to the beginning of the 16th century, listed about 15,000 people right before World War II, including 8,000 Jews. Rosanne saw where these Jews lived and where they were dispersed into two ghettos; and she stood in a field where several hundred Jews were massacred and where 80 residents were later summoned to move the bodies and burn the evidence, only to be shot themselves. The rest of the town's Jews were loaded onto cattle cars and sent to Brona Gora. A by-now familiar story.

But what was unique about Rosanne's Kobrin stopover was going to the home of a 94-year-old man, A. Martynov, the first director of the Kobrin Museum of History, a post he held for 30 years. He was the only witness from the time of Rosanne's last close relative in Kobrin, her grandfather, who left for America in 1911. Although the director didn't remember Rosanne's family, he did recall the World War II years.

Having saved Jews by hiding them, this "righteous gentile" did a lot more. Scrupulously, he recorded their precious history, penning articles about the town's Jews during the war. Perhaps realizing that Rosanne's visit might be a unique opportunity, he did something wondrous. He handed this material, which had been sitting in his closet, to Rosanne.

Yes, here was something substantial for the current Kobrin Jews, between 25 and 100 families, a pittance of the town's 20,000 population. Here was something substantial for those, like Rosanne, with distant ties to Kobrin. Finally, their ancestors have a place of death for the world to know.

When she was back in the States, Rosanne felt that her encounter with the old man was almost a mystical calling, one that assigned her a responsibility to share the information she received. After reading the translated documents, I identify with her commitment. This material not only brings eyewitness testimony about the death of Kobrin's Jews but rare information on what happened to them in their last days.

One of the articles, entitled "Requiem," begins with an explanation of the purpose of his record: "Since the overwhelming majority of our contemporaries have a rather unclear and fragmentary vision of the crimes committed by the fascists, it would not be in vain to restore to our memories, briefly, the events of more than 40 years ago." I already like this man, A. Martynov. He has courage. He has integrity.

His tale evolves from the first days of occupation, when "the town was searched by groups of officers and soldiers with three meaningful letters on their shoulder straps—GFP, standing for Secret Field Police."

These men visited certain addresses that had been provided by the German fifth column, secret agents who had infiltrated the town before the war, many of them posing as Polish refugees, and who created lists of Communist Party and Soviet activists and anyone with antifascist views. Those found from the list faced trial; most were immediately executed, and the others were sent to concentration camps.

The planned mass extermination subsequently began. In July 1941, Gestapo troops conducted a manhunt in the streets. More than 200 Jews were captured and executed in a field. Another large group was executed in August.

A highway slope by the bridge across the canal was frequently used as an execution site. Covered trucks filled with the condemned were sent there. Victims' hands were tied with barbed wire. Forced to kneel by the edge of the slope, they were shot in the head and pushed down, with many falling into the canal. Some victims were coerced into running or tumbling down the slope, whereupon soldiers shot them in the backs. This is how the newlywed Grinyuks were killed, leaping toward their deaths, holding each other's hands. Here is also where a partisan soldier and his family were executed. To intimidate people, corpses were left unburied for several days. Executions were soon moved to a less exposed area—the prison.

A Jewish survivor from Brest heard that in Kobrin, the Germans had burned down the Jewish hospital and the rabbi's apartment. Local firemen were told to ignore the flames. The fire spread to the rest of the town and the Germans threw "living Jews into the flames."

By the fall of 1941, Kobrin became the center of an administrative unit, the *Gebietskommissariat*, headed by Gebietskommissar Pantser, who set up his new government in the local school. One of the first orders of business was to isolate the Jews from the rest of the population by "resettling" them into a concentrated area—the ghetto. In a short period of time, non-Jews who lived in the area designated for the ghetto were given the option of moving into homes left behind by the Jews, primarily in the center of town. The Jews, of course, had no choice at all.

The Kobrin ghetto consisted of two parts. Part A, located in the southern section of the city, was larger in population and territory. It was comprised of those considered potentially useful, such as specialists, workers, the physically strong, and wealthier people who could afford bribes. Any gaps in this main ghetto were enclosed by fences. The smaller ghetto, Part B, was located on Kobrin's western side. With vulnerable borders, residents of this auxiliary ghetto were clearly destined to be first in line for extermination.

As in Volchin and elsewhere in Eastern Europe, Kobrin's ghetto was governed by the *Judenrat,* or Jewish Council, that received orders from the German administration. Headed by a prominent merchant named Angelovich, Kobrin's *Judenrat* had its own police, armed with clubs. They were responsible for supervising the lines of those who worked beyond the ghetto boundaries.

Jews were not allowed to walk on the sidewalks unattended or to communicate with non-Jews. So that there would be no mistake in identification, all Jews had to sew a yellow circle onto the shoulders of their clothing. The Germans called this emblem *Schandenfleck,* or spot of shame.

This was how the Jews lived through the severe winter of 1941–42 until June 2, 1942,[1] when the liquidation of Ghetto B began. According to eyewitnesses, Angelovich addressed those Jews, calmly telling them—though he knew otherwise—to gather food and belongings because they were being transferred to a new place of work. The crowd later was surrounded by SS soldiers and dogs and led to the train station, where Jews were stuffed into tightly sealed cars, each bulging with 200 people, bound for Brona Gora. Half of Kobrin's Jews perished that day.

The Jews from Ghetto A, believing that they would survive the war because of their usefulness, cruelly learned that to the Germans, usefulness was a temporary state. When the ghetto was surrounded on October 14, 1942, some brave Jews resisted by fighting and setting diversionary fires. Out of about 500 Jews who fled the ghetto, many were betrayed by Polish and Ukrainian peasants; about 100 Jews escaped into the woods and joined the partisans.

However, the majority of the ghetto inhabitants were taken to a field in the collective farm Novy Put (New Way), located close to the southern outskirts of town. Previously, 160 men from the village of Hidry had been ordered to dig four 60-by-60-meter trenches. At the time of the execution, the site was surrounded by soldiers armed with machine guns.

The Jews were ordered to undress. According to rumor, the first to go down was the chief rabbi, who told his people to resign themselves to their fate.

Though few Jews survived, the Germans were relentless in their thoroughness. They went through the ghetto, breaking down locked doors, searching through attics and basements. With iron probes, they poked through well-camouflaged hideaways. Those left behind, such as children, the sick, and powerless, were used to uncover hiding places and then were shot. For several days, the non-Jews of Kobrin listened to the occasional rifle shots, machine-gun crackling, the desperate cries of the hunted and tortured. Then, when all was silent, the next chapter began—uncontrolled looting of the property left behind by the dead. For weeks, Hitler's Special Services supervised this phase of the operation. Belongings were categorized. The better and more expensive items were sent to Germany; the remaining things were distributed among the local residents.

Now that the ghetto was liquidated, there were no longer Jews to take the brunt of the Nazis' brutality. Local residents began to fear for their lives; other groups, such as Poles, were killed, often for no apparent reason. Until December 1943, the local administration illegally kept 72 of the most qualified Jews of different trades in the Kobrin prison in case they were needed. They were subsequently also deemed expendable.

Similar annihilation of the ghettos, under the command of Pichmann, the head of the SD, took place in the towns of Divin (1,450 people) and Gorodets (269 people). In addition to having their people massacred, the villages of Kamenka, Borisovka, and Oreyol were destroyed by fire. In September 1942 alone, the same month as Volchin's massacre, there were countless executions of Jewish men, women, and children in villages near Kobrin, followed by the confiscation of cattle, property, and crops.

The relevant published documents include a journal of military activities of the Third Battalion of the 15th Police Regiment from September 11 to November 24, 1942, detailing many of these atrocities. The list of massacres, village destructions, and public executions of partisans continued to grow until the last days of Nazi occupation in July 1944.

The only instance of justice during these times concerned Pichmann, the head of the SD. In the waning hours of 1943, during the last public execution, intended for seven members of the underground, Pichmann circled the execution square in a small plane. Intoxicated by the carnage and the New Year's holiday, he decided to celebrate, dressed in civilian attire, at a Polish friend's house. In the middle of the evening, soldiers traced an indoor light violating the blackout to the house where Pichmann was partying. Forgetting his civilian dress and no doubt thinking he was invulnerable, he confronted the soldiers and pushed one of them. Another soldier, armed with a machine gun, shot Pichmann, who was flown to Brest, where he had surgery but died— before the New Year arrived.

In the spring of 1944, the Germans attempted to destroy evidence of their crimes, forcing prisoners to dig up and burn more than 4,000 corpses along the Divinsky Highway. These prisoners were subsequently shot. In total, the report announces, the Kobrin region lost from 10,000 to 12,000 civilians during the war. Although Martynov carefully includes the ethnicity of the ghetto inhabitants, in his summation, he omits the word *Jew*.

Before the war, my family in the United States enjoyed a rare period of calm. In the late 1930s, Masha and her last child at home, Sara, moved from Woodridge. Taking little more than two valises, she walked out of the Wayside Inn, leaving the 17-room boardinghouse in the hands of her creditors. Heading for Brooklyn, Masha could now be close to her large family, which included her mother; her sisters and brothers (except, of course, Iser); her stepchildren; and her eldest son, Gerson, who was newly married. Masha was not far from Norma, a single, working woman living in uptown Manhattan, and Masha's youngest son, Abraham, who often lived with Norma as he attended City College at night. Only Masha's middle son, Isaih, was away, studying dentistry at the University of Pennsylvania; but he came to Brooklyn often, especially to see his fiancée.

Now a divorced woman, Masha needed to make a living. Seeing a newspaper ad for a night course in practical nursing, Masha enrolled. The way she tells the story, she bluffed her way through the course, pushing ahead of much younger students and, pleading poverty, finagling fee extensions. Moreover, in her version, after she received a phone call telling her of her first job interview, she practiced all night administering injections to oranges. Masha not only got that job but worked overnight shifts for nine weeks, making enough money to pay off her school tuition.

Finally getting her license, Masha was in demand: "Everybody wanted to have a Jewish nurse." She soon went to work for a 60-year-old bachelor, a very wealthy man who owned a bakery chain and several apartment buildings. A short, heavyset, balding man suffering from heart disease (though Masha claimed there was nothing wrong with him except that the doctors wanted his money), Dave Miller was, according to Masha, "The nicest person in the whole world."

Masha nursed Dave back to health, traveling with him to Florida. There she learned how to drive, and together they saw the sights. Before long, Masha Midler Lew was Masha Miller, the same name that her Midler family adopted in this country. Though this was not a marriage of love, it was one of friendship. Most important to Masha, Dave was respectful of her children.

Masha wouldn't settle for being just a wife. Convinced that Dave was being manipulated by unscrupulous relatives and business associates, she began to collect his rents and manage his affairs. And, for the first time in her life, she indulged. She and Dave spent winters in Florida and summers in the country, staying in the best hotels. But her heart was always with her family, especially her children.

This idyllic life, it turned out, was only an interlude. When the war came, everything changed.

During the war years, my family, like so much of the world outside Germany and Eastern Europe, was totally unaware of the systematic extermination of Jewish city and town life. For them, fear and trembling came in more accountable—and countable—forms. There were fewer chairs at Masha's dining-room table on Sunday afternoons; the family frequently received tiny V-Mail envelopes from the War and Navy Departments addressed in familiar handwriting. They were difficult days when these envelopes were missing from the mailbox.

Masha had three empty chairs at her table. Gerson was in the U.S. Army, stationed in Europe, where he fought and was wounded; Isaih was in the Coast Guard; and Abraham, the last to leave, pursued his dream of becoming a pilot. Nicknamed Pee Wee because of his stature as a boy, Abraham grew into a tall and muscular man. Though there were many good-looking males in Masha's family, Pee Wee was, according to his sister Sara, "gorgeous." He had the Midler wavy hair, aristocratic nose, soft brown eyes, and strong chin.

Since I've announced my intention of writing about Masha, on Thanksgiving my mother brings me a huge shopping bag filled with old photos, documents, and packets of letters. Most of those letters are from her beloved brother Pee Wee, written during the early years of the war.

Clipped to the packet is a picture of him. I look at it, and though I've seen it before, it gives me a start. It's a head-and-shoulders shot, clear and focused, without the yellow tint of age. Pee Wee's handsome face is like a classic sculpture—chiseled and perfectly proportioned. I notice that his army shirt collar sports a miniature gold plane, but I come back to his eyes, which seem to gaze above the photographer, holding an expression of warmth and earnestness. I see my uncle Isaih in his nose, my uncle Gerson in his pursed lips, my aunt Sara in his devilish eyes, my mother in his slightly cleft chin. But mostly, I see my dead uncle Iser in Pee Wee's protective sincerity. When I place Pee Wee's photo next to that of Iser with his Volchin family, I see two men unaware of the attractive power of their charisma, two men who reveled in the ordinariness of life, two men whose personal powers could not protect them from the tidal wave of extraordinary events.

Having just read about Kobrin during the war, I leaf through Pee Wee's envelopes, scanning the postmarks to put them in chronological order. While I know Pee Wee was stationed in the American South, I need to corroborate real life in those years. I need to know that while the Jews of places like Kobrin were being prepped for dehumanization, while my uncle Iser was gearing up for death, an American Jew, a flesh-and-blood relative, was getting ready for a rescue mission, if only symbolically.

The first letter I find is dated April 14, 1942. The ghettos of Europe were already functioning. Writing from Maxwell Field, Alabama, where the U.S. Army Air Corps had stationed him, Pee Wee compares his military training to the rigors of West Point. The life of the new cadet had its own kind of forced isolation: "I'm busy as the devil all day. At 5:30 before the crack of dawn, we are dragged out of bed by reveille. We have classes from 7-5 (math, physics, code, military intelligence, combat), then do drills (with guns), and then have athletics. Believe me there's no time to breathe and the sun takes the rest of the starch out of you by the end of the day."

In the next letter, I recognize the family sense of humor: "One day a fellow in the ranks was asked by an officer why he wasn't shaved. He answered, 'It was so crowded in the toilet that I must have made a mistake and shaved my neighbor because I know I shaved somebody!' "

The letter postmarked May 1, 1942, rivets me. "Last night we had a blackout for 30 minutes. It's a cold, eerie sensation. Everything for miles around went black. Only the stars and an airplane circulating the field were visible. I heard there was a blackout in New York. That must have been an occasion."

Suddenly, I think of Kobrin. And I remember what happened to the SD chief, Pichmann, more than a year and a half later, during another blackout. I close my eyes. I see a huge black cloth taped to the barracks window in Alabama, rising and floating in a rippling wave, like a magic carpet, all the way to a Brooklyn, New York, tenement, across the ocean to the village of Volchin, to the town of Kobrin, to the city of Brest. Imprinted on that black shroud is an invisible message: "Anyone with the hubris to let light shine between my folds will be struck dead."

Reading Pee Wee's letters, I'm touched at his reminder to his sister on the importance of mail. "Write soon and often," he implores more than once. "It's our only relaxation during the week and the only thing we have time to read other than our books." Of course, this was another generation, one that relied on the written word. Even though I'm familiar with e-mail, faxes, and all kinds of phone services, I know how Pee Wee must have felt about the mail. Once again, it brings me so much.

I receive the translation of the rest of the 1944 report from the Extraordinary State Commission to Investigate Nazi Crimes Committed on the Territory of the Soviet Union. On the last page, a familiar name grabs my attention: Pichmann from the SD. It must be the same

Pichmann who commanded the ghetto massacres, the same one who dared to outwit the blackout in Kobrin.

I go back to the beginning of this section. It's entitled "Protocol of Interrogation of Witness." The date is October 3, 1944. The interrogator is Major Finiyakin, and the witness is an arrested man named Joseph Pavlovich Schidlovsky, born in 1920. A Polish national of a peasant family, the witness was born in Bereza Kartuska, Brest District, Belorussia. During the German occupation of Brest, Schidlovsky was a policeman. From September 1941 until May 1942, he was a private; he was then promoted to major (the extreme leap is puzzling), a rank he kept until January 1943.

Questioned about the Germans' inhuman acts against Soviet citizens, Schidlovsky says that he was very familiar with the Germans' torture and execution. In May 1942, he reports, a member of the SD named Pichmann arrived in Bereza wearing a police uniform. Standing with the head of the Bereza SS, Oberleutnant Gardes, and the head of the Bereza police, Lieutenant Olshovsky, Pichmann supervised the execution of more than 4,000 Jews.

According to Schidlovsky:

When Pichmann arrived in the morning, he ordered all the policemen to assemble. In addition, he brought 500 people from the Gestapo with him. When we policemen assembled, we were dispatched to watch the homes of the city's Jews. It was organized in such a way that for every policeman watching a home, there was a Gestapo officer watching him. We stood three to five meters from each other in back of the Jews' homes. We numbered 250–300 people. We were ordered not to let anyone in or out of the houses. The watch started in the evening and went on until morning. At sunrise, trucks arrived in the village, and the Jews were put on the trucks and taken to the station. The police force walked there by foot. Once at the station, the Jews were put in a train, and the train was sent to Brona Gora, which is located 15 kilometers from Bereza Kartuska. The police force went in empty cars on the same train.

Schidlovsky was present at the executions in Brona Gora.

The witness also describes the second execution in 1942, also planned by Pichmann. This time, 3,000 Jews were killed, including 50 members of the Soviet underground resistance group. Again, Schidlovsky was part of the police force, surrounding the Jewish homes for the night. In the morning, the Gestapo took the Jews in cars to the village of Smolyarka, seven kilometers from Bereza. Although he was not present at this execution, Schidlovsky heard that Jews were killed about a kilometer from this village.

In the fall of 1942, according to Schidlovsky, another high-ranking SD officer, Gerik, came to Bereza. This man gathered up the town's policemen, including Schidlovsky, put them on a train, and took them to the village of Revyatichi. Once there, the police surrounded three houses. Gerik and five other SD men went inside the homes and came out with a woman and children. The police were then instructed to dig a pit about 100 meters from the house. The innocent victims were led to the pit and shot by one of the SD men. Gerik hanged another man. Besides the police, train operators witnessed these events.

Little by little, I'm getting a picture of the events concerning the murder and destruction of Jews in the area around Brest. Little by little, I'm getting a picture of events leading up to the transport to Brona Gora, from the Kobrin ghetto to the Bereza Kartuska ghetto. By far the biggest transport to Brona Gora came from Brest. Little by little, this information, what life was like in this city ghetto before liquidation, is also coalescing. Eyewitness reports, like those intractable weeds, are wagging their heads at me, daring, daring me to pick them.

I receive two important documents about Jewish life in Brest prior to the ghetto liquidation. Both are from Anatoli Yaroshchuk of Brest-Intourist. The first is an October 9, 1997, newspaper clipping from the *Brest Courier*. It's a full page published on the occasion of the 55th anniversary of the destruction of the Brest ghetto. In big, bold letters, the title is "Catastrophe." As I skim the translation and see the words *Jewish community, genocide,* and *liquidation* in the subheads, my heart flutters, and I'm almost giddy. Can it be that a former Soviet republic is finally acknowledging the identity of the Jews and their history in headline type for all to see?

Statistics for the city of Brest, October 1, 1936, reveal a total population of 51,170, including 21,518 Jews, more than 40 percent of the total.[2] By the start of the war, Brest had about 26,000 Jews; and by the time of the Brest ghetto liquidation, the Jewish population included people from the countryside, increasing the total to 36,000. And then a phrase, though not in boldface, pops out at me: "a catastrophe for the Jewish people." Finally, finally, they are no longer peaceful Soviet citizens; finally, they are Jews.

Even more wondrous, the article doesn't simply recount the tragedy of the Jews. To enhance readers' appreciation for the depth of the losses, the author presents the development of the Brest Jewish community, a history that is "intimately connected with the life, work, and troubles of our ancestors, indeed with the ups and downs of our city."

The second document Yaroshchuk sends was culled from the Lore Museum of Brest. From both sources, I stitch together a historical overview of the city of Brest.

Jews came to the region from Western Europe during the 12th to 14th centuries. Since many Jews were skilled workers, they were shown sympathy by the Polish kings. Brest-Litovsk was first mentioned as a city with a settled Jewish population in 1388. Granted freedom of religion and trade, Jews prospered in the city between the 14th and 17th centuries. During this time, Brest-Litovsk (in Yiddish *Brisk d'Lita,* meaning "Brisk of Lithuania") was acknowledged as the "Jewish capital of Lithuania and of Belorussia."

An architecturally elegant stone synagogue was built during the 15th century. In 1566, 90 of the 743 households in Brest were Jewish, most living in a special quarter of the city. The 16th century was called the golden age of Lithuanian Jewry and was characterized by a multiplying and rich Jewish population. Life deteriorated toward the middle of the 17th century, with worsening relations between Jews and Christians resulting in labor and trade restrictions. A 1637 pogrom swept the city. The fall of the Jewish community intensified in 1648–49, with villages destroyed and people murdered. N. Kostomarov, a 19th-century Russian historian, wrote, "The people exhibited a disgusting attitude toward the Jews. They were doomed to complete extermination, and to pity them was considered treason."

The sacking of Brest was repeated in 1656, and the Jewish population was killed. But Jewish life slowly returned. In the late 18th and early 19th centuries, Brest had 2,840 Jews, 71 percent of the city's population. Drought and famine followed, and the famed synagogue was destroyed. A new one was built, as was a publishing house. However, the late 19th and early 20th centuries were marked by great fires, and half of Brest was destroyed. By the turn of the century, more than 30,000 Jews lived in Brest (65 percent of the population),[3] and the community boasted fine yeshivas, a free ambulance service, and a top-quality secular university. Many famous Jewish literary figures, including Sholom Aleichem, visited Brest.

During World War I, Brest was occupied by German troops, and the Jewish population was expelled from the city. They were permitted to return in 1917–18. The Russian Revolution created new borders, and Brest became part of independent Poland and was known by its Polish name, Brzesc nad Bugiem, from 1921 to 1945. In the 1920s, it again became a Jewish cultural capital, with lectures, concerts, and debates; and it featured a popular trade school, a public library, and many religious schools.

The history wouldn't be complete without a list of some of the city's famous Jewish residents, from a renowned 14th-century rabbi, cabalist, and Talmudic scholar, Yekhiel Lukriya; to Albert Einstein's assistant, Jacob Grommer; to Menachem Begin. Born in Brest in August 1913, Begin graduated from Brest's industrial school and Warsaw University Law School and served as Israeli prime minister from 1977 to 1983. Begin, I remember again, was the best friend of our mission organizer, Louis Pozez.

With the history of Jewish Brest noted for its incredible highs and lows, the final chapter would take the Jewish community to the very depths. By the mid-1930s, anti-Semitism started to escalate. Pogroms became more frequent in Poland and western Belorussia. On May 15, 1936, Brest underwent a pogrom, producing much destruction and two deaths. The attackers, who wore swastikas on their chests, were primed for future "action."

Leonid Smilovitsky of Tel Aviv University's Diaspora Research Institute sends me an article prepared by Z. Zimak, "The Brest Jewish

Community before World War II," that corroborates this information. The pogrom, it seems, stemmed from an altercation between a police officer and a Jewish butcher. Refusing to give another bribe, the butcher stabbed the officer. Organized youth groups and other locals used this incident to inflame anti-Semitism and began to destroy Jewish homes and properties. Wild crowds joined the rampage, which lasted a few days.

The widespread destruction and spontaneous outpouring of hatred was conducted against a group of people who were not isolated from the rest of the local population. Contrary to anti-Semitic opinion that Jews were lazy and avoided physical activity (and paying taxes), Brest's Jews played a major role in the city's economy, representing more than 80 percent of all citizens employed in physical labor. Jews comprised the majority of small manufacturers, carpenters, tailors, blacksmiths, metalworkers, shoemakers, painters, and seamstresses. Many Jewish families owned and operated businesses, stores, warehouses, and factories with small inventories of merchandise ranging from candy to wallpaper. Also against stereotype, Jews were underrepresented or nonexistent in government institutions and constituted a minority in professions such as doctors and lawyers.

Anti-Semitic protests and propaganda continued, but the city's Jews retained their traditions. There were four synagogues; and private Jewish schools included a coed gymnasium (Tarbut, which Louis Pozez and Ida Midler attended), coed Hebrew elementary schools, and a women's religious school. Jews maintained an active social and political life, participating in their own sports clubs, charities, unions, and Zionist-oriented groups. Some of these activities helped locals propagate the belief that Jews were friends—or even spies—of the Soviet Union.

Though the Germans had invaded the city in 1939, it wasn't until their second invasion in the summer of 1941 that the systematic annihilation began. At first, German troops were courteous, but the SS then burst into the city. Posters were placed everywhere ordering all Jews to assemble at the city's main square to receive work orders. The small proportion of Jews who came were taken to the fort, where they were starved and executed by a firing squad. During the next few days a door-to-door search took place, and more men were rounded up and executed at the fort.

On July 12, 1941,[4] more than 5,000 men between the ages of 13 and 70 were arrested. Many of these men were educated professionals. Their execution was organized by an SD squad under Schongart's supervision.

In *Hitler's Willing Executioners*, Daniel Jonah Goldhagen speaks about how the *Einsatzgruppen* began to accustom themselves to the "business" of mass slaughter by concentrating on teenage and adult Jewish males. In Brest-Litovsk, his book states, in July 1941 the men of Police Battalion 307 assembled and killed between 6,000 and 10,000 Jewish males between the ages of 16 and 60.

The atrocities continued in other ways. Men were forced to "register," pay money, and give up their property; leading members of the Jewish community were publicly beaten. All synagogues and prayer houses were turned into stables and garages; religious items were destroyed. According to the Lore Museum, during the war, 30 percent of Brest's brick synagogues and 23 wood synagogues were demolished.

The YIVO Institute sends book excerpts that present more essential details. *The Black Book: The Ruthless Murder of Jews by German-Fascist Invaders throughout the Temporarily-Occupied Regions of the Soviet Union and in the Death Camps of Poland during the War of 1941–1945*, edited by Ilya Ehrenburg and Vasily Grossman, provides chilling eyewitness testimony from Jews and non-Jews.

Grossman (1905–1964) was a prominent Russian novelist, though not well-known in the West, and a leading World War II combat correspondent on the Eastern Front, where the German Army lost a majority of its soldiers and matériel. Grossman's reports for the Soviet *Red Star* provided firsthand accounts of the Holocaust, including the liberation of the Ukraine in 1943–44, where he saw the ravine of Babi Yar and many other smaller massacre sites, and the liberation of several death camps in Poland. After visiting Treblinka, he wrote, "And it seems the heart must surely burst under the weight of sorrow, grief and pain that is beyond human endurance."

Grossman, a Jew, had an even greater personal discovery: the September 1941 death of his mother at a massacre of 30,000 in Berdichev, an important center of Jewish religion and culture west of Kiev. It had been the largest mass shooting of Jews until Babi Yar, which occurred two weeks later.

Ehrenburg, a publicist and popular writer known for his anti-Nazi articles, was responsible for gathering and editing a great deal of the documents contained in the *Black Book*. The impact of his work stayed with him: "I saved the letters, diaries, notes. I read through them again and, although twenty years have passed, I relive the horror, the death-anguish. I cannot understand how we endured it all and found the strength to go on living. I am not speaking about death—not even of the mass slaughters—but about the awareness that these crimes were perpetrated by human beings in the middle of the 20th century, by citizens of a civilized country."

As editors and compilers of the only documentary record of the Holocaust on Soviet soil (accounting for the murder of 1.5 million Jews), Ehrenburg and Grossman encountered a great deal of frustration in the content and publication of the *Black Book*. Although it excludes the participation of locals, except for instances of saving Jews, the book presents startling victim and eyewitness evidence—letters, documents, testimonies, diary entries—of widespread atrocities in cities, villages, forests, and death camps. The implications of complicity were hard to ignore. After the war, Stalin forbade all mention of Jews as the primary victims of Nazi genocide, a ban on the truth that continued for nearly 50 years. Stalin also forbade publication of the *Black Book*. It was never published in the Soviet Union, and was published in post-Soviet Russia in 2014.

In the *Black Book*, Brest's few Jewish survivors tell their stories. From the first day of the German invasion in 1941, the punishments began. Vera Bakalyash says: "Searches were carried out, and people were herded off to forced labor. After work, the people were forced to dance and crawl on their bellies. Those who refused to obey were beaten."

Tanya Gutman adds that the Germans went from house to house, tormenting Jews and confiscating everything. Those who didn't turn over gold were beaten and shot.

Osher Zisman tells about the 5,000 Jewish men who instead of being sent to "work" were taken to the fort, where they were subjected to inhuman conditions and then shot. Many of them were buried alive, covered with earth and hot lime.

"Before shooting my elderly father," he states, "the German beasts pulled out his gray beard. My brother was a dentist. The mad German dogs knocked out all his teeth before the execution. When he fell unconscious at the edge of the grave, they laughed and ordered him to make himself false teeth."

Testimony did not come solely from Jewish survivors. According to an inhabitant of Brest, an engineer named Kokhanovsky, the most prominent members of the community were executed, including physicians, lawyers, engineers, economists, and technicians. "The Germans," he reports, "did not like the intelligentsia. They forced the engineers to clean stables, and publicly humiliated them. Then they were shot, sometimes separately, sometimes entire families at a time. The local Catholic priest was also executed. The Germans were destroying the culture and religion. Those who were physically fit for work were taken to Germany for forced labor. Those who remained were forced to dig trenches."

The intimidation, destruction, torture, and executions were a prelude to the systematic dehumanization and extermination of the entire Jewish population. To accomplish this expeditiously, the Germans had to contain the Jews in one main location. On December 16, 1941, all of Brest's Jews were forced to live in a ghetto that encompassed two separate areas, one small and the other large, divided by the Warsaw-Moscow Highway. Encircled by barbed-wire fences, the ghetto had three entrances with gates and was guarded around the clock by *Gendarmes*. In all, 18,000 Jews were registered.

The German Kommissar, Pandikov, and chief of police, Rode (in German, *Rohde*; see chapter 9) were in charge of the ghetto. Like other ghettos, a *Judenrat* was created to keep order. It was headed by Zvi Hirsch Rozenberg and deputy Nahman Landau. Granted a police force of Jews armed with sticks, the *Judenrat* was instructed to send able-bodied workers to the Germans.

At first, Jews had to wear a yellow, six-pointed star. After the creation of the ghetto, this emblem was replaced by a yellow circle, 10 centimeters in diameter, that Jews were instructed to wear on their chest and left shoulder. It was designed so that a Jew could be spotted a kilometer away.

According to a non-Jewish witness, G. M. Karpuk, recorded in the *Brest Courier*, "Children under 10 years of age did not have to wear the yellow circles. Some of them escaped from the ghetto. They begged for food in the streets of Brest to help feed their families. They were frequently caught and either beaten or shot."

The ghetto had a hospital, stores, and public kitchens, but it was all a sham. The hospital didn't have medicine, the kitchens didn't have food, and the stores didn't have merchandise. Nothing was as it looked. A teenage girl wearing her yellow circle, who could walk only in the center of the street and not on the sidewalk, may have looked like a Jewish schoolgirl with a special insignia. Instead, she was a marked animal, herded into a pen and branded for death.

What was it like for a Jewish father, once a proud and contributing member of the community, to wear this "spot," to be ignored, spat at, cursed? What was it like for a Jewish mother, once an active participant in social affairs, to be snickered at, shunned? What was it like for a Jewish adolescent, once a popular student and neighbor, to be constantly pointed at, singled out, ridiculed? What was it like to be made a social pariah, a leper in a colony of lepers, a person whose disease is present only in the mind's eye of the viewer? What was it like to be branded like Hester Prynne, except that the Jewish "badge" was not scarlet, the color of blood, but yellow, the color of cowardice?

The documents of the German administration between 1941 and 1942 provide evidence of the political attitude toward the Jews. From the beginning of the occupation, Jews were given special IDs and recorded by the Germans. This "passport registration book" lists 12,260 Jews, including teenagers born before 1928, who were living in the ghetto from November 10, 1941, to June 5, 1942. This is the list of Jews known to have been taken from the Brest ghetto to Brona Gora. It's also the list from which members of our delegation, including Louis Pozez and Paula Morgenstern, were able to locate the names of their lost relatives.

Befitting the German bureaucratic administration, there were several lists. Work establishments were required to present names of their employed Jews. Such records show that on July 15, 1942, 7,994 Jews worked in various jobs in the city. The statistics report for the Brest town council on the distribution of provisions indicates that from

March 24, 1942, to April 23, 1942, four bakeries served 17,724 Jews from the ghetto. Bread was distributed from nine posts located inside the ghetto. Every Jew, regardless of age and ability to work, received 1,050 grams of bread a week, which came to a daily amount of 150 grams— barely enough to subsist.

One man who did survive, Sikorsky, comments in the *Black Book* on the food situation: "Living conditions were nightmarish. . . . Even if someone had food stashed away, this was soon confiscated by the police. The people literally starved."

The statistical report also notes that on June 5, 1942, there were 41,395 citizens in Brest, among them were 16,973 Jews.[5] On October 15, 1942, the day that Brest's Jews were transported to Brona Gora, 41,091 Brest citizens were on the list, among them 16,934 Jews. On October 16, records show only 24,162 Brest citizens. From this day until the last notation made on January 7, 1944, the statistics book has no information on the Jews.

These numbers and dates whiz through my brain with the dizzying speed of an airplane performing upside-down stunts. I think again of my uncle Pee Wee, who was feeling his own wings during the summer of the Brest ghetto's lifetime. On July 21, 1942, he writes to my mother, "We have flights and classes morning, noon, and night. We have so much work to do in the air that we don't realize how quickly time goes by. Flying is swell."

Swell—now that's a word from the 1940s. *Swell*—it seems so open, innocent, so American. I wonder if, in the enthusiasm of soaring through the skies of America's Deep South, any of these young men had an inkling of what life was like for those sequestered in the ghettos of Eastern Europe whose futile searches for rescuing American airplanes overhead were anything but swell.

Back in the Brest ghetto, the Germans continued their intimidating campaigns with their frequent "announcements":

It is illegal to buy furniture and other objects from Jews.
Selling anything to Jews is forbidden.
Jews are forbidden from conducting any kind of trade.
Jews are forbidden from being on the street, except during emergencies.

One of the Katsaf sisters, a Jewish survivor who lost 25 members of her family at Brona Gora, recalls, "The announcements caused great shock and were considered extremely demeaning." She says that a Jew entering the marketplace would be driven away with whips and machine guns.

The prohibitions became even more harsh. Zisman notes, "It was forbidden and punishable by death to marry or have children in the ghetto."

Most other city dwellers seemingly remained oblivious to these realities, although they did affect a few non-Jews who were unafraid to protest. To Anatoly Garay, who came to Brest in 1940 when his father was stationed in the army, the Jews were more than strange creatures hunted like animals. In material provided by the museum in Brest, he remembers, "We took up our residence in an apartment on Mayakovsky Street. Opposite us lived my friend Leiba. He visited us very often. He was a bright and joyful kid, about six or seven years old. We played ball together. Jews, Belorussians, Russians, and Poles lived on our street."

Garay then describes how life changed when the war began and his beloved street was divided:

Leiba's house ended up in the ghetto. We came up to the fence and talked, but we couldn't understand why he was there and we were here when we always used to be together. Sometimes Leiba climbed over the fence and came to our yard, but the ghetto was guarded, and climbing over the fence became more dangerous. Finally, the occupiers surrounded the ghetto in the autumn of 1942. Germans ran along the streets. Suddenly, somebody knocked on the door. A German soldier and a civilian ran into the room and cried, "Jews, where are the Jews?" In the morning everything became quiet. When we opened the windows, we saw a terrible picture: destroyed and burning houses, smashed windows—a ruined Jewish ghetto. A policeman was walking back and forth on the street. This was going on for several days.

One day, I saw Leiba. He appeared by the ghetto's gate with a pail. He was looking for the policeman. He needed water. At the time, the policeman turned a corner, and Leiba ran to the water fountain. But the policeman saw a running boy and cried, "Stop! Stop!" but Leiba continued to run. The policeman took his rifle and shot. The boy fell down. I have remembered this incident for the rest of my life.

Garay later became a journalist and wrote a poem called "A Childhood Street" in which he laments:

Why was he shot?
Why was he killed?
Why before his time
Was he buried in the earth?

He gives some possible answers:

Is it really because . . .
His mother, Sarah
Was Jewish
And gave birth to a Jewish son?
Or maybe because he loved matzo?

Then, he accuses: "Ah, the street of childhood! / You are silent, silent."

Karpuk recounts: "Fascists forced the Jews to strip before shooting. A young woman, Fanya Vainshtok, was among them. She refused to strip and her punisher pounced on her and tried to tear off her clothes. She grabbed a brick and hit him in the face. Blinded and bloody, he snatched his gun and discharged all bullets in her. Then he grabbed a machine gun from a soldier and pierced her body with holes, converting it into a bloody jumble."

Though there were between 10 and 20 Jewish survivors of the Brest ghetto, including our Lily Guterman and her brother, Nechamia, their voices were strong and spoke for the many who couldn't.

In a Russian-language documentary, *The Brest Ghetto*, produced in 1995, one such Jewish survivor, Roman Levin recalls: "In September–October, Germans began to put up poles along the highway. We didn't know what for. Mother took me to the village where she . . . earned some extra money by making dresses. When we came back sometime in mid-October, barbed wire had already been laid and people knew it would be a ghetto. We moved there. . . . Right across from our cottage there was a gate. We'd go through to get to the larger ghetto. . . . A short distance from the gate, there were the Jewish market, the *Judenrat*, and the bakery. All activities were in the larger ghetto. I left the ghetto practically every day to get some food. The smaller ghetto spread for about a half a block. I'd lift the barbed wire and sneak away."

Lily Guterman told our delegation about her memories of the German invasion on June 22, 1941. Her house was among the many bombed on that first day. And her sister, Yenta, who had been persuaded by her father to remain in Brest rather than go to the "more dangerous land" of Palestine, was one of the first people killed in the bombings.

With their house destroyed, the family was offered refuge by Peter Golovchenko, a former employee of Lily's father. He said, "Don't worry, I have a place for you. You helped me, and I will take your family." Three weeks later, after the Gestapo rounded up 5,000 males, Lily's family decided it was safer to remain with Peter. There, Lily's family members kept to themselves, working on Golovchenko's farm, praying for an end to the war.

Instead, the ghetto areas were created. According to Lily, "There was not one night that something terrible didn't happen—rapes, taking of belongings, shootings—for no reason." One day, when Lily, who was instructed to clean houses and trains, was beaten up, she asked her father, "Daddy, why am I Jewish?"

With tears and a firm stance, he answered, "We are what we are."

Despite fear of execution, frequent beatings, hunger, lack of medicine and clothing, and isolation from the outside world, some Jews managed to find the willpower to fight back. According to the Lore Museum of Brest, the 1944 Soviet investigative committee determined that at least 500 Jews who tried to escape from the ghetto were shot from the southeastern side of the Motilsky Cemetery and buried in 12 graves. The committee also found three large graves close to Fort 8, near the "Intermediate Barracks," 1.5 kilometers from Rechiza, that contained Brest's Jews "together with people of other nationalities."

Testimony Dov retrieved from Yad Vashem contains information about the atrocities in the forts. Policeman Vasily Timofeyevich Semenyuk, the man who confessed to killing six people in Motikali and other atrocities and who became commander of the Brest District *Gendarmerie* in late 1942 (see chapter 6), says:

I know that near the fort there was a prison camp for POWs, and at the time (1941), I lived close to the camp. Every night, I heard executions taking place there. The prisoners were starving, tried to escape, and corpses were often found dangling from the barbed wire on top of the fences. Others were beaten to death by guards.

People were starving so much that the Germans brought food to the camp in a tank truck and threw fish from the tank into the crowd of starving prisoners, many of whom were trampled to death or run over by the tank. There are thousands of graves near the site of the camp.

I heard that in the fort on the other side of the river, many people were executed. I do not know how many.

Despite the Jews' isolation, resistance groups emerged. Some Jews joined Katowski, a Soviet partisan unit. In the autumn of 1941, the Freedom group was formed in Brest, and, in early 1942, another group called Nekama (Revenge) was created, comprised of young people from the Tarbut. Their main goal was to obtain weapons from the Jews who worked inside the well-equipped fort. They devoted the winter to devising the plot, yet the resistance groups were stopped before implementation. With testimony from informers inside the ghetto, the Gestapo arrested several members.

Arieh Scheinman was a prominent Brest underground leader, maintaining contacts with the Polish and Soviet partisans. Hana Ginzberg was another outstanding partisan.

One eyewitness reports that plans for the Brest ghetto uprising relied on help from Polish and Soviet underground units. When the Germans would begin shooting, the underground would set the ghetto on fire, diverting attention so that the Jews could escape to the forest. However, whether because of poor communication, bad timing, or informants, the revolt did not happen. By the time of the ghetto's liquidation on October 15, 1942, the underground was ill prepared to resist.[6]

Close to that fateful day, rumors began to spread through the ghetto about the destruction of Jewish populations in nearby villages; scattered survivors appeared and told their horrendous stories. Any vestiges of hope harbored by the Jews of Brest were just about gone.

Although their plans were already made, the Germans tried to get whatever valuables they could to the very end. The leaders of the *Judenrat* were summoned to pay for more time—another day, another month, another hour—in gold, silver, precious stones. The Jews came up with only 80 percent of the "ransom."

In the beginning of October, representatives from the German, Polish, and Ukrainian police forces met in a movie theater to plan their final strategies. Guards were placed within a meter of each other. German soldiers went through the whole city, house by house, searching for Jews. Farms close to the city were burned. The entire city was surrounded.

Polina Golovchenko, the sister of Lily Guterman's savior, doesn't remember the exact date but never forgot what she saw. In *The Brest Ghetto* she relates: "We came to the Moscow Highway to watch Jews being convoyed to the power station. . . . They marched in file, holding each other's hands, stretching for a whole block. The file was led by the rabbi wearing a violet skullcap and a jacket. A horrible sight—I can still see it in my mind's eye. Dogs tried to get him. He had long hair, and the dogs caught it. He didn't so much as protect himself with his hands." About a thousand Jews were crammed into freight cars. "Dogs were barking; music was heard. Finally, the Germans took the dogs away."

Karpuk describes the night of October 14 and early morning of October 15, when he woke to the sound of shooting. Out on the streets, he saw a horrible scene: "The road was filled with corpses that we had to step over. When we got to Karbishev, we saw a big pit filled with bodies. We were given shovels and told to dig another pit. Children were led up to the pit and shot by a drunk German officer."

For Lily Guterman, that last day and night before liquidation, October 14, 1942, is etched in her memory. During the day, her father was held by the authorities because of irregularities in his papers. When he didn't come back to Peter's house, Lily waited, becoming increasingly frantic.

Peter's wife, Sofia, said to Lily, "I hear you're going to be killed today." For Sofia, the conflict between the survival of her friends and her family was terrific. "I love you and your family," she told Lily, "but I'm not going to risk my life."

Later on that day, Lily set out to look for her father. As a Jew, she wasn't allowed to walk in groups of fewer than 12 people or with non-Jews. She had to travel in the path of cars and animals because "to them, we are not people, we are animals."

The family members later reunited, although they no longer had a place to stay. With rumors of impending doom, Peter was afraid to keep Lily's family with him; however, he finally agreed to allow Lily, her brother, and her father to stay in his attic, while the rest of Lily's family went elsewhere. "We'll see what tomorrow will bring," he said.

As they waited in the attic, Lily's father tried to reassure them. It's inconceivable, he told them, that the Germans would annihilate 36,000 people, the ghetto estimate at that time.

The next day, Lily's brother and father went to the ghetto. Lily described what she saw as she waited for them at the gate: "All of a sudden, it's like the whole world is dead. Nothing. You can't see nobody. You can't hear nobody. I don't even see a person riding a bicycle." And it was true. Lily's father and brother reported that the ghetto was empty. The Jews were gone.

I note that Lily's impressions are in the present tense. To her, the memories are still strong and fresh. I think of what Hanna Kremer told me when she went back to Volchin in 1946—that eerie, atomic-bomb feeling, the sudden disappearance of all the people she once knew.

The *Courier* ends its account of the Brest ghetto with a list of other ghettos, their life spans, and the number of victims—Jews—killed. On the list, I notice the Kamenets ghetto, which existed for one year beginning in the autumn of 1941. Under number of victims, it says, "5,000 (taken to the city of Visoke and shot)."

As an example of the Germans' mass killings, Goldhagen's book lists 1,400 Jews killed on September 9, 1942, in Wysokie. I'm not sure if this is the same town as our Visoke (Wysokie-Litewskie) or the one near Bialystok (Wysokie-Mazowieckie). He also mentions "the largest single shooting massacre, more than 33,000 over two days at Babi Yar on the outskirts of Kiev at the end of September 1941."

In another section of his book, Goldhagen contradicts this statement, deeming Operation Erntefest (Harvest Festival), the November 3-4, 1943, murders of 43,000 Jews in the Lublin district work camps "the largest single shooting massacre of the war." In *Ordinary Men: Reserve Police Battalion 101 and the Final Solution in Poland*, Christopher R. Browning puts the number of Erntefest[7] victims at 42,000 and says, "It was exceeded only by the Rumanian massacre of more than 50,000 Odessan Jews in October 1941."

Two things strike me. First, Visoke is not only where I stopped but also where Hanna Kremer's immediate family fled, thinking they would be safer than in Volchin. These killings, these numbers, these places involve my people. Second, once again Babi Yar is reported as the largest single shooting massacre, with the Erntefest and Odessan events mentioned almost parenthetically. While it's true that some people were killed at Brona Gora as early as June 1942 and consequent shootings happened there in September, with the large Brest contingent murdered in October, the total killed in that forest was about 50,000. It's certainly a number worth mentioning.

In September 1942, while another transport of Jews from Bereza arrived at Brona Gora, while 1,500 Jews were killed in Yanovo and close to 3,000 were murdered at Luninetz, while the Brest ghetto inhabitants were being starved and beaten, and while his uncle's family was preparing for death in Volchin, Pee Wee was also in a form of isolation—writing from Navigation School in Monroe, Louisiana, where he was experiencing the near-primitive conditions of this swamp country.

In late October, while the earth in Brona Gora was still stained with blood, Pee Wee remained in the part of America known for its slavery, though even American slaves were not generally starved, were not marked for extermination. While those Jews still living in Eastern Europe counted their heartbeats by the stomp of German boots, Pee Wee notes that "the cadence of marching feet keeps the distasteful impression of military discipline always clearly in your mind." And while day and night for Jews were still marked by roll calls and pronouncements, Pee Wee writes, "We are still thrown out of bed to meet the bright, setting stars and the black, fading night."

Some remaining Eastern European Jews managed to record their observations in scribbled poetry and hidden drawings; Pee Wee too summons his powers of artistic observation: "Clouds of brown fire— billowy dust rises about you with every breath you take. It's a good camouflage, if nothing else."

However, in wartime, reality cut quickly through the poetic rhythm, even for Pee Wee: "Our flights are getting tough. For six weeks, we fly celestial flights in which we use the stars for navigation—the hardest part of the course so far."

But most Jews in Brest lacked the heart for creative expression. What happened to them during their last minutes in their once beloved city?

Eyewitness Sikorsky reports: "On October 15, 1942, the whole ghetto was surrounded by SS and SD troops. At 6:00 A.M., the blood started to pour. Nazis burst into the houses and took all the women, children, and elderly outside, and sent them to the firing squad."

Roman Levin tells of his final moments in the ghetto, living in communal housing, sometime after 6:00 A.M., and still dark:

Headlights lit up the barracks. . . . In the next moment, the door flung open. Two Germans stood in the doorway . . . tommy guns in hand. They yelled, "Get out!" The inmates moved backward. No one wanted to be the first. . . . I stood next to Mother, maybe in the front rank—I don't remember. Suddenly there was a sign or a voice, God knows from where. I dashed under a plank bed between human legs. I guess Mother didn't notice I was gone. There was a moment's confusion. . . . Anyway, they shut the door. And I heard Mom saying, "If you manage to flee, go to Aunt Tamara. Don't forget your mom." She knew I was hiding someplace. . . . I realized that if I stayed there, I'd be trapped . . . and I decided to leave the place right away. I flung open the windows and saw a policeman. The [other] windows were being boarded up. As the policeman turned away, I jumped out of the window and ran toward the river.

For those left behind in the Brest ghetto, the situation was bleak. Executions continued as the police and Gestapo caught Jews hiding in attics, basements, and other places. Survivors, many of them recorded in the *Black Book*, tell harrowing tales filled with personal sacrifice and the witnessing of atrocities.

From a ventilation shaft, Zisman saw how the Germans tortured their victims before killing them: "Threatening people with being buried alive, they stripped them naked. Since they did not have enough bullets for everyone, they poured dirt and hot cement on the naked people. I got sick with dysentery and could not get up anymore, but I could still see how the Germans raped young girls before killing them. I heard one of the girls call for help. The Germans buried her alive for hitting her rapist in the face."

One of the Katsaf sisters remembers: "On October 15, 1942, at six in the morning, we took Mother and my sister's child . . . and we went up to the attic of our house [126 Kuybishev Street], where 16 of us huddled in a boarded-up corner for five weeks. It is hard to imagine the conditions: hunger, cold, filth all around us. But this could not compare to the horrors we didn't see but could hear though the thin walls of the building. . . . In the first three days, Jews were taken to Brona Gora, and there was a lot of traffic. The Germans did all of these things with a sense of fulfillment, as if they had accomplished something great. There was a lot of music and singing after the executions."

The woman continues, "Every day, 70 to 100 people were taken to a nearby square, stripped, shot, and buried right on the spot. Early in the morning, workers came to dig graves. Once we heard a child scream, 'Mother, it is so cold. Why can't they shoot me sooner?' . . . Mothers undressed children and then undressed themselves." On the night of November 20, 1942, the hidden Katsaf family was discovered by the Ukrainian police. Fortunately, they were "only" robbed, but they had to flee.

During this time, Commander Semenyuk of the *Gendarmerie* was more than the passive observer he was when he had previously lived near the fort. His statement, recorded in 1945, includes perhaps the most honest and incriminating evidence I have yet received: "In November 1942, when the Jews started to run away from the ghetto in Brest, I was ordered to capture them, especially women and children. Once we executed 47 Jews, of whom I personally killed eight. Before shooting them, we took away their clothing and put them into graves in rows. Each one was shot in the back of the head."

Again, as in his confession about murders in Motikali, I am shocked at his testimony. Surely, now there will be some retraction. Or perhaps remorse. But there is nothing more.

Also in November, across the ocean, my uncle Pee Wee continued his preparations, anxious to complete his training so he could join the war as soon as possible. Meanwhile, he enjoyed his own ironic reality, having been elected officer of the day and chalking up flying time learning navigation. At month's end, he writes: "We flew around 4,000 miles in the past week from Texas to Kansas to Florida." Flying was not always smooth: "We ran into storms. . . . Our radio went blank. . . . My roommate went into a spin, but recovered."

My mother saved the invitation to Pee Wee's graduation from the Army Air Forces Navigation School on December 5, 1942. Pee Wee had attached a business card that read, "Abraham Lew, Lieutenant Air Corps, United States Army." Underneath, he jots, "I did it."

In a letter from Orlando Air Base, Pee Wee describes his transformation to lieutenant: "They put a few puny little bars on your shoulders, and put a pair of wings on your chest and lo and behold, you become a gentleman. . . . My squadron was lucky enough to get Flying Fortresses. They fly like a dream and are really the safest ships in the air. We will move our squadron to Brooksville."

Comparing Brooksville, Florida, to Woodridge, New York, where he spent his boyhood and adolescent years, Pee Wee notes, "The movies, gossip, hunting and fishing are the greatest pastimes." Not so different from Woodridge.

The Jews hiding in Brest had no such pastimes. For those who survived, there were sorrows on top of sorrows, miracles after miracles. According to Gutman: "Me, my sister, and our children hid under the house. We saw how the other Jews were led to their death. . . . For two weeks, we ate raw grain, beets, pickles. The children literally dried up from the hunger. After two weeks, I left the ghetto to see what had happened. I brought back some bread, gave it to the children, and left again. I did this for five weeks, coming and going. One day, I came back, and the children were gone. I aimlessly walked around, not knowing where I was going. Late at night, I decided to go to a Russian family who felt sorry for me and hid me in their shed. Thus, I spent the whole winter, sitting in a hole in the ground, covered by straw. I was saved by the Red Army. I saw the sun again, the soldiers fed me, and I became a person once more."

Zisman recounts his long ordeal: "Me, my wife, and 12 other women were hiding in a pit under the shed. Some of the women lost their minds. When my wife and I got sick, we gathered up the last of our strength and moved to another place, an attic. We moved around like that for 17 months, going from attic to attic, basement to basement. By the time the lucky day, July 28, 1944, came, I couldn't even talk, much less move around."

The Katsaf sister reports how her family endured over two years in assorted attics, sheds, and basements. "It is a miracle," she says, "that we did not freeze to death. For six months, we did not change our clothes or eat cooked food. If this had gone on for two weeks more, we would not have survived, but the Red Army saved us."

Bakalyash describes how she, her children, and her sister hid in her basement, which had a secret passage to an upstairs room. The entrance was blocked by a bookcase and guarded by her elderly mother, who was later taken away by the Germans. For about two weeks, the family sub-sisted on raw beets, cabbage, grain, and flour mixed with salt. Hunger forced them out of the space. Bakalyash hid in a nearby village while her son went back to get the rest of the children, unaware that they had already been caught by the police and killed.

Delirious with fever, Bakalyash spent some nights in an abandoned field and hid under the floor of a local man's house, then under an old church. Finally, near death, she came to the forest and collapsed. A kind woman fed her some bread and led her to an area of the forest occupied by the partisans, where she lived until the Red Army arrived.

Frequent police checks made it difficult for Lily Guterman and her family to remain in Peter's attic. After a month, they moved to another attic in the area, a very high place reached by a narrow ladder. There, they lived in floor-to-ceiling straw, with only a small hole for exiting and entering. "Straw was our sheets," Lily says in an interview videotaped on the bus during our trip. In a voice that seems choked with the sharp, dry grass, she continues, "Straw was our pillows, was our blankets, was our towels—we had absolutely nothing."

Filthy and infested with lice, the family remained there, working at farm chores when possible. Every few days, Lily says, they got a little bread, which was, "so thin you could see yourself."

But, as ever, Lily's family was resourceful, making holes in the roof to see the surrounding area. And what they saw were soldiers with dogs. Although Peter was able to buy the soldiers off with some schnapps, it was time again to flee. They went back to Peter's original attic and this time, Lily's father recited Kaddish, the prayer for the dead. "Forgive me," he told his children. "This is the end."

Luckily, they were able to remain there for several months. Then the Gestapo returned with German shepherds, searching for Jews.

Even though the war was going poorly for the Germans, they were still obsessed with their hatred of the Jews.

This time, the frantic threesome did what they hadn't done before—they separated. Lily's father and brother hid in a neighbor's shack, and Lily spent 24 hours huddling in an outhouse waiting to hear if her loved ones were shot. After dawn, Lily joined her father and brother, and they vowed that whatever happened, they would never again separate.

The group eventually went back to Peter's attic, which seemed "like a castle." There, they heard airplanes and bombs. The last night before the war ended in Brest, the city was on fire. To Lily, it looked like the end of the world.

Then, there was an incredible sound. Lily thought she must be dreaming. She heard Russian male voices cursing. Before long, Lily ran into the arms of a Russian soldier. "Thank you so much," she gushed between hugs and kisses. "You know, I'm Jewish. I'm Jewish, and you liberated me."

In total, Lily and her family hid for 22 months. What saved them was their vow to stay together, their resiliency, their willpower, and, of course, the selfless and humane acts of their non-Jewish friends. As the fewer than 20 Jewish survivors of the Brest ghetto prove, however, these righteous gentiles were far too few.

Polina risked her life by keeping two Jewish children in her flat. In *The Brest Ghetto*, she tells about one, a boy named Misha, from a family she knew well, who came to her at the end of October 1941: "There was no one in the ghetto at that time. Some were hiding in basements and attics. But the ghetto was practically nonexistent. The boy Misha asked me, 'Is Mom here?' I told him, 'No,' and he stayed with us. There were many people living at our place, including kids 10 to 12 years of age. . . . One day, five Germans were passing by. One of them stopped and said, pointing to Misha, '*Jude* [Jew].' The boys with whom Misha were playing, Sasha, my nephew, and others, they shielded him and said, 'Run for your life!' Misha took to his heels, while the boys kept saying, '*Mein Bruder*,' meaning, 'He's my brother, not a Jew.' Meanwhile, Misha managed to hide in the back garden."

And so some survived. Too many others didn't. In a war noted for its unprecedented barbarism, death came in many ways. Sometimes the survivors weren't those who underwent torture, but those who waited.

My mother's packet of letters from Pee Wee contains an envelope with some documents. I open the first, a letter dated October 5, 1943. It's from the War Department, Commanding Officer, First Bombardment Squadron, Ninth Bombardment Group, Brooksville Army Air Field, Florida, and signed Mack McKay, Major, Air Corps. Addressed to my mother, the letter reads, "It is with deepest regret that I must inform you that your brother was instantly killed in an airplane crash at Brooksville Army Air Field, Brooksville, Florida, at 6:10 A.M. on October 3, 1943."

After expressing his sympathies, the major concludes, "Abraham was held in high regard by all members of the Command and his loss will be deeply felt by his many friends. He was a splendid soldier and an outstanding character."

Then there's a letter from the Tarpon Springs Insurance Agency, addressed to my grandmother and signed by Manuel Johnson: "Abraham and I became very close friends, as I gave him a lot of lessons in shooting as I hoped one day if he went across it would do him some good. . . . I feel that I have lost a good friend as well as the friendship of a real boy."

The date on the letter is October 15, 1943. October 15, exactly a year from the day that the Jews from Brest were sent to Brona Gora. October 15, exactly a year from the day the executions began. October 15, a day I shall always remember. October 15, my birthday.

There are some death notices, one from a fraternal Jewish organization in New York: "First Lieutenant Abraham Lew, Born January 7, 1920, died in the service of his country, October 3, 1943. Killed in the crash of a Flying Fortress, at Brooksville, Florida."

A letter dated October 22, 1943, provides me with a glimpse into the personality of my uncle Abraham, my namesake. It is his personal effects: 41 pairs of socks, 16 handkerchiefs, two dumbbells, one photo album, 35 cents, six rolls of Kodak film, six golf balls, one cigarette case, five pipes, 50 yards of silk fishing line, and a book, *The Strategy of Terror*.

A December 3, 1943, bill of lading from the Orlando Railroad lists one box of personal effects, weighing 176 pounds, valued at 10 cents per pound. To the U.S. Army, my uncle's belongings were worth $17.60. The box was received in New York on December 28, 1943—my grandmother Masha's 50th birthday.

My mother, not one for idle sentimentalizing, never got over the death of her precious brother. She often spoke of his funeral: the blocks of mourners, the attendant officers, the flag-draped coffin, the folded flag handed to her devastated mother, her involuntary scream when the coffin with her brother's remains was lowered into the ground.

And through the years, she depicted him as "lovable, charming, always ready to help anyone with a task." She described his chores around the boardinghouse in Woodridge. He used to take care of the chickens. To him, they were creatures with distinct names and personalities. It was Pee Wee who awoke at five on bitter-cold winter mornings to start the heat; it was Pee Wee who was never scolded by his authoritarian rabbinical father.

In particular, my mother described Pee Wee's love for his little black dog, Soccy. One day in Woodridge, the puppy strayed, and the whole village helped in the search. Soccy was finally found in a remote corner of the backyard, flung against the fence, barely alive, mutilated and castrated by some sick fiend. This, my mother said on more than one occasion—each time with fresh bitterness—was Pee Wee's first introduction to human cruelty. Even this experience, she noted, didn't make him a bitter person. Instead, he was mischievous and daring, sweet and popular, the favorite of teachers and neighbors. The village of Woodridge named a street after him.

Also fresh in my mother's mind was that October day when she heard her doorbell ring in Brooklyn and there stood a boy with a telegram. I have a phone interview with her reciting, again for me, the key words: "Search mission . . . two of the other men just went along for the ride . . . lost wing . . . only 80 feet from the ground . . . one giant conflagration . . . 13 young men incinerated." Like a mantra, whenever she says these words, she adds, "Pee Wee among them."

I am prepared to take advantage of a rare opportunity to quiz Pee Wee's surviving siblings during a post-Thanksgiving visit at my aunt Sara's home in Woods Hole on Cape Cod, Massachusetts, where she retired after working as a psychologist and raising two sons. Seated at the dining-room table with my mother, Uncle Gerson, and Aunt Sara, I take out my tape recorder and begin a series of questions. These family elders are only too happy to speak, unintimidated by the whirring machine.

"Now that you're all here," I begin, "something has bothered me for years. Pee Wee always came across as a perfect person. I never felt like he was a human being. I know he was glorified in death, but could he have been so wonderful?"

My mother says, "He was truly good, the kind of person one says doesn't have a bad bone in his body."

"He was only a kid," Gerson says, as if Pee Wee had been too young to develop bad traits.

Overweight and depleted from a long battle with diabetes, Sara's drawn face crinkles, revealing a hint of her adolescent tomboyish features as they appear in old black-and-white photos. She returns to the subject of Pee Wee's chickens: "He had 12 of them and a coop in the backyard. He would go there every day and get four eggs and bring them to my mother. He was very proud. One day, he came back and the eggs had holes in them, like a weasel had come and sucked them out."

"How did it happen?" I ask.

Sara answers: "He was all ready to set a trap. He caught my father red-handed. My father took a pin, made a hole, and sucked out the fresh eggs."

As I listen to this story, I smile. Finally, I can see Pee Wee as he must have been, a young boy of maybe eight or nine, heartsick over his eggs, naively setting a trap only to discover that the culprit was none other than his own father. I see a boy whose beloved puppy was sadistically massacred. I see someone who knew deep hurt, who, naturally of a sweet disposition, must have understood at an early age his role as family arbiter. Though his siblings didn't want to admit it, even after all these years, nobody is too good. Even good people pay a price.

As I think of Pee Wee, I picture him in his last days. Though exhausted by his rigorous schedule and frightened by the uncertainties of flying, he still managed to think the world was "swell."

I think of other families during those war years, thousands of miles away—the families of all the Jews isolated into ghettos—beaten, raped, tortured, starved, and transported to uncertainty. I think of those lucky few who survived, including Lily Guterman, spending 22 months hiding in an attic.

And I think of all those who didn't survive—the 50,000 killed at Brona Gora; the nearly 400 Volchiners, including my uncle Iser and his family; and finally, the 13 unsuspecting American men on a peaceful search mission. My uncle Pee Wee among them.

Chapter 8

Annihilation

Incrementally, I have been preparing myself to present detailed eyewitness reports about Brona Gora. I managed to gather personal material on ghetto life and subsequent liquidation; I got to the point of train arrival at the forest site. Then, I skipped to opening of the pits in 1944. I even tackled the horrific slaughter of my own people in Volchin. Somehow, in my unexpressed thoughts, I kept putting off the inevitable Armageddon. It was one thing to witness the murders in an isolated village; one could always rationalize that this was an aberration. But the premeditated annihilation of 50,000 people required the complicity of hundreds, if not thousands, of Nazi professionals, German soldiers, local auxiliary police, railroad personnel, church officials, government figures; and farmers, villagers, and city residents—average citizens of every type. This is too overwhelming to contemplate.

What can't be properly expressed finds a way to insinuate itself. Not surprisingly, I begin to have nightmares of wild chases through dark and damp mazes. In my dreams, I'm running naked through forests, and I awaken right before catastrophe with a palpitating heart and drenching perspiration.

The other night, the dream was so unbearable that all I can remember is sitting up, mumbling to myself in a strangulated mantra, "Forget this now. Forget this now." I must have been frozen in horror for some time because for a few days, my head pulsed with an excruciating pain probably attributable to extreme muscle tension. Certainly the terror I felt was nothing like what the victims felt. I tell myself, over and over, that this is something that must be told—for them.

So I begin with the first information I received about the actual massacre: the report from Kobrin. The record keeper, A. Martynov, presents the testimony of a railroad worker who witnessed the entire execution:

> Beforehand, 300 local peasants had been ordered to dig out eight holes in the ground—each was 40 to 60 meters long, six meters wide, and four meters deep. The sector was surrounded with a barbed-wire fence. In specially prepared places, the victims were told to strip themselves naked. Then through the use of hitting and dogs, the guards made the victims go down the ladder into the holes and lie down, in lines, facing the ground. The people were driven to such levels of despair and torpor that they followed the orders without protests. Probably they were affected by some kind of "hypnosis of inevitability." Machine-gun rounds poured down on the people lying down. The next lines of people, in the same submissive way, lay down upon the dead and nearly dead until the hole was filled with bloodied human bodies. More than 50,000 people from Kobrin, Gorodets, Bereza, Brest, Drogichino, Yanovo, and Pinsk were slaughtered in this meat grinder.

I wonder at the phrase "hypnosis of inevitability." Were these the actual words of the railroad worker or, more likely, an interpretation by the historian, Martynov. I can accept this concept, that the Jews had been so dehumanized, tortured, starved, that this shooting was the inevitable next step. All hope had been lost. Yet I don't like the word *submissive*. Somehow, this implies that they were giving in, agreeing in some way to yield, to surrender to another's will, that they were complicit—that word again—in their own death. I don't think they were surrendering or yielding. I think they were actively ending their misery.

I also wonder if these 50,000 really were so "submissive." Other massacre witnesses, including those from Volchin, reported the sounds of crying, screaming, begging for mercy. There were those victims shot beforehand—my own cousin Ida—because they protested. I wonder if those who watched, or if those who could have done something, wanted to believe the victims were submissive, that they were merely fulfilling their fate, or, as the women in Volchin thought, being punished for killing Christ.

These thoughts bring to mind a story my uncle Gerson once told me about one of his strongest childhood memories, from when he was eight years old, in 1920. He was on the train with his father and stepsister Esther, on their way to join the rest of the family in Warsaw during the Russian conflict. Half of the railroad car was filled with Hasidic Jews and the other half with wounded Polish soldiers. The soldiers began to needle the Jews, threatening to cut off their beards with their swords.

My grandfather Isaac, a handsome and imposing figure, stood up and addressed a lieutenant: "You are patriots. You are fighting for your country. These people are also citizens of Poland."

And then, a frightening thing happened, Gerson related: "One of the soldiers hit my father over the head with his knapsack."

I wonder if these Polish soldiers, when telling their stories to their families, forgot my grandfather's gallant act and instead talked about the submissive Jews.

I recall my grandmother's story, from about the same time, of putting flour on her face to fool the Cossacks into thinking she was an old, undesirable woman (see chapter 1). I wonder if the Cossacks thought my grandmother's grandmother (who outwitted them by getting them drunk and pretending that there was a quarantine) was submissive. I wonder if they had seen my grandmother, pale-faced in the woods, would they have thought her another passive old woman?

From those days in Eastern Europe, through the hardships in America and raising a family, Masha could never be described as submissive. Even in her more relaxed middle years, she brought sheer determination to every situation. And always, she longed to go to Palestine, the land of her people.

After her second husband Dave Miller's unexpected death at the hands of a disgruntled tenant in 1948, Masha fought with his family over the inheritance. "I'll never forget," Norma says on one of my tapes, "my mother eventually got some money and immediately bought herself a $5,000 mink coat and went to Israel."

Of course, Masha doesn't tell it that way. She says, "Many times I went to Israel. I was [there] about eight months a year and three months I would come back to Brooklyn to see everybody. I couldn't stay there. My heart was in Israel." Masha had realized her dream.

The official word on the Brona Gora massacre can be obtained from the 1944 report by the Extraordinary State Commission to Investigate Nazi Crimes Committed on the Territory of the Soviet Union, based primarily on eyewitness testimonies and a special investigation carried out by members of the commission at the site of the mass murders. I receive the translation of the sections previously deemed untranslatable, having obtained the original report from the United States Holocaust Memorial Museum. Among repetitions from other commission reports, there is also new and more specific information.

The first section, entitled "A Report on the Atrocities, Robberies, Harassments, and Destruction Caused by the German-Fascist Invaders in the Region of Bronnaya Gora, the Brest Region," includes the names of the members of the commission[1] and their conclusions:

In May–June 1942, the Germans started to dig pits, 400 meters northwest of the Brona Gora station. This took place over an area of 16,800 square meters. In order to dig the pits, the Germans mobilized inhabitants of nearby villages, about 600–800 people per day. Explosives were also used.

In mid-June 1942, when the graves were dug, the Germans started transporting trains to the Brona Gora station. The trains contained Russians, Belorussians, Jews, and Poles, ranging from infants to the aged. The trains arriving at the station were guarded by a convoy of Germans wearing SD and SS uniforms. The trains came from assorted parts of Belorussia: Bereza, Brest, Drogichino, Yanovo, Gorodets, etc. People were also taken to Brona Gora on foot.

The trains arriving at Brona Gora were extremely overcrowded. As a result, some people actually died during the trip.

Arriving trains were diverted from the main track onto an auxiliary track, running past military warehouses, 250 meters from Brona Gora. The graves were also nearby.

Contained in the commission report are protocols of witness interrogations. The first is from a Polish national whose residence is listed as Brona Gora Station, Brest District. Born in Warsaw in 1891, Roman Stanislavovich Novis was in charge of the Brona Gora railroad station before the war. During the occupation, he was demoted to railroad worker while a German named Heil took over Novis's former duties. Novis worked there until liberation by the Red Army. In his position, Novis had a unique insider's view of railroad activities during the time of the massacres, and he took scrupulous notice. His testimony, recorded on September 12, 1944, provides a chilling account:

In June 1942, five trains arrived at Brona Gora carrying Soviet citizens. The first came from the Bereza Kartuska station, Brest District. It had 16 cars, all of which were filled with Jews. There were more than 200 people in each car. The train was extremely overcrowded. All of the people came from Ghetto B in the village of Bereza Kartuska.

The second train had 46 cars. It contained Jews from the Drogichino, Yanovo, and Gorodets stations. The majority of the people were Jews. The cars of this train also contained over 200 people each.

The third train had 40 cars and came from the Brest-Litovsk station. The train was extremely overcrowded. The citizens were Jews.

The fourth train came from the Pinsk and Kobrin stations, and had 18 cars full of Jewish-Soviet citizens.

The last train also came from Brest-Litovsk. It had 13 cars. The train contained people from the Brest prison (Belorussians, Poles, Jews).

According to Novis, the Germans killed more than Jews. The locals did not escape punishment and were "silenced" for their complicity: "During the month of July 1942, the Germans executed the 800 workers who were brought from military warehouses to dig the pits. The workers were shot and thrown into a pit not far from the barracks and warehouses. The barracks are located 400 meters from the Brona Gora station, near the Warsaw-Moscow Highway."

Novis then describes the rest of the transports, corroborating much of the Kobrin testimony:

In September 1942, another train of Soviet citizens arrived. This train had 25 cars and came from the Bereza Katuska station. In the beginning of October 1942, another such train arrived, containing 28 cars from Brest-Litovsk. Both of these trains were diverted onto the alternate track, the same one that was used for the trains that arrived earlier that year. These people were stripped, led into the pits, and executed in the same manner as before. Among these people were women, infants, teenagers, the elderly, and grown men fit to work. The executions were accompanied by blood-curdling screams.

At this time, I found out from local residents that the Germans were also executing Soviet citizens . . . near the village of Smolyarka. . . . I do not know how many people died there. The victims were buried at the scene.

Although Novis's account differs considerably in the size and in the number of pits from the Soviet commission's findings and other sources, his knowledge of the train arrivals should be accurate.

He summarizes the tragedy: "In all, 186 railroad cars came to Brona Gora, and the passengers were executed. The trains, now containing the clothing of the victims, were sent back to the originating stations. I had friendly relations with the German Heil, in charge of the station, and he told me some things about the murders. He said that 48,000 people had been killed here. He also told me that in 1943, two automobiles full of gold and other valuables confiscated from the victims were transported back to Germany."

The enormity of the statistics is indeed overwhelming. But even Novis cannot forget the human carnage: "When the victims came out of the cars, some corpses were also dumped out. These people probably died of malnutrition, overcrowding, and bad ventilation of the cars."

The surviving passengers were unloaded onto a special platform, surrounded by barbed wire. Novis continues, "They were forced to strip—men, women, and children alike. After this, the people's fingers were inspected, and all rings were confiscated."

Then, through a narrow corridor enclosed by barbed wire, the victims were led, one by one, to their graves. Each went down a ladder into a pit, lay side by side, face down, and had to wait.

Novis reports, "When the bottom of the pit was filled up, the Germans shot all of them. Without removing the corpses, they would force more people into the pits to lay on top of the dead. Thus, the pit was filled up layer by layer until it was completely full. While the executions were carried out, the air was filled with screams and moaning, that of men as well as women and children. From my booth near the main track, about 250 meters from the pits, I could easily see these horrible executions."

The commission named some of those responsible:

The coordination of the arrival and departure times of the trains was carried out by the head of the Brona Gora station, Heil, and station guards Pike and Schmidt. All three were German.

To conceal traces of their crimes committed at the Brona Gora station, the Germans executed more than 1,000 people living in the vicinity of the military warehouses, where the original executions took place.

Although eyewitness testimony differs, the commission members, through on-site investigations, determined the exact measurements of the pits, all of which were between 3.5 and 4 meters deep:

No. 1–63 meters long, 6.5 meters wide
No. 2–36 meters long, 6.5 meters wide
No. 3–36 meters long, 6 meters wide
No. 4–37 meters long, 6 meters wide
No. 5–52 meters long, 6 meters wide
No. 6–24 meters long, 6 meters wide
No. 7–12 meters long, 6 meters wide
No. 8–16 meters long, 4.5 meters wide

The commission concluded that between June and November 1942, the Germans killed more than 50,000 people at Brona Gora.

As victory against the allies became more uncertain, the Germans grew anxious. In March 1944, they began to destroy evidence of their crimes: "The Germans took more than 100 workers to the crime site. The workers, who came from different parts of the Brest District, were forced to dig up corpses and burn them. The burning of the corpses took place on the site of the graves in six areas of the location. The fires burned for 15 days and 15 nights. To facilitate the burnings, the Germans ransacked 48 military warehouses and barracks located near the scene. Also, a lighting liquid was used that gave the flames a bluish tinge."

Novis notes that the burnings produced an "unbearable stench throughout the village of Brona Gora."

One of the few to give names, Novis says, "Among the people who were forced to dig up the corpses, I can identify two: the first had the last name of Racha and came from the village of Segnevichi. The second is Mikhalyak Martzeniy, from the Oranchitsi village." The commission determined:

When the work was done, the Nazis also shot and killed the workers. Their bodies were also "cremated."

At the site of these inhuman atrocities and suffering, the Germans planted trees, but they could not completely hide what they had done. Items later found there included charred bones, a hair clip, a set of shoes, Soviet coins, a shoulder bone, and a child's arm of 18 centimeters long.

The above actions were witnessed by Roman Stanislavovich Novis, Grigory Grigoryevich Yatskevich, and many others.

As discussed in chapter 7, the commission also investigated the mass executions on a plateau near the village of Smolyarka, Berezov District. This site was six kilometers from the Brona Gora station. In October 1942, the victims arrived in automobiles from the city of Bereza and several villages in the Berezov District. They were tortured and executed in much the same way as those at Brona Gora. More than 1,000 people were murdered. The commission found five graves there, each 10 meters long, 7 meters wide, and 2.5 meters deep.[2]

The matériel devastation in the area around the Brona Gora station was considerable. The Germans demolished many railroads and depots. Squads known as the *Pimashtzug* destroyed tracks using a special machine with a metal hook that broke both the rails and the cross ties. Depots were totaled with explosives. The person in charge of the brigade responsible for this destruction was a German, Captain Sporberg. Total damage to the Brona Gora station was estimated at 1,152,000 rubles.

What makes Novis's testimony even more unique is that, unbeknown to the Germans, he was fluent in their language. Therefore, the Germans spoke freely in his presence. Other than Heil, who returned to Frankfurt in 1943, Novis didn't know the names of those who supervised the executions. The trains had been guarded by a special deployment of SS and SD troops. These people came in cars, dressed in military uniforms, and left when the shootings were over.

However, the commission was able to pinpoint some of the guilty, with most names repeated in other sections of the findings, and charged SS and SD troops with the executions near the Brona Gora station and the village of Smolyarka. The list included the names of those commanding the troops.[3]

One can only wonder what went on in the minds of these murderers. As the soldier poked his rifle into the neck of the terrified little girl, did he think of his own child, her hair carefully braided, her dress perfectly starched? Was he nauseated by flying bits of bones and body parts? Was he annoyed by spattered blood and brain matter staining his uniform?

Was he bored and exhausted, only waiting to finish this unpleasant duty? Was he thinking of the celebration afterward when he would brag about the number of Jews he killed for his homeland? Had he already been so brainwashed by generations of inbred hatred that the writhing, wailing people beneath him were no longer considered human, worthy of compassion?

And the Jews, as they crouched and huddled, breasts smashed into the dirt, blinded by pressed flesh, gasping for air, calling out, in strangled sobs, the names of loved ones—did they curse the men above them? Did they find any solace in their faith? Did they believe their God had something better waiting for them?

Another railroad worker, Ivan Vasilievich Govin, corroborated Novis's testimony, although Heil had ordered both men to keep everything they saw an absolute secret. A Ukrainian by birth, Govin was head of the repair brigade at Brona Gora station before the war. Like Novis, the Germans demoted Govin to the position of a regular railroad worker; as such, he remained in a position to witness the atrocities. His account begins with the events of May 1942, when the pits were made, he says, by "firing heavy artillery into the site and by forcing local residents to help dig." His estimates of the size of the pits differ from those of Novis and the commission.

Although the Germans didn't tell the workers the true nature of their labors, it wasn't necessary. Govin says, "It was common knowledge among workers that the pits would be used to hide the groups of people who would be shot there."

As the trains came from early June 1942 through October, Govin watched the gruesome events. In particular, he notes the response of the victims: "I witnessed how the people inside the cars, before they were let out, begged for a drink of water. I could not come close to the trains because they were heavily guarded. As each new train arrived, I could hear screams and moans issuing from within . . . which continued until the last person was shot."

In addition to the German chiefs—Heil and his successor, Pike—Govin names two other Germans working at the station, Schmidt and Schiller.

These "eyewitness" railroad workers could be considered collaborators in the sense that they cooperated—willingly or not—with the occupying force of their country. Whether they can be considered perpetrators is probably a matter of semantic interpretation. By collaborating, they were certainly committing a crime. Though they were not initiating the acts, their actions helped in the commission of the crimes.

Other locals undoubtedly took more active roles, volunteering their skills and resources, relishing their importance, happy to rid their land of the "subhuman" Jews. Whether these locals were forced physically or psychologically is also a moot point. A moot point to those on the receiving end.

Railroad workers were not the only eyewitnesses to the killings. Local policeman Joseph Pavlovich Schidlovsky, who had already testified about German torture and execution in Bereza Kartuska, accompanied the Jews on the train to Brona Gora. He stood 250-300 meters from the place of execution. "Out of curiosity," he watched the Jews being killed. "I saw that the Jews were taken out of the train and told to strip," he reports. "After they finished, about 10 people per car were left to collect all of the clothing into the car, while the rest were forced to go into the pits and were shot. . . . Then the Jews who loaded the clothing back into the trains were also shot."

Although Schidlovsky claimed he didn't witness the actual shooting because his view was obstructed by a hill that had been dug out of the pits, he said that after the killings, the Germans covered the pits with earth and ordered the police back onto the trains. When he returned to Bereza, he saw trains arrive with the victims' clothing, which was taken to the German barracks.

At SD headquarters, Pichmann told the policemen through a Russian interpreter named Ivan, "Do not tell anyone what happened today. If anyone tells, I will find out, and the same thing will happen to you."

Villagers also saw and heard. In the Belarusian documentary, *The Brest Ghetto*, a woman named Zhenia says, "We lived in the village of Zarechye. My father was a trackman. It's a short distance from Brona Gora to Zarechye. I was grazing cows then, and I saw Jews being shot to death. There was a huge pit not far from Brona Gora, and they filled it with corpses. . . . I heard little children crying and groaning."

An interviewer in the film asks another eyewitness, Alexi Kovalevich, about the pits. He points to an area in the forest and says, "See one over there? That was a pit too. . . . They'd strip to the skin and move along the track lined by barbed wire right into the pits so there was no getting away. . . . Nice, good strong people they were. Did nothing wrong."

In an excerpt from a volume, *The Crimes of the German-Nazi Occupation of Belorussia, 1941–1944*, provided by YIVO and containing some of the Soviet commission's findings, there is testimony from one worker who survived his participation, recorded on September 15, 1944. Ivan Geitz, a resident of the village of Smolyarka, Brest District, says: "In September 1942, I was forced by the Germans to dig pits at Brona Gora station, where I worked for seven days. There were more than 600 people digging. We were closely watched and forced to work from sunrise to sunset. . . . The Germans told us that the pits were for potatoes, but they were really for the concealment of corpses."

And again, the terrible sounds reminds us that the Jews did not go to their deaths silently. According to Geitz:

In October 1942, my wife and I were digging up potatoes near the Warsaw-Moscow Highway. We saw Soviet citizens in automobiles being taken to a place near a few pits in the ground, which were 100 meters from the road and 600 meters from our house. We heard crying and screaming. We heard the sounds of hundreds of gunshots. It went on for three days. I do not know where the people were from, or how many of them died.

I also witnessed how bodies were brought there from the village of Bereza. This also took place in October 1942. The pits were dug one day before the people were brought there. The inhabitants of our village, including my wife, were forced to dig the pits.

Also, I know about the execution of the family of Peter S. Poznyak, numbering nine people, three of them small children. They were buried in a pit near their house. I do not know why they were executed.

Perhaps this Peter S. Poznyak was one of those who said "no" to the Germans. I'd like to think so.

Saying "no" saved my grandmother and her family. My grandparents said "no" to more persecution, determined to flee Eastern Europe. When Masha waited for my grandfather Isaac, who arrived in America, to send enough money to bring over his family, she said "no" to starvation. She and her children survived on meager supplies, often finding respite in her mother's Volchin home, also loaded with children.

And survive they did. If Masha hadn't been able to cope with her large brood in Eastern Europe, if she hadn't been able to outwit the authorities, hide illnesses from the officials at Ellis Island, she would have remained in Europe, probably drifting back to Volchin. If the family had stayed in Volchin and grown up with the other Midlers, Masha and some of the older children, and their new families, would have undoubtedly been killed in the village massacre. If the family had stayed in Volchin, the youngest children would have been the proper age to have been sent to Brest for "work" purposes. If the family had stayed, these children would have probably been killed at Brona Gora. Of course, if the family had stayed, all the progeny would have not been created; this account would not have been written.

Some lucky Eastern European Jews escaped to friendly countries, and others fled eastward. Yet countless unlucky ones remained, for varying reasons. Historically, many Jews had managed to survive Soviet roundups and deportations and believed they could do the same with the Germans. Of course, Soviet censorship prevented news about the atrocities and acts of resistance from reaching the Jewish communities.

My relatives, the Midlers, loved life in a small village; they loved their traditions. It's inconceivable that so many people like them, thousands on thousands, were transported and massacred. In one location alone, 50,000 human beings.

Just imagine, Toronto's SkyDome stadium (since renamed Rogers Centre), seating capacity 50,000. A game in full swing. A cheering audience. The old man with his grandson on the right. The beautiful young woman in front. The class of second-graders in the row below. A family of four to the left. Every person there murdered in cold blood.

Railroad worker Govin reports that local residents told him of a wounded woman who escaped from one of the Brona Gora pits during the executions and was later caught and taken away by the Germans. He didn't know what happened to her and assumed she was killed. I receive an account from the Brest Lore Museum that makes me wonder if this is indeed the same "woman." At 12 years old, Esfir Manevich was the only survivor of the Kobrin Jews taken to Brona Gora. Here is her miraculous story:

> I was standing at the hole's edge. A soldier with a machine gun was apparently aiming at my head, but he hit my arm and touched only my skin. I fell down, but not into the hole, and pretended to be dead. After that, I started unnoticeably to crawl away, and then I ran. Busy with shooting people, the Germans didn't see a running girl. But the officer in charge of shooting, who was on the hill, saw me. The pursuit started. I ran into the forest, where I fell down. I was lying in blood. The dog for some reason started to lick the blood and didn't touch me. When the Germans ran up to me and saw that, they said, "Kaput," and ran away. I lay for a long time in a bloody puddle, and then I stood up and went away, avoiding people so that I wouldn't be caught by the Germans.
>
> After that, I met a woman from Kobrin. She said to me, "Come with me. Live through the war. Very soon I will have a baby, and you will baby-sit him." I agreed. She brought me to her house and handed me over to the Gestapo. I refused to confess that I was a Jew. I was a fair-haired girl, and I made up a story that I was an orphan and that I was allegedly a maid for a Jewish family in Kobrin. I said that I was Polish, but they took me for a Jew.
>
> Several times I was taken from my cell to the shooting, together with other prisoners, but time and again, the Germans took me back to my cell. The prison's chief was the one doing that. I was like a target for a game. However, he probably pitied me. He released me from prison and handed me over to the cloister. There I waited for the Red Army.

Out of the carnage of blood and bones, someone at the edge of the pit survived. With what she saw, what she experienced, Esfir was still able to run, to have enough wits about her to want to live. Even at such a young age, she must have known that she would have to tell her story many times. She had to survive any way she could. And, there, at that period in history, there was only one way to survive—to deny that she was one of those hated, reprehensible creatures: a Jew.

I hope that Esfir never regretted that denial. I hope that in her later years, she repeatedly announced that she had been a girl who once stood at the edge of the pit, a girl who ran away, a girl who survived, a Jew—one of 50,000—who lived.

Worshipping in Volchin, 1997: the old synagogue, now a trade school; the Russian Orthodox church; and the Catholic church. Courtesy Dov Bar.

Volchin, site of the former ghetto, 1997. Courtesy Dov Bar.

Volchin, 1997. This building may have been constructed from Jewish cemetery headstones. Courtesy Dov Bar.

Hannah Williams on the killing fields in Volchin, 1993. Courtesy Hannah Williams.

Shmuel Englender says Kaddish at
Volchin's Jewish memorial, 1997.

Two houses on Midler
property, 1997. Author
and Shmuel stand in
front of original site.

Left to right: Anna Gagarina, Hannah Williams, and Svetlana Kuntz by Volchin's riverfront, 1993. Courtesy Hannah Williams.

Rosanne Lapan and historian A. Martynov in Kobrin, 1997. Courtesy Rosanne Lapan.

Lily Guterman and Nechamia Manker's attic hiding place in Brest, 1997. Courtesy Sara Sanditen.

Louis Pozez at memorial to
Brest ghetto, 1997. Courtesy
Louis and Ruthann Pozez.

Ruthann and Louis
Pozez, late 1990s.
Courtesy Louis and
Ruthann Pozez.

Entering Brona Gora, 1997.

Monuments at
Brona Gora, 1997.

The new Volchin family at Brona Gora, 1997. *Left to right*: Drora, Shmuel, author, Dov, and Esther.

Nechamia Manker, Lily Guterman, and Sara Sanditen with Belarusian locals at Brona Gora, 1997. Courtesy Sara Sanditen.

Belarusian locals at Brona Gora, 1997.

Author and Hanna Kremer go
over photos of murdered family
members, 1997.

Mike and Hanna Kremer, 1997.

Volchin memorial in Holon Cemetery in Israel. Names of Jewish families are engraved on panels.

After Dave Miller's death, Masha traveled to Europe and Israel, often luxuriating on ocean voyages, wining and dining with the ships' captains and other international characters. In Israel, she made lifetime friends and, of course, visited her relatives, Dina and Shoshana, the wife and daughter of Masha's stepson, Jack. Masha was finally in her element—the vivacious and enviable American widow, ever on the lookout for adventure and romance.

In 1950, she was in Tel Aviv, staying with friends who convinced her to spend the evening at a nightclub owned and managed by a pal of theirs, a handsome Russian émigré named Michel Hiro.[1] When Michel asked Masha to dance, she remembers, "I thought he was a god. We started dancing, and he didn't let me off the whole evening. Dancing and dancing. And in five or six weeks, we got married."

Masha telegrammed the news to her children. Frantic with worry, they suspected the motives of a 45-year-old bachelor suddenly marrying a wealthy American widow of 57. Although I was only five, I can remember the family fights, the phoning back and forth. But nothing could dissuade Masha when she wanted something.

For several years, Masha maintained a transatlantic marriage with Michel, and the family slowly began to believe that he truly loved his wife. Then, as a result of new German laws, Michel, a former concentration camp inmate and resistance fighter, moved to West Berlin to collect reparations from the government. Immersed in the bureaucratic maze of restitution, Michel settled in for

Response

the long run. He bought and managed a nightclub, Chez Nous, that featured entertainment by female impersonators, and a more upscale Russian restaurant called Troika. The irony of perpetuating the victims' indignities by having to prove suitability for restitution—as if anyone could be compensated for such atrocities—did not prevent Michel from adapting to his new environment. Having survived scraps of mythic proportions, he was a master of adaptability.

However, Masha—also a survivor par excellence—was not happy. She didn't like Michel's late and long hours. She didn't like her husband's extravagant gestures to all types of disreputable hangers-on. Most of all, she hated Germany.

In 1960, my family moved from a small tenement apartment in Brooklyn to a big house to accommodate the inclusion of my cousin Arlene. My age and the daughter of Masha's—and Iser's—youngest sister, Ida, Arlene was suddenly orphaned when her parents died from unrelated illnesses within months of each other. With my father clinically depressed and my mother the major breadwinner, we could barely pay the mortgage.

On one of her trips to America, Masha lent moral and financial support by giving up her coveted Ocean Parkway apartment, cramming her most precious possessions into a small room in our new house. During the days when I was in high school, I'd come home and after doing my household chores, I'd join Masha in the television room, where she loyally followed her "stories," cursing at and crying with her favorite soap-opera characters.

I loved snuggling with her on the couch, gossiping about these people as if we knew them. But my time with Masha was limited. Soon Michel "called"—sending a dozen, long-stemmed roses and a recording of "La Vie en Rose"—and Masha was off again to Germany.

Her return was almost as sudden. During that first year in our new house, she appeared unannounced on our doorstep, valises of every shape and condition assembled around her like a circle of tired children. After rushed greetings, she shed her clothes with the rapidity of someone infested with bedbugs. Around her waist were several silk scarves; on each wrist was a 24-karat gold bracelet; around her neck, hidden under her sweater, were five strands of gold, each bearing a different charm. Three Omega watches were taped to her midriff. But it was her big-bosomed bra that held the most treasure. How she managed to hide several pairs of gold earrings, German gold coins, and two pearl necklaces in those giant cups—and still keep a smooth bustline—was the biggest wonder!

At the time, I was home with my sister, Barbara, and her fiancé, Tommy, who later moved into our crowded household. This was the first time Tommy met Masha. Barbara still remembers the occasion, "Just imagine Tommy, an only child with spartan parents, brought up in a lower-middle-class housing project. There was my grandmother stripping in front of my boyfriend. I almost died."

Masha developed a modus operandi for smuggling her contraband. In her slumpiest stance and shakiest voice, she asked the airline representative to provide her with a wheelchair as her "latest heart attack left me a bit breathless." No customs inspectors, she gambled, would stop an elderly woman in a wheelchair. She was now free to "unload" her questionably obtained and undeclared "goodies" on her children and grandchildren.

Who was this man who had the power to summon my grandmother to live in a country she hated? I wanted to see this man for myself, and I finally got the chance.

In 1964, Masha sent money for my mother and me to visit her in West Berlin. I was 18 and this was my first trip outside the tri-state area, certainly a far cry from Brooklyn's Flatbush Avenue or the Catskill village of Woodridge, my previous reference points. An introspective dreamer, I was so excited to be traveling to such an exotic destination—and to visit my grandmother and meet her debonair husband—that I put aside any uneasiness about setting foot on German soil.

On the plane there—my first plane trip!—I tried to picture Michel, the one who, from his photos, looked like David Niven, the European bon vivant, the concentration-camp survivor, the successful restaurateur, the sender of romantic presents, the man who could never come to America.

The instant we got past customs, I heard Masha's voice among the crowd. "Darling, here," she yelled. As if in a movie, the crowd seemed to fade away, and there emerged a tall woman in a mink stole and matching pillbox hat. To her side was a man only slightly taller, broad-chested and paunchy, wearing a rust-colored suede jacket and cap. They looked like a sophisticated, moneyed couple in their prime, not like a thrice-married grandmother around 70 years old and her 12-years-younger husband, the man an uncle swore was a two-timing gigolo.

By the curbside and in the taxi, I took a closer look at Masha and her husband. Some people hide their life histories, and others wear them. Masha's face was smooth and rosy, barely lined; her short, upswept thick hair was only tinged with gray. Michel's puffy cheeks were sallow; his mustache and hair were thin and gray; he had dark bags under his watery eyes and deep horizontal lines across his forehead; and his cleft chin cut an arrow to his jowls. He looked like a man who had once been gaunt and malnourished, who now ate and drank too much and slept too little. But when he smiled, it was broad and long-held, an unfolding world of charm.

On the drive, Masha did most of the talking, carrying on about the "bastard" who was managing Michel's Russian restaurant and, as far as she could tell, stealing her husband "blind." Michel didn't say much. His English was scattered with French and German words, and his accent included Russian and French intonations. By the time we reached their modern and smartly decorated apartment, I decided that this man was not only infuriated by his nagging wife but adored her beyond reason. I knew exactly how he felt.

I have so many memories of that trip, including a tour of the bombed-out streets of East Berlin and an evening at Michel's cabaret, Chez Nous, a long, narrow space jammed with rowdy customers howling at the antics of female impersonators. Many of these customers, I heard my mother and grandmother say, were Germans who had held high positions—in other words, ex-Nazis. This fact didn't seem to bother Michel, at least outwardly.

Of his customers, the Schwankes[2] became my grandmother's good friends. Herr Schwanke was a famous judge in his 60s and his wife, who apparently loved my grandmother, was not much younger. Frau Schwanke called Masha every day and often came for short visits. My grandmother, who had never studied German, spoke to the Schwankes in her own concoction of Yiddish, English, and the German Michel taught her or words she picked up from the entertainers. Even though I didn't speak German, I understood Masha's version—and so did the Schwankes. The only thing I could say to them was "Danke schön," so they called me Fräulein Danke Schön.

One day, we were invited to the Schwankes' for coffee and dessert. They lived in a large apartment. The living room had dark paneling and a brick fireplace. The mantle was lined with double picture frames, fanned open like butterflies. As I looked at the photographs, I heard my mother ask, also in broken English-Yiddish, "Judge Schwanke, what did you do during the war?"

Michel and Masha cleared their throats and tried to change the subject. Finally, the judge gave a long answer, of course in German, translated by Michel. He said that naturally he was in Germany during the war. He was an officer, stationed in Berlin.

My mother must have been emboldened by the coffee. "Ask him then," she continued, looking at Michel to translate, "about the Jews, the *Juden*. Did he notice them disappear? Where did he think they went?"

Michel refused to translate, but the judge must have understood the word for Jews and spoke softly. He said that at the time, he didn't know what happened to the Jews. He believed what he had heard, that they were sent to work camps and were properly clothed and fed.

"But he was an officer! Don't tell me he was ignorant." My mother aimed her outrage at the fireplace.

Again, Michel didn't translate. Nobody spoke. Frau Schwanke got up, left the room, and returned a few minutes later with a different picture frame. She held it up so we could all see. It was the face of a young woman, about my age, with long dark hair and dark eyes. It looked like something cut from a magazine or the printed face of a model that comes inside a frame sold at Woolworth's. Frau Schwanke pointed at the woman and said something to Michel, who blanched. She repeated her remarks, again tapping the glass.

"What is she saying?" I asked.

"She wants you all to know this is a Jewish girl they saved during the war." Michel's voice didn't hide his disbelief.

I don't think my grandmother ever saw the Schwankes again.

———

I think of this incident when the mail brings me an intriguing envelope, postmarked Ludwigsburg, Germany. This is the town near Stuttgart where my brother-in-law, Tommy, was stationed in the late 1960s, the ugly army base where I had stopped during my postcollege tour of Europe. The envelope must contain a response to a letter I sent to the German Federal Archives. Inside, I find a letter, an official-looking document, and a photocopy of a magazine article. While they are all in German, I can make out Brona Gora and Brest-Litovsk in both the letter and document; and I don't need a translation for the article's title, "Das Massaker." This package contains the previously untold side of the story: the German version. Finally.

As I await the translation, I familiarize myself with other German accounts. *The Einsatzgruppen Reports*, edited by Yitzhak Arad, Shmuel Krakowski, and Shmuel Spector, contains selected dispatches of the death squads' murderous activities against the Jews in occupied Soviet territories from July 1941 until January 1943. Although there are reports of massacres in countless communities, including those in western Belorussia, there is no specific reference to the October 15 liquidation of the Brest ghetto or to the killings in Brona Gora.

Can this new German correspondence be different? Does this letter-writing official, like so many others in Eastern Europe, merely tell me there is little or no information about Brona Gora? Does this official, like Frau Schwanke, present the party line—the phony picture of sanctimonious innocence? All I know is that my search must include the German source. Something deep within me wants to say, "Danke schön."

I receive the translation and first read the letter. It's from the main office of the Judicial Administration in Ludwigsburg, signed by District Attorney Wacker. Responding to my request for information on Brona Gora and Volchin, Wacker says, "It was impossible to find any indications on a massacre in Wolczyn, dated September 22, 1942. Maybe you can give us a source that will be accessible to us."

However, he does have information about a massacre that recently appeared in the January 24-25, 1998, *Nürnberger Nachrichten*. A copy of this article is enclosed. This massacre occurred on September 23, 1942, a day after Volchin's, and the place was called Kortelisy.

I interrupt the letter to read the translation of the article. A boldface blurb explains that a recent film reminded the author of an almost-forgotten mass murder committed by the police company Nürnberg during World War II in which 2,875 people[3] were killed in a Ukrainian village called Kortelisy. The article represents the author's investigation of this massacre.

In evocative prose, the author, Gerd E. Haida, describes the scene: a procession of Ukrainian policemen from the town of Mokrany moved through the fog-enshrouded forest in a convoy of horse-drawn wagons, reaching an area about 60 kilometers southeast of Brest-Litovsk. Following German orders, the convoy continued another 16 kilometers to its destination, the village of Kortelisy, which they reached before dawn.

The rest of the story is all too familiar. The police surrounded the village, made a door-to-door search, and assembled all the inhabitants in front of the church. Meanwhile, the Nürnbergers, a reserve police company composed of about 100 active and older policemen from Nuremberg and Fürth, plus 50 Polish police from the Brest area, arrived from their headquarters in Brest-Litovsk. The Nürnbergers handed spades to the Ukrainians and ordered them to dig five pits in the middle of the village. There, amid shouts and beatings, some Nürnbergers shot victims; others pressed the trucks' gas pedals to drown out the noise as bleeding bodies reddened pond waters. The Germans were killing faster than the Ukrainians could shovel. The work was finished by 4:25 P.M. In total, 2,875 people were killed, including 1,624 children. The village of Kortelisy was emptied.

Years later, a Soviet report stated, "The inhabitants of Kortelisy went to their deaths silently, prepared, and with dignity." Wouldn't it be nice if everything were so neat.

The article goes on to report the by-now-expected aftermath of the massacre: looting of victims' belongings, burning of their homes, followed by executions of partisans and other prisoners. The company was also accused of atrocities in other villages. A few perpetrators are identified, mostly by their first names and last initials.

Only when I get past these other crimes do I see Brest mentioned again and realize why the district attorney sent me this article. Although the Nürnbergers' responsibilities supposedly included fighting the partisans and guarding several properties, the author states that the company helped "clear" the Brest ghetto in September 1942[4] and forced "the Jewish people" together.

In 1960, a disgruntled policeman, Ernst W., reiterated this charge, along with other atrocities, in a letter to officials. Ernst said that after clearing out the Brest ghetto, he saw a nine-foot-high hill of dead and almost-dead children. Ernst later retracted all his accusations, except for the Kortelisy massacre. The author concludes that although it is known that many atrocities occurred in "clearing" the Brest ghetto, it is not established that the Nürnbergers participated in any place other than Kortelisy. In 1972, 12 years after Ernst W.'s accusations, the German court dropped charges against 60 members of the company. Reason: "All 60 members said that they didn't take part in these atrocities."

But a Soviet court reacted differently. In 1959, it handed death sentences to two Ukrainians who helped the Germans in Kortelisy. Both denied participation, blaming the Germans, although one of the accused admitted that he shot people in another village.

Although it presents an interesting picture of how the "ordinary" soldiers rather than elite troops contributed substantially to the killing of Jews in occupied Soviet territories,[5] this article only hints at possible involvement in the Brest tragedy. As can be expected, most last names were omitted; all accusations were denied or retracted.

I return to the letter, expecting little more but still hoping—my usual stance. My hopes are short-lived. Regarding Brona Gora, the letter states, "The names of the victims are unknown in this case."

Though disappointed, I'm not surprised—another familiar stance. Nothing on Volchin. And now no names on Brona Gora. The Germans must have misplaced their list of 12,260 names of Jews over the age of 14 living in the Brest ghetto before the liquidation, those presumably sent to Brona Gora.

However, they must have something, because of the five-page report I hold in my hand. I read the explanation. This is an excerpt from a cessation order concerning the Brona Gora massacre, issued by the district attorney's office in Dortmund. I'm not quite sure what such an order means, but I continue.

The letter says, "The court procedures had to be abandoned because none of the persons who committed the crimes could be indicted." These people were killed in the war, died from other causes, or were missing. How convenient.

The author must have known the lameness of this explanation and continues: "The possibility could not be ruled out that an unknown mobile SS and SD special force performed the killing of the Jews of Brest-Litovsk in Brona Gora in October 1942 and that the preparation of this mass extermination had been supported by the staff of offices or units stationed in Brest-Litovsk. This resulted from testimonies. The efforts that have been made to investigate the special force were unsuccessful." What the letter doesn't say is that these efforts were as lame as their explanation.

The letter ends with another apology: "Unfortunately, we cannot send you any photographs since their authenticity is very often disputed." The creativity of excuses never fails to amaze me.

These are much the same kind of excuses that the State Department gave Masha during her numerous attempts to secure an American visa for her husband, Michel. She paid several thousand dollars to various sources to expedite the paperwork but ran into a wall of silence and procrastination. Some relatives said that Michel must be a Russian spy; some said he was an Israeli spy; others said he was both. Everyone generally agreed that Michel's customers spanned the spectrum of the notorious.

My mother's sister Sara felt she had the definitive story of what happened to Michel during the 1950s. I recorded it during my interview at her house in Cape Cod.

Sara's husband at the time, a physicist and an expert on gas diffusion, had to fill out a government form to work for a VA Hospital as an unpaid consultant. "One day," she says, "there was a long letter from the

government saying, 'You have not been given clearance for this job!' "
There were many reasons, Sara recalls, among them her and friends'
naive college affiliations with the Communist Party and Masha's marriage to what the government called "the leader of a Russian espionage
ring in Paris."

Sara confronted Masha, who flew to Israel where Michel lived at the
time. After many curses, Masha said to him, "You got my children in
such serious trouble. I'm not going to stay with you anymore." She came
home and filed divorce papers.

Now, some of my grandmother's papers stored in a box in my closet
take on new meaning. There's an Israeli marriage certificate for Masha
and Michel, dated 1950; an Israeli religious certificate of divorce (called
a *get*), dated 1956; and an IOU dated West Berlin, 1967, from Michel to
Masha for 300,000 Deutsche Marks.

When Sara tells me this story, I question whether Michel really was
a leader of a spy ring.

"Well," Sara begins, "Michel denied the whole thing. He said
it was all a mistake. What actually happened was that he was in a
concentration camp and Marshal Zhukov liberated the camp. Michel
could speak all these languages—German, Polish, Russian, French—so
he became Zhukov's interpreter. As a thank-you, Zhukov asked if there
was anything he could do for Michel. And Michel answered, 'If you
can help me find my mother and sister. The last time I saw them, they
were in Latvia.' So Zhukov found his mother and sister, and Michel
was very grateful."

"Then what happened?" I ask.

Sara continues, "Some years passed, and Michel went to Paris and
opened a nightclub there, and Marshal Zhukov visited. Michel took him
around the city and splurged on the finest food and entertainment.
Zhukov told him, 'We're having an Officers' Ball at the Russian embassy
and you come and be my guest, but you need a uniform to get in.' So
he gave Michel a uniform. On the way to the ball, they were in a car
accident, and there was Michel in a Russian uniform. And that's how
they thought he was a Russian spy."

Though I heard many stories about Michel over the years, ranging
from his heroic stint in the French resistance to his dealings with

profiteers, I couldn't hear them often enough. I became convinced that whatever the truth, he was a survivor to the nth degree, that Nazis, Russians—even the transvestites he hired—were people like anyone else. He didn't judge, he survived.

Years later, when Michel and Masha lived in West Berlin, they often visited Michel's mother and sister in Riga. On one occasion, they took two of my cousins, all of them dragging suitcases stuffed with medical supplies for Michel's sister, a doctor, and appliances, jewels, and other merchandise negotiable in the black market. To ensure that they had equal weight at the border crossing, they returned with their luggage filled with loaves of Russian bread.

Though Masha willingly accompanied her husband, enjoying the role of "wealthy and glamorous foreigner," she always resented his exaggerated generosity.

"Wherever there were kids crying," she once told me, "Michel ran to get for them something. He'd leave me alone outside on the sidewalk and run with a bunch of kids and buy them anything they wanted. *Nu!* Is this normal? It's not normal."

No matter how much Masha complained about Michel, she was a lot more like him than she admitted. Shocked to discover that the "female artistes" at Michel's club were really men, Masha nevertheless became their best friends, enjoying their flamboyant femininity—and probably thankful they didn't present a sexual temptation to her handsome husband. Though capable of reusing a tea bag for a week, Masha was also financially extravagant, especially when there was an audience.

Her husband always remained a mystery. "Why wouldn't they let him come to this country?" I ask Masha at one of our interviews.

" 'Til today, I don't know," she says, even though she had heard the rumors and the Marshal Zhukov story. "They wouldn't tell me why. I went to the big shots and they said, 'We're awfully sorry. Go to your husband, let him tell you why.' I asked Michel, he said he didn't know."

The report I hold was written when my grandmother lived part-time in Germany. It is with extreme skepticism that I turn to the translation of the cessation order, dated December 8, 1965, and titled "The head of the main office in the German state of North Rhine-Westphalia, dealing with the mass crimes committed by the German National Socialists, at the supreme district attorney in Dortmund." The report covers two subjects. The first concerns: "The killing of approximately 10,000–15,000 Jews from Brest-Litovsk in Brona Gora, near Bereza Kartuska (Russia), in the fall of 1942." The second subject is blacked out. I hold it up close and pass it under the light. I can't read the writing. Were these lines eliminated because they're irrelevant or too relevant? Before I read the report, I'm already suspecting gross omissions.

The introduction presents its case against the heads and staff of the German offices in Brest-Litovsk and in the Ukraine office of the commissioner of the German Reich. Those investigated include: the commander of the security police; the police force; the local constabulary; the head of the SS and chief of police; the Brest-Litovsk regional commissioner; the SD in Rowno (Rivne, Ukraine); the police in Nuremberg; and the commanders of the *Gendarmerie* and police, head of SS, and commissioner general of the Wolhynia District. In addition, the accused include Karl Bauernfeind, the former first lieutenant and aide-de-camp of the police cavalry, and Josef Blings, the head counselor of the *Gendarmerie*.

Well, here are some names after all. The list of the investigated seems comprehensive. However, because of the lack of indictments mentioned in the letter and the short length of this translation, I don't expect much in the form of proof.

The first section of the report presents a brief geographical introduction: "Brest-Litovsk, which is today the regional capital [Minsk is the capital] of the Soviet Belorussian Republic, is situated on the banks of the Bug and Mukhavets and is a very important traffic and railway junction. The city was alternatively and repeatedly under Polish and Russian control." What follows is a brief history of the city from World War I until the end of German occupation in 1944. During that time, Brest and its surrounding areas were administered by the general commissioner's office of Wolhynia, which "was under the control of the commissioner's office of the German Reich in the Ukraine, with headquarters in Rowno."

According to a city plan of March 10, 1942, the report states, "The region of Brest-Litovsk, which was involved in the war, had an area of

2,600 square kilometers and 200,000 inhabitants. At that time, the city had a population of approximately 54,000. These people were of different nationalities and religions. The highest percentage was Ukrainian, followed by Polish and Belorussians."

Just when I become outraged at the omission of Jews, there is further explanation. "At the beginning of the campaign in Russia, the number of Jews could not be exactly determined; however, their number was considerable. According to statistics from the year 1931, more than 32,000 Jews were living in the surrounding area of Brest-Litovsk. According to a Polish community register from 1921, the Jews comprised around 50 percent of the total population of Brest." While these statistics differ from the ones I obtained from Brest and other sources, given the difficult nature of such facts, they are not outrageously inconsistent.[6]

During the occupation, many German offices and units were stationed in Brest. Their leaders included Schoene, the head of the SA (Storm Troopers) and supervisor of the general commissioner's office for Wolhynia until the spring of 1942; Wappenhans, SS chief for Wolhynia-Podolia until the end of August 1942, and his successor, Willi Günther (declared dead); Colonel Dressler, commander of the office of "order-keeping" police until September 1942; Major Friedrich Wilhelm Rohde, head of the SS and chief of the Brest police; and Ernst Berger, head of the SS and SD in Rowno.[7] The only name I recognize is *Rohde* (spelled previously as Rode; see chapter 7). These are names of those stationed in the Brest area, but these men are not necessarily guilty of any wrongdoing. No one was indicted or prosecuted. I remember the letter stating that the court procedures had to be abandoned.

The next section describes the living conditions of the Jews from the German occupation on June 22, 1942, until the liquidation of the Brest ghetto on October 15 of that year. A few days after the occupation, members of Police Battalion 307 selected 5,000 Jewish men from Brest, loaded them onto vans, transported them to the outskirts, and shot them in previously dug pits.[8] The head district attorney had initiated preliminary proceedings against a man named Salzinger and others for this crime.

Again, since no indictment was made, I assume the proceedings didn't go beyond the preliminary stage.

Life for Brest's Jews became more and more harsh. Jews from the surrounding area were brought to the city. Later, the Jews were ghettoized, though the report can't determine the exact date but assumes that it was the fall of 1941. The report states that according to Jewish testimony, approximately 25,000 people were forced to live in primitive conditions, restricted to a confined space, often with three or four families sharing a room. Within the ghetto's barbed wire, under strict surveillance, the Jews received inadequate amounts of food and no real medical care and were ordered to work—conditions leading to many deaths.

In the beginning of the occupation, supervised groups of Jews could leave the ghetto during the day to work in factories and German sick bays. Each Jew had to wear a yellow patch and armband and would be killed for leaving the ghetto without permission. Jews were arbitrarily required to contribute cash and other valuables. Only those capable of work could ask for bread, distributed in meager amounts. The rest, mostly the old and children, faced starvation and death. Later, all Jews were restricted to the ghetto. The report says, "The Jews became certain that their extermination could only be a matter of time. Only a few managed to escape and hide with Polish friends."

So far, this account, though thin and simplified, is basically accurate. There is nothing new here, although I'm glad to see the admission of the horrors inflicted on the Jews. I wonder, though, how the authors of the report knew that the Jews became "certain" of their extermination when so many Germans themselves claimed to have no real knowledge of this fate until after the fact.

To a woman such as Masha, used to "letting everything out," the lack of honesty that she encountered with many of the Germans surely ate away at her insides. While she couldn't hop on a plane or take an ocean voyage whenever she was angered, she accompanied Michel on any business or personal trip, big or small, and found individual spontaneous distractions.

My sister, Barbara, tells one such tale. One afternoon in 1966, she was at the kitchen table in her apartment on a U.S. Army base in Ludwigsburg, Germany. Suddenly, she heard, "Bar-bar-a, Bar-bar-a, Barbar-a," outside her window.

"I couldn't believe it," my sister reported. "There we were having lunch, the kids throwing mashed potatoes at each other, when I heard that unmistakable voice calling me, 'Bar-bar-a, Bar-bar-a, Bar-bar-a!' "

At first, my sister thought she was hearing things. Though living in West Berlin, Masha had never mentioned any plans to visit. Masha didn't even know where Barbara's husband was stationed. All she knew was that they were somewhere near Stuttgart.

This strange voice continued calling, "Bar-bar-a."

My sister opened one of the fourth-floor windows of the redbrick dormitory-like building and stuck out her head. She couldn't believe what she saw in the street below. A taxi driver opened the passenger door, and there was Masha, stepping out, her long mink coat sweeping the curb—quite a contrast to the barren barracks around her. Still in shock, my sister continued to stare.

"Darling, it's me!" Masha shouted. "Make a *glasseleh* tea. Your grandma has come for a visit."

The final section of the report is entitled "The clearance of the ghetto of Brest-Litovsk in October 1942 and the killing of the Jews." Finally, this is what I have been waiting for:

In the early hours of October 15, 1942, the ghetto in Brest-Litovsk was abruptly shut down. German and foreign units blocked the streets and entrances to the ghetto and, by densely posting themselves next to each other, formed a ring, eliminating any opportunities for the Jews to escape. At the same time, other troops entered the ghetto. They systematically combed the lodgings and forced the Jews on the streets, disregarding their age, sex, and health condition. Jews who put up even the least resistance were shot on the spot, according to orders. Bodies of Jewish men, women, and children were lying in the streets. The noise of gunfire could be heard all over town.

The Jews, who had been taken from their lodgings, were put in bigger groups and led to the streets under heavy surveillance. Women with their children, as well as the old and weak, were selected from the line of people, which was moving, with repeated beatings, and brought to a big, open area surrounded by German police. On the police officer's command, foreign volunteers brought these people to a yard behind a building, near the open area and not far from the Mukhavets River, where they were killed by shots in the neck. At this execution, the newly arrived Jews had to lie down on their fellow sufferers, who had already been killed, and were then shot in exactly the same way. In the late hours, the bodies were transported in a car to an unknown destination.

The great majority of Jews, however, was not included in this selection. On the march, thousands of Jews reached a siding, which was far away from the regular railway station. At almost summery temperatures, they were forcefully crammed into waiting freight cars and cattle trucks and were transported to Brona Gora, near Bereza Kartuska, on the Brest-Litovsk–Baranovichi line.

Immediately after their arrival, execution commandos pushed the victims to the prepared site. The Jews of Brest-Litovsk were shot at this site. The details and the course of the killings are unknown, despite extensive investigations. However, it is certain that the clearance of the ghetto and the killing of the victims in Brona Gora were carried on for several days.

Despite the seemingly extensive liquidation of the Brest-Litovsk ghetto, some Jews managed to hide in inaccessible places, such as basements, tunnels, and chimneys. In the following weeks, systematic persecution measures against these Jews were undertaken by German units brought there for this purpose and by foreign volunteers. The Jews were discovered in their hideouts and either shot on the spot or brought to the jail. Approximately 300–400 Jews were removed from a freight car en route to Baranovichi by unidentified SD members. It can certainly be assumed that these people were killed as well.

The total number of Jews killed during this action of mass extermination cannot be exactly determined. However, it is assumed that approximately 10,000–15,000 people fell victim to this.

Several things strike me after reading this section. First, it is noteworthy that the blame is attributed to "German and foreign units," "the German police," "foreign volunteers," and "execution commandos"; and equally noteworthy is the omission of specific names. The details of the killings at Brona Gora, the report says, are unknown ("despite extensive investigation"). From my own research, I know this to be untrue.

The report focuses primarily on the Jews from Brest-Litovsk who were killed, ignoring the large numbers that came from nearby towns and villages. In this way, the report implies all the Brest Jews were killed in one action, limiting the total number killed to 10,000–15,000 and the time of the killings to several days. We know from railroad worker Novis and investigating committee reports that transports from Brest and other places came to Brona Gora as early as June. By focusing on one action, the report minimizes the protracted process of the killings, requiring the participation of thousands, and greatly reduces the true number of those killed at Brona Gora: 50,000 Jews.

Perhaps, I think, this is my error. Perhaps when I wrote to the German authorities, I restricted my inquiry to Brest's Jews. I look back at my letter. It clearly said: "I am also doing research for a documentary on the Brona Gora (alternate spelling Bronna Gora, Bronnaya Gora) massacre, which occurred in the forest between Minsk and Brest on October 15, 1942. For this research, I am also interested in life in Brest and other villages from where the Jews were transported to this massacre site (Kobrin, Bereza, Gorodets, Bielsk-Podlaski, Drogichino, Yanovo, Pinsk). This would cover conditions leading to the war, the ghettos, liquidation of the ghettos, the transportations to Brona Gora, and anything surrounding the massacres in Brona Gora in the summer and fall of 1942."

One thing I have learned for certain during this search is that I am thankful for small things. I am thankful that there is a report, any report. I am thankful that the report mentions the perpetrators as Germans and the victims as Jews. I am thankful that when there are still people who claim the Holocaust never existed, many of whom would never believe otherwise, there are reports that corroborate that Jews were sequestered, starved, tortured, and exterminated.

I think back about my first trip to Germany, when Frau Schwanke brought out the picture of the supposed Jewish girl and was greeted by silence. Out of the need to ameliorate the tension, I said, "The girl is very pretty. *Schön*." Frau Schwanke was the only one to smile. Michel brought us our coats, and we shook the Schwankes' hands and said good-bye while I repeated my "Danke schön." Frau Schwanke grabbed my shoulders and gave me a hug, mumbling, "Mein Fräulein, Fräulein Danke Schön."

Yes, for some small favors, I am still thankful.

Chapter 10

Atonement

The primary motivation behind my pilgrimage to Volchin was to find something that would help explain my grandmother's dominating and provocative personality. Instead, I found troubling facts, overbearing tragedy, and little of what remained from Masha's time. Though I now have a sense of the physicality of her village, the distance between towns, the lifestyle and values of Iser and his contemporaries, I learned little more of the background that shaped Masha's early years. But with my enhanced visual context and by meeting people of her next generation, I can use more of my imagination to fill the gaps.

Still, I keep returning to the sources I know best—her closest living relatives. My mother and I go to Brooklyn to visit Masha's sister Ray. "What do you think happened in Masha's childhood to give her such *chutzpa* [guts]," I ask Aunt Ray over bagels and lox.

"What made her, I don't know," Ray answers. Then, as if it were 75 years ago, she says, "She was my father's favorite."

The oldest of eight children from her father's second marriage, Masha had to contend with the demands of three half-siblings and those of her young mother, who was barely a teenager when she married.

Ray saw her family from the perspective of a much younger female sibling: "My father used to travel all over Russia and come back and bring my mother the most gorgeous things. And you know what? Masha hated our mother because he bought more stuff for his wife."

Listening to this description, my mother comments, "Masha was a manipulator. She manipulated the environment, her family, whatever she wanted. That's how she survived."

I remember a photograph I took of Masha about four years before she died. On the side of a small table rests a menorah with three candles lit, its silhouette looming on the wall. Above the shadowed image is a painting of a bearded rabbi, wrapped in a *tallis* (prayer shawl) and blowing the shofar. On the other side of the photo, Masha bends slightly as if she's about to blow out the candles. Only a small section of her profile shows, revealing still-thick dark hair framing her wrinkled cheek and a dominant nose beaked with age. Around her head and draped over her shoulders is a dark, fringed shawl, embellished with intricate floral designs. Although the photo is black and white, I remember that the soft wool shawl had a black background with vividly colored flowers, predominantly reds and purples.

Anyone looking at the photo would think that this is a very religious woman, someone who holds tradition with reverence. No one would suspect it was a setup. I was the one who moved the menorah under the painting of the rabbi. I was the one who arranged the shawl around my grandmother's hair. I was the one who suspected that Masha's old age—I didn't know then it was Alzheimer's disease—would give her the right amount of confused expression that would appear as devotion. I was the one who knew that my grandmother, though she did retain a deep respect for her religion, couldn't pass up an opportunity to be the center of attention.

My reward for this little "ruse" was a fabulous picture and, of course, a story. This one was about the long shawl, brought to her, she recalled, by her father during one of his business trips throughout Russia. "When he brought it to me, my mother ripped it from my hand," Masha said. "She didn't want he should bring me any fancy things."

But life has a way of changing perceptions: "Then, afterward, during [World War I]," Masha recalled, "my mother came to see me. She went where nobody could go through. I was afraid to go from one city to another. Her house—it wasn't a house, it was burnt. She left the kids and said, 'If they kill me, let them kill me. I'll go and get Masha.' She went to godforsakes places—a nice couple of cities to go through—at night, in the woods, where people were getting killed. She came to me.

She lost everything, whatever she had . . . but this she kept over her head . . . and later she held it here in the bosom. She brought me my father's shawl."

Many of Masha's stories were distorted and fabricated. I believe this one. From what I knew of the women and their historical context, I believe that sheer determination is as powerful as desperation. The thought that you might never see a loved one again, that you might be forever deprived of atonement, this is what drove Masha's mother, Osna (Anna) Midler. Osna Midler, also the mother of Iser, the next one born after Masha.

The shawl story is what comes to mind as I read an article about Louis Pozez, the organizer of our mission to Eastern Europe. In 1938, when he was 17 years old, conditions worsened for the Jews in Brest-Litovsk. His mother, fearing war, managed to obtain two visas through political connections. She sent Louis and his sister, Irene, to live with an uncle in Kansas, while she remained with her husband and their 11-year-old son, Aron, plus 20 other members of their family.

For all the many years since, Louis had been haunted by one image: his mother running after the train that took her two children on their journey. Basia Pozezinska sensed not only that the world she lived in would undergo irreparable turmoil but also that there was a distinct chance she would never see her children again. Just like Masha's mother.

Basia was right. Eight months after Louis left Brest, World War II erupted. For two years, Louis received censored letters from his family. On June 22, 1941, however, the Nazis invaded, and from that day on, Louis had no word, a silence that lasted for the next 53 years. He believed that some of the family he left behind must have died in the beginning days of the invasion when he had heard about thousands of Jews massacred. If he couldn't find out his family's exact fate, he needed to return and say a formal good-bye.

For more than 40 years, Louis tried to get a visa to visit his homeland. Finally, in 1989, he was able to take that journey—a trip of a lifetime. Thirty-three members of his family, including his sister, Irene, and his aunt, Luba, who also had left Brest, made the pilgrimage. For Louis, it was an extremely emotional time, trying to recognize sights in a city that had been 90 percent rebuilt and joining his fellow travelers in saying Kaddish for Brest's Jews.

Five years after that journey, through contacts he had made in Belarus, Louis learned that the Brest archives had "internal" passports captured by the advancing Soviet troops in 1944. Also captured was a ledger recording the distribution of these passports, including the signature of all those recipients. This letter-sized, spiral-bound book, more than 500 pages long, had been created from a census taken by the Germans and contained 12,260 names of Jews over the age of 14 living in the Brest ghetto in November 1941. There, Louis found the names of his parents and brother.

The front page of the volume is entitled "Brest Ghetto List, Administrative Department of the Municipality of the City of Brest, Book of Records of Distributed Passports, Started November 10, 1941, ended June 5, 1942." The list is divided into columns for an identifying number, the person's name, name of parents, year of birth, date of issue, and signature.

In August 1997, Louis received an important package from Yad Vashem. From the passport records themselves, it contained photocopies of a paper called a *Protokol*. This form, for the issuance of a "personal identity card," included the date, first name, last name, mother's name, father's name, date and place of birth, nationality, occupation, and passport number. Even more remarkable, each *Protokol* had a fingerprint and photograph. The most personal proof of Louis's loved ones.

The documentary *The Brest Ghetto* contains footage showing the Police Investigation Department's former headquarters. The camera zooms in on aisles and aisles of ceiling-high boxes, jammed with the *Protokols* for issuing passports. Whether by design or neglect, no one working here supposedly knew what these boxes contained. Not until the film was released in 1995.

In the film, Brest survivor Roman Levin picks up a pile of *Protokols* and in an excited but controlled voice, as if he can't quite trust his luck, tremulously exclaims, "Mama! It's her. Right. And they say she's not in the files. I picked out the files with the letter *L*. I just leafed through them. . . . That's Mom. I can't say when the picture was taken.

There is my name in it as those passport lists, . . . they had no columns for children. See, 'Roma Levin.' "

Roman's voice softens, "Mama. Sima Moiseyevna, born 1905. Sure, it's a wartime picture. Mother was really cute. Here she looks drawn and older. But she wasn't really. She was 30-odd years old."

As I watch this, my throat closes when Roman says simply, "Mama." I can only imagine the conflict in discovering this document—joy mixed with unbearable sadness.

The next *Protokol* in the film is that of Chasia Begin, Menachem Begin's mother. According to the film, the former prime minister never saw this photo.

A cousin of Begin, Brest-born Shlomo (Shleyma) Weinstein survived the war by serving in the Red Army. In the film, he sits at a desk piled with papers. Like Roman Levin, Weinstein's discovery is emotional yet restrained. "This is Mom," he says. "Look, she signed her name in Yiddish. It was her way of protesting. And that's my father, Osher. And my younger sister's name. Her name was Golda. She was born in 1928. She was 14 at the time. Dad signed his name in Russian. O. Weinstein. And that's a place for a fingerprint. My father's print. And my sister was to leave it on the other side. She dipped her palm in ink and left all five fingerprints. They were suspicious even of children."

Interspersed in the film are photos of Brest Jews before the war, before they were murdered: robust young adults sprawled on the grass during an outing, virile men from a swimming team, two carefree bicycle riders. There are many close-ups—all so full of life.

The most touching is a portrait of a lovely young woman with large, intelligent eyes and stylish bangs, teasingly biting a long strand of pearls. Is this a present from her fiancé? Is it a family heirloom? Is she taunting the photographer, daring to break the delicate string and scatter the precious gems? Then, she could afford such playful behavior; she thought the world was hers, and she had all the time in the world.

At Brona Gora, there is a large, fence-enclosed boulder with a plaque that reads in Russian, "At this place, the Nazis killed 50,000 Soviet citizens and others." There is no mention that these 50,000 were Jews.

However, in post-Soviet times, there is some restitution. Another Brona Gora memorial, erected in large part as the result of Weinstein's efforts, shows an engraving of a railroad car inscribed in Hebrew and Yiddish: "Remember Brest, Kobrin, Bereza, Drogichino, and the surrounding area. Here are buried 50,000 holy victims from many of the Jewish communities. Killed and buried alive by the Nazis—let their memory be erased—in the time of the Holocaust."

And the most moving memorial, a sculpture of railroad tracks dramatically reaching skyward, honors the victims while recalling the central role the trains played in the massacres. In Russian, this plaque finally acknowledges the ethnicity of the victims: "More than 50,000 Soviet citizens of Eastern Europe primarily of Jewish nationality were brutally murdered by the fascists during the Great Patriotic War, 1941-1945." An official national recognition that these people were Jewish. Finally.

In the city of Brest, official recognition was also years late. On October 15, 1992, on the 50th anniversary of the destruction of the Brest ghetto, a memorial plaque in honor of the Nazi victims was placed on Kuybishev Street, on the spot where 5,000 Jews were killed. (Their remains had been exhumed and moved. See page 225.) The plaque was paid for by donations from Brest's Jewish community, including Shlomo Weinstein.

In 1993, the Municipal Council of Brest decided that from October 13 to October 17, the city would pay homage to its dead with five days of protest against international discord. A roundtable discussion, "Genocide of the 20th Century," included democratic proponents, former political prisoners and others from the Nazi camps, and Ukrainian witnesses. The group called for unity against national chauvinism, remembering the tragedy of Brest's ghetto.

On hand during the discussion were also former prisoners of the Minsk, Grodno, and Mogilev's ghettos. Brest ghetto survivor Roman Levin expressed gratitude for the efforts of his savior, a Polish woman named Florya Budishevskah. A noted Jewish activist, Yakov Basin, said that anti-Semitism was still very much alive. Turning to current newspapers and magazines, he read frank anti-Semitic propaganda. The level of civilization in the world, Israeli and Russian representatives agreed, could be defined by its relationship to minorities and to the Jewish people.

The last event of these days of memory was held at the Palace of Youth. Opening the ceremony was a unique prelude—a prayer delivered in Hebrew. Local participants expressed sorrow that they didn't do anything for those killed from the ghetto.

A memorial was unveiled, built by volunteers in 22 days. Topped by a Jewish star, it lit up "The Way of Sorrow," the path the Jews once took.

On May 12, 1995, another significant event occurred in Brest: the opening of its Holocaust Memorial Center, 50 years after the end of the war. Louis Pozez sends me a video of this momentous occasion, marked by prayers and the lighting of candles and attended by a predominantly elderly audience, including men and women wearing hard-earned medals. The speakers are eloquent and personal: the youngest remember dead relatives, the oldest recall wartime experiences from the perspectives of both victim and eyewitness.

Some of the orators are familiar to me: Shlomo Weinstein, still haunted by the whereabouts of his relatives' burial place; and Gresorily Obramovich Shuldman,[1] leader of the Brest Jewish community, calling for the immortalization of Jewish victims and the preservation of Jewish culture. Three unidentified female speakers bring their relatives back to life: one describes her grandfather, who became a spy in the army; the second discusses her grandmother, who escaped Brest as it was burning and joined the army, earning many medals; and the third talks about her grandfather, still living, who served as a field doctor in the army and provided her with the names of 17 doctors killed in the Brest ghetto.

For the non-Jews, the memories are vivid, though not always specific. Although he's unclear as to the year or exact location, a man remembers "a single day of horror" in Brest:

> I was 17 years old. That night, we heard a lot of screaming and shouting in the city, so we thought that we were being liberated. Suddenly, German soldiers kicked in the door and told us to line up outside. There were about 50 people [Jews], guarded by Nazis. Then . . . we were moved away from the city and came to a place where around 150 Jews were crowded together, guarded by Nazis. We thought they were going to shoot us, but they didn't. They led the Jews to the left and us to the right.
>
> While we were walking, we passed a horrifying sight. We saw a lot of older Jews lying on the ground. They couldn't keep up with the pace, so they

were shot right there on the street. Their bodies were stacked in a huge pile. This was the first time I saw something like that. As we came closer, I noticed that their eyes kept looking up at the sky. They seemed alive.

We were told to dig a hole, where we would later put the bodies. While we dug, the Germans were selecting children from the crowd. They were 9, 10, 11, 12 years old. The *Gendarme* took each child and shot him in the head. He then threw them in the hole that we just dug.

When the first part of the day was drawing to a close, the grave was almost full. We were trying to move the bodies carefully, but my hands were still covered in blood. A woman's body slipped out of my grasp and the *Gendarme* saw it. He tried to shoot me, but lucky for me, he missed. At that moment, someone tried to escape, so his attention was diverted away from me. The only thing that saved me was the arrival of some high-ranking Nazi.

Then, I saw something I'll never forget. . . . A group of wounded German soldiers appeared. The Nazi in charge took a tall woman, holding a baby, and the woman's mother. They were dressed in all black. The Nazi asked the soldiers if anyone wanted to shoot the group. None of the soldiers volunteered, so the *Gendarme* said he would do it. I turned away so I wouldn't see, and I noticed that most of the soldiers also turned away. We were all waiting to hear the shots. The first one was a misfire. The second one too. On the third time, the shots came and it was over.

We were then led to a prison. It was getting cold, and the ground was hard and partially covered with frost. There I saw a woman who had worked for my father. I knew her well and saw how bravely she met her end. It was truly heroic. Again, I saw a hole in the ground. The Jews were told to strip and jump in. They were then shot and covered by a layer of dirt mixed with blood. This way, more people could follow. This woman refused to undress. A soldier kept telling her to, but she firmly refused. Then she picked up a rock and hit him on the side of his head. He started bleeding. He pulled out his gun and kept shooting at her until he ran out of bullets. He then ripped a rifle from the hands of another soldier and continued shooting. So you see, she didn't undress. I'll always remember her.

This startling testimony debunks several theories: one, that most of the perpetrators were "willing volunteers" and that the Jews were mere "passive" victims. Of course, the orator's recollections could have been "clouded" by aging and vested interest, but there was certainly little incentive to remember Jewish resistance.

Some speakers addressed the issue of complicity, blaming local populations and singling out the few righteous among them. A Jewish doctor, Yan Natanovich Zanovich, born in 1937, tells how his parents performed in the Brest Drama Theater, hiring a Polish woman named Mehelena Antanovna Voytovich as a nanny. In 1941, Zanovich's parents went to perform in Grodno and were unable to return to Brest. The Polish nanny christened the boy Yanok and took care of him until his mother returned after the war.

Arcady Blacher, in charge of the Holocaust Center and the Brest archives, presents the center's goal: to create a "Yad Vashem in Brest" by keeping records not only of the Jews who were killed but also of those non-Jews who helped the small number of survivors. He says that of the 34,000 Jews who lived in Brest during the war, only 19 survived.[2] He presents a gift to Palageya Philipovna Makarenko, responsible for saving six of those surviving Jews.

Echoing his thanks to such brave locals, Israeli Ambassador Eli Valk reports that in Belorussia, 251 people risked their lives to save Jews, with another 150 cases being investigated. To the daughter of Nikolya and Fidosiya Navodich, who saved Jews during the war, the ambassador presents a certificate recognizing her parents as "Righteous People of the World."

Accepting the award, the daughter tells her poignant story:

> When the pogroms began, we found a Jewish man on the street, beaten almost to death. In 1942, we hid him and his two brothers in our barn. Our house was in the middle of the city, so we were surrounded by Germans. We had to be very careful so that no one would find out that we were hiding Jews. We had to sneak food to them in buckets that were supposedly filled with food for the pigs. Eventually, we found a way to send them out of the city to the troops hiding in the forest. Only one of them survived.
>
> After the war, he lived with us for a little while until he contacted his parents and went to live in Israel, where he stayed until 1993. He wanted to visit the monument to the Jewish people in Ivanovo very much, but his health didn't allow it. He went through difficult heart surgery and died in 24 hours. He left a large family behind. We're still in contact with his relatives and children. That's all.

That's all.

As discussed in chapter 7, on October 9, 1997, the *Brest Courier* published a full-page memorial entitled "The Catastrophe." According to the article, this word is the Russian equivalent of the word *holocaust*, complete destruction.

On our trip to Brest, in the Trishan Catholic Cemetery, I listened to our tour guide say that on June 28, 1941, 6,000 Jews were killed in the city center.[3] In the 1960s, when digging to construct an apartment building, workers unearthed the remains of those Jews, which were moved to the Trishan Cemetery. The tour guide pointed to the original memorial on a tombstone, which reads, "To the victims of the Nazi occupation." Another memorial was later erected, this time by Jews. In Hebrew, it says, "To the sacred memory of the thousands of victims. From the Jewish community of Brest and the survivors, to those who were killed and buried alive by the Nazis—let their names and memory be erased—from the time of the Holocaust. Let their memory be forever."

At the Holocaust Memorial Center in Brest, our delegation crowded into a narrow hallway, pressing against poster boards displaying various lists of the city's Jews. There we stood, peering at names, waiting for someone to translate the few words of description. Occasionally, someone located a relative. Occasionally, a voice uttered, "Yes, yes, that was my aunt." One of the delegates, Gerry Tumarkin, found his family name and whispered, as if to himself, "Isn't that something?"

These modern symbols of atonement—or less reverentially, retribution—though refreshing and certainly welcome are, of course, too little and too late. The real question that should be answered by the Belarusian people is one I have asked myself repeatedly during my research: How was it possible, for so many years, to hide the deaths of 50,000 human beings? Fifty thousand—the approximate population of East Providence, Rhode Island; 50,000—most of the population of the island of Bermuda. How was it possible?

How was it possible for so many people's disappearance to be unaccounted for, to go unnoticed? How was it possible for so many people to vanish without a trace?

The answer, of course, is complex and beyond the scope of this book. Much has to do with the fact that the archives containing the Soviets' extensive investigations of Nazi atrocities were not made available until 1991. Although the official conclusions of the Soviet Commission hid the ethnicity of the victims and the local collaborators, many of the eyewitnesses recorded in these documents did not. The truth lies within the pages.

The original documents are located in the Russian State Archives in Moscow. Yad Vashem in Jerusalem has microfilmed large portions of these archives and sent copies to the United States Holocaust Memorial Museum in Washington, D.C. Some of these documents have been quoted in this book. The Library of Congress has also received copies of the archives. However, most people still don't know about the contents of these archives; much of it has yet to be translated into English.

Mass shootings of Jews, particularly in the Soviet Union, have not received as much attention as the extermination camp atrocities perpetrated in other areas. Yet the Germans killed between 40 and 50 percent of their Jewish victims by methods other than gassing, and more Germans and their collaborators were required to carry out the mass shootings. Hopefully, significant historical gaps will be filled with the opening of the archives and the publication of books and articles on the subject.

According to *The Holocaust in the Soviet Union*, edited by Lucjan Dobroszycki and Jeffrey S. Gurock, by the beginning of the war, about one-third of all Jews killed in the Holocaust lived under Soviet rule. The majority was killed in mass shootings. Proportionately, Belorussia suffered more losses than any other Soviet republic, with 81 percent of its Jewish population murdered.

Clinging to the rationalization that it was improper to differentiate Jews from other ethnic groups who also lost many, the Soviets lumped all wartime victims into one category: "peaceful Soviet citizens." Communist policy created "blank spots"—intentional factual omissions or falsifications of horrific events in everything from school textbooks to popular culture.

An essential ingredient to the Holocaust story had a gap as deep as the killing pits.

The secrecy of these atrocities is inextricably linked to one undeniable fact: the victims were Jews. No one missed them, no one wanted to think about them, and no one wanted to be blamed for their absence.

And though the Holocaust was fed on centuries of inbred anti-Semitism and orchestrated and carried out by the Germans, it could not have been implemented as smoothly and efficiently as it was without the complicity of the local populations. Since Eastern Europeans were also generally imbued with generations of anti-Semitism, they could naturally deny or ignore the basic barbarism of the acts around them.

In Belorussia, the Jews faced unique problems. Historically, Jews were affected by Belorussia's lack of national independence as the region experienced changing boundaries and disputes involving Lithuanian, Russian, and Polish forces. The majority of Belorussian Jews were denied middle-class status and were often outcasts, subject to restrictions. From 1791 to 1917, the Jews of Belorussia were literally banished to a demarcated area called the Pale of Jewish Settlement, aimed at keeping them out of Russia's interior. Consequently, the Jewish population remained isolated and could not assimilate as Jews did in other countries.

Changing boundaries also plagued the territory in the early 20th century, as the Pale area was included in a partitioned Poland, returned to Russian influence, and subsequently was encompassed in the Second Polish Republic from 1921 to 1939. A popular joke comments on the area's frequently switching nationalities: "Poland, Russia, Poland," a man says. "I'd rather we were part of Poland. I hate those Russian winters."

This period of Polish independence aggravated anti-Semitic attitudes among the region's non-Jews, including Belorussians, Poles, Ukrainians, and Lithuanians. Cultural differences between Jews and non-Jews worsened during the Soviet regime, 1939–41. The majority of the Polish population supported Polish sovereignty; other minorities, including Jews and Belorussians, identified with the Soviets, helping to intensify Polish anti-Semitism. Whatever Belorussian-Jewish bond was created by this common dislike of the Poles, however, quickly dissolved. The Soviet policies of repression and collectivization eliminated and redistributed employment opportunities, creating new sources of competition.

In one instance in Volchin, E. S. Rosenblatt of Brest State University reports, a system for the distribution of products such as sugar caused rivalries between the Jews and Belorussians. After the products came to the village, Jews would line up outside one store, while Belorussians waited at another. Arguments as to whether a Jew could enter the Belorussian store were not uncommon.

For the Belorussians, the new object of hatred was an old one: the Jews. And as the Soviets banned traditional religious customs and trades, Jews too began to lose their livelihood, their identity—and their allegiance to the Russians. As always, the Jews were utterly alone. And the consequences were lethal.

Martin Dean's book, *Collaboration in the Holocaust: Crimes of the Local Police in Belorussia and Ukraine, 1941–44*, contains reports revealing the widespread and active collaboration of indigenous police forces in the mostly rural districts of Ukraine and Belorussia, particularly during the Second Wave of killings in 1942. The local police (*Schutzmannschaft*) swelled to about 300,000 men. (In the Brest district, the majority were Ukrainians.) Comprised initially of volunteers and later conscripts, these local policemen's duties centered on ghetto liquidations—rounding up and escorting Jews to execution sites, sometimes participating in the killings, and searching for and executing hidden and fleeing Jews, many attempting to join the partisans. Hundreds of villages were burned and razed in massive antipartisan sweeps. According to Dean, "In 1942 and 1943 German police organizations and their collaborators killed in excess of half a million Jews, mostly by shooting, within the 1940 borders of the Soviet Union."[4]

Motivations for collaboration included alcoholism, expectation of rewards, and anticommunism. (Nazi propaganda depicted Jews as Communists.) Yet the primary impetus seemed to center on such basics as regular food and wages. Whatever the reasons, the collaborators couldn't have succeeded if Belorussia had a strong national identity and military establishment rather than being weakened by ethnic rivalries among the Poles, Ukrainians, and Belorussians and, of course, anti-Semitism.

In *Holocaust in Belorussia, 1941–1944*, Russian historian Leonid Smilovitsky points out another unlikely source of local antagonism: the partisans. While partisan units composed of Poles, Belorussians, and others often welcomed escaping ghetto Jews, many refugees were also rejected because they were seen as burdens, suspected of being German spies, or thought to be fabricating ghetto horrors or simply because of anti-Semitism.

Acts of attrition and atonement are always necessary for the healing process. Truthful history must be taught to the young. But it's difficult to believe that anti-Semitism no longer prevails in Eastern Europe, particularly since the current Jewish population in countries such as Belarus is so small.

In post-Holocaust times, most Jewish people have personally experienced or known someone who has experienced anti-Semitism. In some countries, like Israel and the former Soviet Union, it has taken more violent and repressive forms. In many other places, the forms have been more subtle.

Numerous personal examples leap to my mind. A Connecticut contractor, not suspecting my religion, told me "not to Jew him down"; a neighbor listed all the Jewish friends he had over his lifetime; an accountant discussed financial investments and mentioned that with my background—he could only have meant my Jewishness since I had little financial experience—I would understand this subject.

Thinking it a compliment, many people have told me that I don't look Jewish. I never know how to react, but I refuse to say thank you. This happens to me in Greece and Cyprus, since I am there often to visit my husband's family. The Greeks seem confused that I'm a Jew but look more "Greek" than many of them. They often ask why I don't live in Israel.

Even with the opening of the Soviet archives, there is still so much more that remains unknown. Thankfully, there are people still alive who generously share their stories. Like Lily Guterman, who survived hiding in the Brest ghetto. In Lily's direct way, she provides her lesson to young people: "I hope you never know what I know."

When we went to Brona Gora, I took long, hard looks at the faces of the locals. All the adults around the memorial were women; most were overweight, their bodies thick and large—bold figures set against the tall, thin birches seemingly sprouting from the tops of their heads. Most had prematurely lined faces, faces of women whose lives didn't come easily.

At one point in the ceremony, I wandered over to Lily, who was standing near these women. An older one, dressed in a green sweater, her head covered by a white scarf, seemed agitated. In a barrage of Russian, she spoke to Lily, who translated: "She says that it's not because the victims were Jewish or not Jewish. [The local women] wanted to come here. They come here very often. They want their kids not to forget what happened. They wish us never, never again to be like it was before."

I watched this local woman speak, shaking her head vigorously. The others, younger and more modern, nodded slightly. A man from our delegation held the woman's hand, and Lily touched her cheek. Between sobs, the Belarusian woman repeated, "It's not because they were Jewish. Because we could have been next."

Lily said, "That's true."

And then I looked again at the healthy, cherubic faces of the school-children, most of whom probably couldn't fathom why they were standing where they were.

The Belarusian woman's words echo in my mind. Yes, they could have been next. But were those like her moved by that fact or by the intrinsic nature of these barbaric acts, acts against the essence of humanity, acts against the Jews? I wish I had thought of it at the time, when I heard her say, "It's not because they were Jewish." I wish I could have answered her, "It was because they were Jewish. And that was the only reason."

I want to believe this woman was sincere. I want to believe that she will continue to bring her children and grandchildren to this site. I want to believe this will never, ever happen again. But, I also remember that the next stop after Brona Gora was Mir, the place where a local man said to me, to the smirks of his friends, "Heil Hitler."

Chapter 11

Survival

About 25 years ago, my friend Penny and I embarked on a minivacation to the city of Quebec to break up the monotony of our then-single lives. I don't remember what month it was, only that the weather was wet and raw. At the airport, something had delayed our flight; I have vague memories of a rainstorm. I don't remember much of Quebec itself except that to escape the downpour, we went to see *Gone with the Wind* and were amused at the southern Americans dubbed into French. What I do recall in vivid detail is my wait at the airport. At each announcement of a further delay, I was unperturbed even though our three-day sojourn was being quickly decimated. Leaving the latest novel unread on my lap, I spent hours staring out the drippy windows; watching passengers rushing by; welling up at farewell embraces; overhearing travel chitchat and deeper disturbances; and generally submerging my psyche in the comings and goings of everyday people, interspersed with my own random daydreams. I was having a fine time.

Penny, generally good-natured, was getting agitated at the wait that was becoming, she thought, "interminable." Noticing that I seemed perfectly fine, she said, "You probably would be happy living in a jail cell."

That line has stuck with me all these years. What Penny said was true. Well, maybe not "happy," and maybe not a jail cell. But I am basically happy when I have time to sit quietly and think. Delayed airplanes certainly are not adequate tests of one's mettle. Yet my response that day so long ago was indicative of my main coping mechanism. Whenever something traumatic happens to me, I retreat internally, often detaching emotionally. Not the healthiest way to deal with problems, but my way of survival. I am a person who lives "in my head."

Perhaps it's a natural consequence that I write. I'm fueled by a need to observe, to understand human nature and, by association, myself. All those unprocessed internal musings have a vehicle for expression; I must make sense of them.

As I wind down my search for material on Volchin and Brona Gora, I think of survival techniques. I think of why this search has preoccupied me, why it has transported me across geographical and time barriers. I think of my obsession with my grandmother's life—how and why she survived, what she inherited from her mother, what she transferred to my mother, what my mother transferred to me, and what I have transferred to my daughter.

These thoughts used to terrify me. I'd worry that I, like the generations of women before me, would pass on guilt and anger. How would I be able to break this chain? At the same time, I'd worry that the strength and determination displayed by these previous generations of women would bypass me completely. I need to look again at the chain of command.

I review the basic facts of Masha's life: her idyllic early childhood in Volchin, persuading a tutor to help get her a teaching certificate, rare for Jewish women of the time; petitioning her parents for permission to work for a distant cousin in Warsaw; becoming the first female teacher at the school; insinuating herself into the affections of Isaac and his children; becoming a wife and young mother; outwitting the Cossacks; foraging in the woods; caring for nine children in steerage on the boat to America; raising a family and helping to establish a Hebrew school and teach; owning and operating a boardinghouse; fighting poverty to become a practical nurse; overseeing her second husband's business affairs; traveling around the world; living in West Berlin and befriending female impersonators; and managing to be the matriarch of a sprawling and spirited family.

Beginning life as an indulged older child and growing up in relative prosperity, Masha was thrust into a world of discrimination, loss, flight, hunger, and fear. Her survival techniques were reactive and required cunning resiliency.

———

December 1997

Discrimination, loss, flight, hunger, fear. The life of so many Jews, over so much time. The life Hanna Kremer had when she also left home too soon. I think of this as I prepare for my videotaped interview with Hanna in December, almost six months after my trip to Eastern Europe. In October, when I first told her about the proposed documentary and asked her to participate, she appeared reluctant. But for me, she would think about it and eventually agreed. After getting to know Hanna and learning how she kept much of her pain private, I realized what an act of generosity she gave with this interview, and I will always be humbly grateful.

The local videographer hired for this interview looks forward to hearing Hanna's story. His ancestors, he explains as he tests Hanna's skin tone and voice, were from Pinsk. Hanna relaxes her shoulders. With my people from Volchin, the videographer's from Pinsk, there is family in this room. I don't tell Hanna this is no coincidence. I don't tell her it's *bashert*.

The videographer needs a while to set up his equipment in the living room. Hanna and I step into the den and sit on the couch, next to a coffee table piled with books, papers, and maps. Hanna tells me that she just returned from her apartment in Florida, where she found something I might want. "Here," she says, handing me a Priority Mail envelope. Inside is a light brown booklet, its splotched and frayed cover written in Yiddish; the only thing recognizable to me is the date, 1948. I turn the page and read in English, "Entertainment and Ball Given by the United Wisoko-Litowsker and Woltchiner Relief on February 7, 1948, at Beethoven Hall, 210-214 East 5th Street, New York City." This is it—the *Yizkor* book I had been searching for, the only book memorializing the dead of Volchin and Visoke! And there it was all this time, amid the boxes of memorabilia in Hanna Kremer's Florida apartment. *Bashert. Bashert.*

The Kremers and the videographer's coworker, fluent in Yiddish, look over my shoulder, calling out translations. The first page of the thin booklet reads:

> *In Memory!*
> *Dedicated to the Holy Memory of the Martyrs of Visoke-Litovsk and Volchin.*
> *I weep for those mishaps, my eyes are dripping with tears, for the destructions.*

Yes, as I fondle this worn memorial, my eyes are dripping with tears.

The first few pages of the *Yizkor* booklet take care of business. There is a list of officers and executive committee members and a financial report representing the years 1944–47. In the description of the organization, one date pops out at me. The United Wisoko-Litowsker and Woltchiner Relief held their first meeting on October 15, 1944. October 15, 1944, exactly two years after most of the Brest Jews were killed at Brona Gora. October 15, 1944, exactly one year before I was born.

I flip through the book. Interspersed between articles written in Yiddish are memorial messages, photos, greetings, and best wishes to those establishing a homeland in Palestine. There is a half-page message, plainly reading, "In Memory of the Widler Family from Woltchin." I stop and rest my palm on the page and feel Hanna's hand on my shoulder. "There were no Widlers," she says. "This was a typographical mistake. It's the Midler family."

The Kremers insist that I take the booklet and get it translated. At first I equivocate, fearful of assuming responsibility for such a valuable document. But when Hanna slips the booklet back into the envelope and hands it to me, I know it's not up to me to protest.

After several light testings, the videographer is ready for Hanna. During her interview, she remains anxious but very focused on her story. There is a rehearsed quality to her narrative; her words are rushed and barely animated, as if she's delivering a speech to her teacher for a final grade. Many elements in her story are, by now, familiar to me—her family composition, her early years of carefree play, her first awareness of anti-Semitism, and of course, most touching to me, her friendship with Sala and her time spent in the Midler household. As these memories unfold, Hanna's voice slows, and she allows herself a moment or two of nostalgia.

I hear more about the social activities of young people, particularly their participation in the Zionist organizations. This must be around the same time that my uncle Jack, born and raised in Eastern Europe, was also active in Zionism in America. Hanna says, "Everyone had one goal—our own homeland."

As Hanna goes into the beginning of the war, her voice picks up speed, and she recounts the first German invasion and her family's fears, which relaxed temporarily when the Russians took over. From the point of her moving to Visoke for school until her liberation in 1944, Hanna observes the tight format of her story, her emotional equilibrium showing cracks as she recalls her last farewell to her mother, the pronouncement of her five-year prison sentence, and her reunion with her uncle.

When she was finally allowed to travel, she set out to join her uncle in Minsk. At the train station, she had only 90 rubles. Starving both emotionally and physically, Hanna saw a woman at the station selling ice cream. Hanna spent everything—on nine ice cream cones. She didn't care if she had money for the train ticket; at that moment in her life, the only thing that mattered was that she was alive and there was ice cream.

After relating her wartime ordeal, Hanna becomes more associative. Again, she recalls her surreal visit to her desolate hometown and, with a quaking voice, retells the story she heard about the massacre and the brave protest of my cousin Ida Midler.

It's time for those end-of-interview questions: the summing up, the moral lessons. What kept her going, she repeats, was the hope—as other survivors have reiterated—that she would see her parents, her family, her town again. And while that hope was savagely quashed, Hanna is not one for needless self-pity. "I am the luckiest," she says. "I don't have too much hatred. I see what hatred can bring. And I see what's going on in Israel today."

For the first time during the interview, I worry that Hanna can't continue. She wrings her hands, her accent thickens, her lips tremble. She speaks about the dead, her dead: "They gave their lives for Israel. If there wouldn't be a Holocaust, there would be no Israel, and the Jews would still be without a country. It's still going on, struggles with struggles. I only wish and hope," Hanna takes in a breath, "that no children should have to go through what I went through and, worse, what [the Volchiners] went through."

At the end of our interview, Hanna and I go over a stack of photos— some hers, some mine. Again, we fondle the faces of our families and linger over the picture of the one with both of our uncles. For a second, my hand remains on hers.

When the photos change from black and white to color and we come into modern times, Hanna again proclaims her luck, thanking her husband for his support. Showing me a photo of her children and grandchildren, she says, "This is what I'm thankful for. God didn't punish me completely. He let a new generation come." She smoothes her fingers over the faces of her loved ones and says in one small gasp, a gasp tinged with unshakable recurring images, "That's why I survived."

After the videotaping with Hanna, into the new year, I receive the translation of the *Yizkor* booklet and discover the treasures in this fraternal society's journal. The first article of interest is entitled "Summer in My Small Town, Visoke" by Faigl Shatsky-Yudin. Although these memories are not about Volchin, they come from nearby and reflect the pre–World War I childhood that overlapped my grandmother's time.

As the town awoke on a typical summer day, Shatsky-Yudin recalls, the men went in one direction toward the synagogue to say morning prayers, after which each went to make his daily living—the artisan to the workshop, the storekeeper to the shop, the merchant to buy bargains (a chicken, a basket of eggs, a sack of corn, a cart of wood) from peasants outside town.

As for the rest of the townspeople: "The women were busy from early morning with their housekeeping, preparing and cooking meals. . . . We children were free of all these chores. The boys left for *cheder* [Hebrew school]. The girls, who were not required to learn, who didn't need to know too much, were free. One grabbed a cup of chicory, a piece of bread or a roll, and went in the street. . . . Some would play *tchaiches* [a game with bones], others hide-and-seek; some made ovens out of clay; or we would all go to the river and disappear for the day. When the sun began to set and the children didn't show up quickly . . . the child would first receive several hearty slaps from the mother, several ear twists from the father, and then was sent to sleep in tears, without supper."

Although this was day-to-day shtetl life, everything changed on the Sabbath. Shatsky-Yudin says, "As soon as we finished eating the *cholent* [Sabbath stew], we children would leave either to walk . . . or to the fields where we would find our older brothers and sisters who called themselves *sistzialistn* [socialists] and they would conduct secret meetings."

These innocent years did not last long, interrupted by World War I. Shatsky-Yudin describes what happened:

> War broke out, and the Germans conquered the czarist army and also occupied our town and began to bully us. And we, who were still kids, had to work like adults, removing rocks from the fields . . . cutting and drying nettles, and digging potatoes. For this we were promised one mark per day. But when they had to pay us, these miserable Germans always found fault with our work and never paid. They called this "voluntary work," which was quite different from forced labor, when they would grab people off the street without giving them the opportunity to get their warm clothing or say good-bye to their families and would send them off to either dig peat in the swamps or chop wood. . . . In the greatest frosts, barefoot and naked, they were forced to obey the Germans. . . . Nobody survived this. . . . I remember many a time when I would see a young man run across the street disguised as an old woman to avoid being caught for forced labor, which meant certain death.

Finally, Shatsky-Yudin recounts the end of the German occupation and how the Poles replaced the Germans, causing different troubles. The villagers, already worn out from the war, had to endure the newly established Polish state, its abusive army, and a host of new taxes, penalties, and humiliations. The Poles, Shatsky-Yudin says, "took sadistic pleasure in tearing off Jewish beards, throwing Jews off moving trains, or just beating them at every opportunity." Many young people ran away to relatives in America, and those who remained struggled for a life of freedom—a difficult and often elusive goal.

So I have a personal glimpse into the life my grandmother and her family must have led in Volchin. Some of it reminds me of my aunt Ray's memories of her brothers Bernard and Iser, who hid in the neighbor's house to escape army conscription; some of it echoes my uncle Gerson's memories of anti-Semitic Polish soldiers on the train.

The next article in the *Yizkor* book is called "From Darkness to Light," by Rabbi Abraham Shmuel Samuels. The rabbi recalls his last visit to Volchin, as a child, in the winter of 1915. One evening, he went for a walk with his aunt Etel (the Volchin rabbi's daughter). At the time, Volchin had no streetlights. By mistake, they walked into deep mud, covering their shoes. Samuels turned to his aunt and said, "Well Etel, I am leaving and will not return until there are lights on the streets of Volchin."

This remark stayed with Rabbi Samuels throughout the ensuing years. He writes, "I will never be able to return to Volchin. Maybe because in the Volchin of my childhood, that Volchin of beautiful Jews, her holy synagogue, her house of worship, home of the prayer houses, is now dark even in the daytime." The memory of "our lost ones," he prays, must "motivate us and give us strength to bring light to our people and to the whole world."

Another childhood sketch, "A Yom Kippur Night in Volchin," comes from Morris Gevirtz. All year long, on every Sabbath and every holiday, Gevirtz's father, Shmuelkeh Michel, prayed in the Orthodox synagogue, where his "seat" was located near the eastern wall. On Yom Kippur, however, Shmuelkeh prayed in the wooden synagogue because this world-renowned place was about 500 years old, had a very high ceiling, and had walls and the ceiling covered with historically inspired paintings and inscriptions.

A naturally cheerful and witty person, Shmuelkeh would become serious and tearful on this holy holiday. He would rise from the table, put on his *kittel* (white linen robe), *tallis* (prayer shawl), and overcoat. Then he would give wishes to his wife, kiss the mezuzah (a small container, including verses from Deuteronomy, affixed to doorways to bless Jewish houses), and, accompanied by his 10 children, head to the synagogue for Kol Nidre, the plaintive prayer ushering in Yom Kippur.

Morris Gevirtz tells what happened on one Yom Kippur, when they reached the massive synagogue door:

We are greeted by a flood of light from . . . many lit, white candles . . . long and massive . . . placed in a special casket filled with sand to prevent a fire. The candles are memorials for the deceased. A sea of white linen robes are already swaying in the air . . . a prelude to Kol Nidre. All, especially the older people, have their prayer shawls thrown over their heads, their faces buried in the machzors [holiday prayer books], and are crying silently and see nothing around them. They are deeply involved in the uncertainty. . . .

Suddenly, three sharp blows are heard as Noah Mordechai Rashkes pounds his iron-strong hands on the bimah [platform], which heralds . . . the cantor, Reb Moshe Chazanovitch, who . . . is already at the pulpit, wrapped in his prayer shawl and white kittel, surrounded by a dozen choir boys, lined up by size. His stately appearance is framed by his thick gray beard. . . . The great musician, composer of hundreds of compositions . . . everyone is totally imbued with the beauty of his singing and his masterful conducting of the choir, as he quietly, almost humming, begins Kol Nidre. . . .

Right after the singing of Kol Nidre, Noah Mordechai Rashkes reappears in full height and again strikes three sharp blows, calling for silence to listen to the rabbi's sermon. The crowd sits erect, prayer shawls are removed from their heads, tear-stained eyes are dried, and the people sit motionless. The Volchiner rabbi, Reb Chaim Tuvia, who has served for many years but is not so old, only in his late 50s, but long renowned in many places as a sage . . . begins very quietly, as though speaking to himself, describing in simple language, the seriousness of Yom Kippur and the importance of atonement. The rabbi proves that by our deeds, not only are we responsible for ourselves and our families, but also "all the Jews are responsible for one another."

The rabbi then cries out, questioning responsibility and fate: "In view of our many sins, a great fire is burning; we are submerged in sin, and there is nobody to intercede for us. Woe to us!"

Gevirtz continues the narrative: "The rabbi wrings his hands and weeps out loud; and his cries mingle with the terrible spasmodic lament from the women's section of the synagogue, making it feel as if the balcony is splitting. And suddenly, the rabbi turns, facing the Holy Ark, and, with all his might, pulls at the curtain covering the scrolls. Hastily, he flings open the Holy Ark, falls with his face on the scrolls, and screams with all his might, 'Holy Torah, our Mother, have pity on your children. . . . Do not forsake us in this difficult hour.' "

The rabbi finishes his sermon; the cantor finishes his singing; and the crowd is drained of tears, exhausted, and feeling purified. But for Gevirtz, one memory stands out above the rest: "Soon something occurs that most of the crowd did not expect. From somewhere Rafaelke Esties appears. He approaches the platform and strikes it, calling attention that he plans to take over the command; and screams out in a 'lion's' voice: 'Happy is the man who does not walk in the counsel of the wicked, and does not stand in the way of the sinner, and does not dwell with evil.' "

Not only is this man's voice strong and clear despite hours of praying, but the large chorus responds with the same high spirits. Together, they exchange verses, completing all the Psalms—a task that lasts more than two hours.

As I absorb this translation, I am transported back in time. Again I assume that this childhood incident occurred sometime around World War I. This is the closest I have come to feeling as if I am back there, in the village of Volchin, with my grandmother, her parents, and her siblings, especially her dear brother, Iser.

I close my eyes. I feel the heat of the candles. I hear the choir's chants. I absorb the prophetic words of the rabbi's pre-Holocaust plea: "Do not forsake us in this difficult hour." I am filled with the enormity of all that was lost. My eyes are dripping with tears.

For those who stayed behind, no Jew survived the massacre in Volchin. In nearby Visoke, a miracle occurred.

Shortly after the Liberation, Visoke native David Wolf wrote two letters to relatives in America depicting his harrowing tale of survival. Both are reproduced in the *Yizkor* book. To his uncle and aunt, he describes how he felt when he received their letter: "When I realized I survived to find my real relatives, I began to weep like a small child." So filled with emotion, Wolf had to delay reading his relatives' letter several times while he tried to contain himself. For him, the ability to cry—repressed for such a long time—was a "pleasure."

When the war broke out, Wolf was in the Polish army. By the time he was released and returned to Visoke, the entire area was occupied by Russians. And then everything changed: "As soon as we were invaded by the Germans, we were cut off from the whole world. . . . We were immediately incarcerated in a ghetto . . . on Bod Street. Three families were tossed into one room. . . . We could not go out into the street, and sending letters, . . . one could not even dream about that. . . . Everyone was forced to wear a yellow patch on their lapel and on their back. The greatest pleasure for these bandits was to conduct raids with the excuse that they needed people to take to work. The routine was generally as follows: You were locked into a dark cellar for three days, no food, merciless beatings or attacks by wild dogs who would tear off chunks of flesh. More than one person died in this manner. Many were shot in the street for no reason. In this way, Bod Street changed into a cemetery. Since one could not leave the ghetto, we buried them right on the spot."

After listing those killed, Wolf then describes a day he would never forget: "On November 11, 1941,[1] at 5:30 in the morning, the Hitleristic bandits ordered all the Jews to be out on the street by 6 A.M.—in just a half hour. Those who didn't come out would be shot on the spot. With clubs, they began to chase the men and women separately. At that hour, we were separated from our wives, children, sisters, mothers, and friends. Accompanied by the most ignominious heckling and murderous beatings, we were herded to the train. We were loaded onto freight cars like animals, and in that way we were sent to Treblinka. What happened en route—the lamenting and cries of desperation . . . and the heartbreaking cries from the women and children bemoaning their uncertain destiny—certainly split the heavens. The worst, however, were the inhuman cries of the little children demanding their mothers, their little sisters. Many of us went mad."

For Wolf, his destiny diverged from the others. Others, like Hanna Kremer's parents and siblings, who had gone to Visoke because they thought it would be safer than Volchin, were probably on that train. Late at night, not far from Treblinka, Wolf and three other young men managed to dislodge several boards from the railroad car; and when the train slowed, they jumped. Wolf recalls:

The Germans noticed this and opened fire. Two were shot immediately. A bullet hit me in the left part of my behind. With the help of my companion, we managed to disappear into the woods. For two days, we lay in hunger and cold. Added to that was the pain of the open wound. On the third day, we headed toward the countryside. In the day, we hid in the bushes, and at night we knocked on doors of peasants to ask for food. Some gave, others angrily said, "Jew, get away from here!"

I dragged myself around this way for 15 days. I lost my friend on the way. He either joined a partisan group or was betrayed by a peasant. I never saw him again. I was able to reach a town not far from Visoke. There, I was familiar with a family I had befriended when I worked for the Germans digging peat for heating purposes.

I knocked on their door in the middle of the night. They recognized me, took me into their house, gave me something to eat, and made a bed for me in the hay in the barn. These gentle people were as much to be pitied as I. Had they been caught hiding a Jew, the entire family could have been shot. . . . But these decent Christians compromised themselves. . . . They dug a pit in the barn, covered it with boards on which the cow stood. . . . They created an opening through which they could bring me food, and late at night, I was able to go out, wash myself, and get a little fresh air. These noble people even risked getting me medicine from the dispensary to ease the pain from the wound, which was not healing.

In this way, I spent a total of 23 months in the pit until the Germans were defeated and the Russians took over the area.

Like Hanna Kremer, who was obsessed with returning to her hometown, Wolf had one thought only—to reach Visoke and find someone else who had survived. But Visoke, like Volchin, was a ghost town. The Germans had obliterated 3,500 Jews. Wolf wandered, in shock: "I went into the *bet midrash* [synagogue], sat there for a few hours, and wept. I walked by the house where we had lived and didn't dare go inside. I just stood outside, observed, and wept."

Wolf continued past the homes of his relatives and friends, stopping by the grave of 120 killed, weeping the entire time. In his letter, he says, "Even now as I write about this, I am weeping."

Unable to remain in Visoke any longer, Wolf returned to his Polish saviors, who had been offered a farm in Silesia. He joined them in their new undertaking.

In another letter to America, dated May 20, 1947, Wolf presents a more reflective view: "To this day, I cannot forget, and I often think and imagine for the thousandth time, asking the same question: Did this really happen or was it simply a wild nightmare?"

He wonders why he avoided death so many times and recalls an incident when he was in the pit under the barn and his Polish saviors were digging potatoes in the field:

Before they left . . . these good people always warned me: "We are going to the fields. If someone should call to enter the barn, do not reply. . . . One morning, . . . a vehicle with eight soldiers drove into the yard. They got out and went to the house. The door was locked. They made their way to the barn. Searching every little place and not finding anything suspicious, they cursed. . . . For me, however, these minutes were like a painful eternity. Hearing the German language, I was certain they came because someone had informed about me. I was sure this was the end. My heart froze. But I did not panic. I grabbed a handful of hay and blocked the opening. . . . I was lucky. The murderers left.

The Polish family . . . observed from a distance. They were petrified. . . . At night, the housewife told me that when she first spotted the Germans driving into the yard, . . . she immediately fell to her knees, stretched her arms to the sky, murmuring, "Holy Mother, hide him with your cloak so that these murderers and defilers of God may not spot him."

When he wrote this letter, Wolf was 35 years old, with no real plans for the future. His only hope was to eventually immigrate to America, where he had relatives, where he could find some warmth and consolation.

How did this man survive, cheating death many times? Clearly, luck was on his side. Perhaps it was *bashert*. But, there was something else, something deeper and probably inchoate, operating in an unconscious, primal manner, giving him the will to survive.

Several themes are common to many of the survivor stories I have heard. One is the hope, no matter how unlikely, to see family, someone—anyone else—from the hometown who also survived. The other is the longing to go to another land, America or Palestine—a place to begin again, start a new life as a free and breathing Jew.

Inadvertently tackling this issue was one *Yizkor* book correspondent, Mendel Refkovske, who wrote to an American relative from Paris on January 12, 1948. It's not clear from this excerpt how Mendel heard about the fate of Volchin's Jews, but he describes incidents with the emotions of someone who must have been there at some time or who had heard reports from eyewitnesses.

As soon as the filthy German boots crossed the Volchiner soil, they imprisoned all the Jews into a confined, narrow little street, and their fate fell into the hands of the infamous Ukrainian, Theodore Maluta. Just one glance at the animalistic features of this human being was enough to cause all blood to freeze in fear. This obese ruffian with his leaden pistol, which never left his hand, inflicted injury on Jewish bodies at every opportunity.

The young men, as well as the young women, were sent to work in Brisk [Brest-Litovsk], and they never saw their families or Volchin again. Those who remained lived in great pain and poverty. This wild Ukrainian managed by various means to extract every groschen or piece of jewelry. Many Jews paid with their lives when they went out into their gardens. . . . I still remember the name of one who died when he went out to get a few potatoes. That was Itzl Englender from the bakery.

This is the same bakery that Shmuel Englender so fondly recalled. Itzl Englender, Shmuel's father.

Refkovske then tells about the day of the massacre, beginning with a foggy dawn when trucks arrived and the Jews were ordered to take their valuables and get on the trucks (others say carts), bound for the Visoke ghetto. At the village gate, the trucks were diverted to a side road, where large ditches had been dug. Heartbreaking pictures fill this letter: mothers pressing children to their breasts, kissing them for the last time, tears streaming; mothers undressing themselves and their children. Driven to the ditch by angry dogs and soldiers with canes, machine-gun fire drowned out the agonizing screams of the dying people, whose last words were mixed with pleas to God, "Shema Yisrael" ("Hear, O Israel," the opening words of a Jewish deathbed prayer), and revenge.

Through the years, my uncle Gerson filmed many family outings. He had a movie camera long before most people had still cameras. Every once in a while, he'd pull out the old screen and show some footage, and I'd be delighted to see any proof that we were the children of my memory. In 1991, Gerson gave me a compilation video of his old movies. Something about the *Yizkor* stories jogs my memory of this film.

I dig in my closet, retrieve the video, and put it in my VCR. Again, I am entranced and stunned by the transformation of my oldest relatives into youthful, vibrant, and shockingly beautiful people. In the footage, they are gathered in Woodridge, at parks, at homes of relatives, in the late 1940s and early '50s. There are baseball bats, long tables with food, rowboats, birthday parties, Adirondack chairs, big black cars and wood-paneled station wagons, felt cowboy hats with drawstrings, card games, men covering their bald spots with towels, halter-clad women bouncing crying babies.

There are so many young children that I can't find myself, though I must have been in attendance. There are many beautiful women, my mother the most glamorous. With her hair swept back, wearing sunglasses and an Eisenhower jacket, she looks like a movie star. All the women, in almost every frame, are smoking. Hovering in and out of the pictures is Masha, who is barely older than I am now at 52. And as I am now, she is past her time.

Contrary to memory and family lore, she is not the prettiest. She is overweight and almost mannish in her gestures. And contrary to memory, others host these family events—unlike years later, when the family became assimilatingly busy and only Masha was the hostess, serving steaming platters of tangy-sweet stuffed cabbage and butter-soaked onion rolls.

In these movies, we are all so young. Were we really so happy? Or is the video merely carefully edited snippets of the best moments? Come to think of it, there are few men around; I don't see one shot of my father or my uncles. Where are the scenes of our family house in Woodridge, of my apartment in Brooklyn?

In these movies, we are all so playful. If I didn't know better, I would think these "actors" are part of a Kennedyesque clan, accomplished, close-knit, good-looking, and loving. Were we really so happy?

When I first watched the film in 1991, I was so saddened about my mostly dispersed family that I decided to host a get-together at my country house. On the invitations, I pasted a photo of Masha, dead for nearly a decade, standing tall in her mink coat. In a bubble above her head, in a mixture of Yiddish and English, she "orders" her extended family to the first of her posthumous family reunions.

Some of my relatives thought this was a wonderful idea. Some wondered why I wanted to bother with such an undertaking. Some claimed they wouldn't speak to so-and-so; others felt threatened that they'd be called on to host a sequel. But, as it turned out, about 40 people came, some from as far away as Israel. We had a wonderful time, longing for another reunion as soon as possible.

During the party, the talk, especially among the elderly, drifted to Masha, focusing on her later life, back in her old apartment on Ocean Parkway. After many years of traveling to Germany, Masha was becoming too old and frail to travel. She was in her 70s when she made her last trip to Berlin. Michel's letters—and pleas to visit—became more infrequent and eventually stopped. We heard from mutual friends in Israel that he had lost his business; some said that he had moved and might have remarried; some said he had been sick and had probably died. My mother wrote to him, but the letters came back marked "Addressee Unknown."

Now that I am involved in recording survivor stories and family history, I am more curious about this elusive character. I am profoundly sorry that I did not question him more about his past. When I met him, I was only 18 years old, but there were certainly opportunities to write him over the following years. Regretfully, he will remain, like many of his time and experience, a figure of romance and mystery—out of reach forever.

I can console myself with fragments of memorabilia. I am the family keeper of letters and official papers. I am the family keeper of Masha and Michel's many photos: their marriage ceremony; their life in Israel; his nightclub in Berlin, posing with Shirley MacLaine, Ella Fitzgerald, Jayne Mansfield, and gorgeous female entertainers who were really men; his family in Riga. I wish there were more.

At that 1991 reunion, we recorded our individual family histories and included facts from those unable to attend. These have become the basics of our family statistics: Masha's nine children have produced 15 grandchildren and 36 great-grandchildren. As of this printing in 2002, there are two psychiatrists, three psychologists, two dentists, two physicians, two artists, one professional writer (and numerous "authors"), three businesspeople, one principal, one engineer, one physicist, one social worker, and one rabbi. As the offspring age, the next generations promise fascinating life choices. If professions count for anything, Masha spawned an accomplished family.

I soon learn that my meeting Hanna and the discovery of my Volchin family were even more fortuitous than I had thought. A fellow mission delegate Sara Sanditen, Lily Guterman's daughter, visits me in New York, and we have a lovely time reminiscing and catching up with the latest news about our respective "relatives." Sara relates how the meeting with my Volchin family evolved.

When she was in Israel, about four months before our trip, one of her friends mentioned an elderly man she had met during a business transaction. This man, Sara's friend learned, was from Brest. She gave Sara the man's name and number. A few hours before her flight back to America, Sara called this man, who told her that other Israelis he knew from the Brest area had been planning a trip there in May. Sara contacted the group leader and other members and persuaded them that it would be a more powerful visit if the Israeli and American groups could overlap their visits. The rest, she says, was history. Or more likely, *bashert*.

And it was Sara, I remind myself, who also told me about the couple from New York who had planned to join our trip but had canceled at the last moment. The Kremers. Without Sara, Volchin would have been a remote village where my relatives could have died. And without Sara, I would not have learned of the connection of the two Hanna(h)s.

Hannah Williams from England wrote that when she was at the Volchin gravesite, she had promised her ancestors that she would do everything in her power to erect a memorial stone in Israel. Back in England, she wrote to her cousin Shmuel Englender, and asked him to contact the rest of the Israeli and American survivors of Volchin. This led to a phone call to England from Hanna Kremer. Both Hanna(h)s wept as they spoke about their once-beloved village.

Months later, Hannah Williams received plans for the memorial stone. She said, "Without the help and generosity of Hanna and Mike Kremer, it would still be a dream. . . . It's hard for me to find the right words to thank them."

In October 1994, 52 years after the Volchin massacre, Hannah Williams and her husband met the Kremers and other friends and relatives from Israel and the United States at the Holon Cemetery in Israel for the stone unveiling. Each stood and admired the engraving of the Volchin memorial. Each scanned the names of the Jewish families of

Volchin, eyes resting on those they recognized. On that occasion, there was no one to focus on the last name on the right panel: "Family Midler."

"I was delighted," Hannah Williams said, "to see so many people—the survivors with their children, grandchildren, and relatives. For me, it was the happiest day of my life."

When she was in Volchin, she filled a bag with sand and stones from the mass gravesite. In Israel, she buried these remains under the earth by the memorial stone. "The survivors were crying," she said, "thinking about their families. But these were also tears of happiness that after 50 years, they were alive to see a memorial stone in Israel to their families." Since then, on each Holocaust Remembrance Day, Volchin family survivors meet at the Israeli memorial.

The memorials to Volchin continue. Just when I accept that the "gift"—the *Yizkor* book—from Hanna Kremer is probably the last "official" Jewish record of life in Volchin before the war, I receive yet more testaments, this time on the wings of air mail—fittingly from Israel. Dov, my intrepid chronicler, sends me an envelope with several papers.

The most intriguing item is a large document, folded in half. Before I open it, I read Dov's note: "Shmuel called and told me that his memory from childhood suddenly came back to him with great clarity, and he plotted a map of Volchin, including all the houses, with the names of the Jewish owners. . . . And I, Dov, received it as a treasure and amended it very carefully."

Dov explains that this map depicts Volchin as it looked in the late 1930s, with later ghetto boundaries. Although it contains inherent distortions, particularly in the compression of the outlying village areas, Dov appreciates its rarity. "The important things," he emphasizes, "are the houses and most of the center, including the ghetto." After reducing the document to fit a photocopy machine, Dov was charged with sending it to me. "You, Andrea," he writes, "are in a position of first priority."

As always seems the case in my search, the last line contains the icing on the cake: "Your family's house—Midler—is on the map, no. 13; Midler's orchard is no. 14."

Carefully, I unfold the map, ever-mindful of my "position of first priority." While I'm aware that the original document was larger, I am nevertheless shocked at the minuscule, scrupulously rendered shapes, symbols, and lines as well as various titles and lists—all handwritten in Hebrew. The village itself is crudely depicted in a whalelike form, the center bulging with Jewish life, the ends tapering off the main road—the north leading to the killing fields and Visoke, the south pointing toward Brest and places beyond. In the dense middle, little squares representing buildings are placed in the appropriate positions and labeled numerically. On the bottom, a copious legend lists every remembered Jewish family—more than 50 names. As if I'm touching the fluffy head of a dandelion before it flowers, I pat nos. 13 and 14. Yes, Dov, I hold in my hand a true survivor, a "treasure."

It seems that Shmuel's map served as a catalyst that unlocked more of his childhood memories. Shortly after receiving the map, I rejoice in another of Shmuel's handwritten survivor treasures—29 pages containing sketches of Volchin's families, structures, and landmarks identified by their numbers on the map. I flip through the pages of perfectly rendered Hebrew, flawlessly recopied by Dov, hoping I can recognize something besides the numbers. But no such luck; I'm still a language removed. I balance the pages in my palm; the weight of a lost world rests in my hands.

Days later, when I receive the English translations, I'm again awestruck by the precision of Shmuel's work. From the map, I get the lay of the land, from the southern end of Old Volchin, where the Russian Orthodox lived—many of their houses spread along the main street—to the northern end of New Volchin, home of the Polish Catholics, the Catholic church (not far from the massacre site), and the palace. In the middle Jewish section, Shmuel delineates the ghetto area, with its entrances and exits. Extending its northern and eastern borders to the Pulva River (which led to the Bug River), the ghetto was bordered on the south by the Christian homes of Old Volchin and on the west by the main road, marked by a wooden fence. Shmuel identifies four entrances and exits: (1) across from the administration offices, for officers and guards to enter the ghetto (through an alley leading from the main street through Iser Midler's property); (2) near the bakery, the main entrance, for wagons and work details (ghetto residents), cows, and horses; (3) a passageway from the ghetto to the well in the market square, for ghetto guards and *Judenrat* members; and (4) near the post office, where the *Judenrat* had an office, a passage for food distribution and from which bodies of the Jews who died from hunger and disease were moved during the night to the Jewish cemetery. There, a pit would be dug—its size determined by the number of bodies brought over that night. The "buriers" left no grave markers.

The bulk of the map's legend, in numbers from 1 to 136, identifies every recalled physical structure, from the flour mill to the alfalfa field, from the tile workshop to the slaughterhouse, from the schools to the stables, from the palace to the statues, from the synagogue to the churches, from the *mikva* (ritual bath) to the policeman's house, from the barbershop to the bakery, from the Christian pig seller to the Jewish butcher, from the priest's house to the rabbi's—and, of course, including every family home, Jewish and non-Jewish.

As I hungrily read the translated memoir and map notes, names—so familiar by now—and landmarks come alive as they were an elderly man's lifetime ago. These are not the fragmented snatches of nostalgia. These are the painstaking replicas of humans and their artifacts, systematically pinpointed in geographical location and sociological import—all from the vantage point of someone who was frozen in youth. Each person, each object appears suddenly before me like a child's pop-up book; I'm jolted by the sudden impact and soothed as each then recedes to its rightful place in the overall scene.

The ghetto walls disappear, and I begin to see Volchin before the war enforced artificial boundaries. I follow the exact route, in and around the same places as Shmuel passed during his daily routine: the grade school he attended, Christian and Jewish children together, taught in Polish; the Polish Church, the adjacent palace (then converted to a monastery), and the nearby public park, where he joined other young people on the Sabbath and Jewish holidays. Within the eventual ghetto, I see the Jewish school—financed by American relatives—where classes were taught primarily in Yiddish and subjects included Hebrew and the Torah. When Shmuel gets to the synagogue, I feel his reverence, so similar to that of Morris Gevirtz's as recorded in the *Yizkor* book.

Remembering the large brick building, Shmuel describes the walls covered with paintings and biblical verses. He relishes the lost details: the carved handrails flanking the steps leading to the *bimah*; the ark housing the Torah scrolls, draped by a curtain embroidered with artistic images. The town elders and well-to-do members of the community paid for the more expensive seats, facing east, on both sides of the Holy Ark; the rest of the congregation sat in assigned family seats. The women prayed behind a wall in the back of the synagogue.

On the Sabbath and Jewish holidays, all the village stores were closed, and everyone went to the synagogue to pray or socialize. Following services during the more revered holidays, Jewish residents were invited to the rabbi's house to give, according to will and ability, a donation to the community board of directors.

Ironically, the Christian Orthodox church physically dominated the center of the village and the Jewish section. The priest prayed daily with a small group of elderly villagers. But on Sundays and holidays, many people from the surrounding areas would come to the services. A large number of them would get drunk and get into fistfights with the Catholics, who also came to attend church services. Although these groups hated each other, they were united in one thing: they hated the Jews more, a hatred often manifesting in violence.

The market square surrounding the community well was a large bustling center of village life.[2] On one side was a line of stores, connected to a passage leading to the synagogue and Jewish school. The other side of the market led into the main street. Monday was market day. Shoppers and peddlers from all over would roll in their carts. Merchants would put up stalls. On the other days of the week, farmers brought in carts with firewood. In Volchin, the furnaces were made of clay, and firewood was used all year. Farmers also brought in seasonal fruits and vegetables.

The square was also used for weddings. It was the custom to have the wedding on a Friday. The *chuppah* (wedding canopy) would be erected in the square on a Friday afternoon and the entire village would join in the celebration. Klezmer musicians from nearby Visoke would entertain. Even enemies would come, using the occasion to patch up arguments.

Across from the church, a large multiuse facility served the Jewish community well. It was the headquarters of the volunteer Fire Brigade, and its large hall and stage was the setting for theatrical performances and balls. Almost every week, the young Volchiners—Jewish and Christian—attended dances there. Zuberman's restaurant was directly opposite this building. With a permit to sell alcoholic beverages, the restaurant was also the scene of a great deal of vodka drinking—and Sunday fisticuffs.

The Jewish cemetery was also centrally located, not far from the other side of the main street. A large area, surrounded by a stone wall, it was completely destroyed during the occupation; all headstones were removed and used elsewhere in the village for building materials.

Shmuel writes about his visit to this once-sacred site in 1997: "We—Dov, Esther, and Drora—left the cemetery with a great ache in our hearts. Not only did the murderers slaughter all the remaining Jews of Volchin, but they did not spare the dead. They intended to erase all memory of the Jews and Judaism from the face of the earth." Of course, no one suspected that so many years later, Dov and Shmuel would find a building on the village's main street with Hebrew letters—fragments of the Jewish cemetery's headstones.

Shmuel is also meticulous when he describes the villagers. I learn about Eli, the cart owner, who traveled to Brest to pick up merchandise for Sobelman's store. During the occupation, the Germans enlisted Eli to harness horses to his cart and provide the transportation to a wedding. Once at their destination, they forced Eli to become drunk; ordered him to dance in a circle; and abandoned him to recover in the snow, an action that caused him to lose his toes. There was another Eli, the cattle merchant, who during the Soviet regime, when trade was forbidden, would buy and sell secretly until he and his son were caught and spent several years in prison.

A Polish family, Kuzshenyovsky, had a unique status by living among the Jews. Before the war, the father was a peaceful neighbor; however, he subsequently became the mayor and assisted the Germans. He was one of the few to know beforehand that September 22 would be the massacre date. He organized local laborers to clean out the death pit, recruited horses and carts to carry the weak and old Jews to their deaths and to transport their belongings afterward, and was a witness to the executions. His son, Shmuel's former classmate, was in charge of the guards surrounding the ghetto.

The cobbler, Rief, and his family lived near the cemetery; his son, Shmuel, was Shmuel Englender's best friend. Before the war, both Shmuels enlisted in the army. At the recruiting center, they were given uniforms and awaited orders. A cart was provided to take them to the train, where they would travel to their army units. When Shmuel Englender heard his name called, he got into the cart. The other Shmuel's name was not announced because there were enough volunteers. Shmuel Englender was jealous that his friend could return to the safety of their village. He writes: "He went back home, and I became a soldier. My destiny was to fight in the war, get wounded many times. I was meant to die, but I survived. . . . As to the fate of my friend, within a few months the Germans entered Volchin, and he was taken into forced labor, to build the Brest-Chernavchich road. Shortly thereafter, he was massacred together with all the Jews from the Brest ghetto." At Brona Gora.

Two families in particular helped retain Jewish traditions. The town butcher, Shulklafer, lived near the synagogue, off the main street. In his home, he ran a *cheder* where children studied the Torah and other sacred texts. He also tutored boys for their bar mitzvahs. On the far end of Volchin's main road was the Mandelbaum house. Many of the family's five sons and five daughters were intellectuals. Young and old would gather at their house to read Yiddish newspapers and discuss social and political events.

Like many such Jewish villages and towns, Volchin participated in the Zionist debate. The Laufer family, living in the center of the village, had two sons. Both were active (the elder was the commander) in the Betar, the Zionist militant youth movement whose most accomplished member was Menachem Begin. Shmuel remembers vicious arguments between Betar members and those of opposing groups.

Shmuel devotes a page to the Stabeskys, Dov's family. I recognize the name of Dov's grandfather, Yerachmiel, who was, according to Shmuel, "one of the respected people in town." Not only did he sit facing east in the synagogue, next to the Holy Ark, but he was a cantor, read the Torah, and blew the shofar during the high holidays. Distinguished by a pointed beard, Yerachmiel was a font of proverbs and jokes. One of his four daughters, Dov's mother, Tama, was an active figure among the Volchiners; and his only son, Berel, who married Shmuel's oldest sister, was also very social and talented, often sitting outside and playing the mandolin as young people sang along.

When portraying Dov's people, Shmuel allows himself a rare moment of divergent interjection. "Dov Bar," he says, "is a very active and central figure among the Volchin immigrants in Israel. Without him, not much would have been done. There is a 'chemistry' between Dov and me. Everything I do for the people of Volchin has been inspired by him. We collaborate in our writing about Volchin and provide material to Andrea Simon, a descendant of Volchin, in New York."

Another large section of the memoirs presents Shmuel's family and house, occupying a prominent place facing the main road. The house contained the family bakery, where they sold bread, rolls, and challah. "My mother and I would get up very early Friday morning to braid the challahs in preparation for the Sabbath," Shmuel writes. "I worked in the bakery after I finished school while the war was going on and before I enlisted." His mother, Hinda Leah, also ran a restaurant. "She was an excellent cook," Shmuel says. "Gentiles would come, particularly on Sundays, holidays, and market day to celebrate with food and vodka. They loved her herring and pickled fish, for which she was famous."

Of the fate of Shmuel's loved ones, I read with a heavy heart: "We were four brothers and four sisters. I was the eldest. . . . All [the others] were murdered by the Nazis—the older ones were sent to the Brest ghetto; the younger ones were killed with my mother . . . and thrown into the communal pit." As previously noted, one of Shmuel's brothers was killed after the massacre, and Shmuel's father was shot and killed by a ghetto guard when he climbed the fence into a garden to get a few potatoes to feed his children.

Shmuel poignantly describes Rachel Stoler, the woman he married in December 1940: "We were married until April 1941, less than half a year, when I left Volchin. I never saw her, my parents, or the rest of my family again. . . . According to the locals, after I left town for the army, she moved in with my parents. I don't know if she lived in the ghetto and ended up like the others who were shot and thrown into the death pit . . . or maybe she was taken with the other young people of Volchin to forced labor . . . and massacred together with the Brest ghetto residents."

"Sadly," Shmuel says, "this was the fate of my family. I am the sole survivor. I have braved battles, injuries, the tides of war, and camps in the Soviet Union, Germany, Austria, and France. When I was in Siberia, I married and had a son, who grew up to be a doctor. We finally arrived in Israel, where, with the help of God, I rehabilitated myself. We have a grandson and granddaughter, and they bring us great joy."

Close to Shmuel's home, and next to the water well, was the home of Avrum Kupershmidt, Dov's grandmother's brother (the *Judenrat* member mentioned in chapter 6). A good man, Kupershmidt took great care of his fellow Jews in Volchin's ghetto. In fact, he was instrumental in saving Mendel Kaplan, the fabric store owner, who had been captured outside the ghetto. Before the war, Kupershmidt was a popular and active leader. As such, he was one of five members of Volchin's Jewish community council, serving in the role of "foreign minister," whose responsibilities included the issuing of official documents. Another prominent council member was Iser Midler, captain of the Fire Brigade. Shmuel says that Kupershmidt and Midler were the "nonreligious members of the board."

The Kupershmidt home also played a role in one of Shmuel's most vivid childhood memories. One Friday night, when Shmuel was about 11 years old, his family heard loud banging at their restaurant's front door. Shmuel's father came to the door and the Polish policeman, who lived nearby, barged inside. He was drunk and could barely stand. He yelled for vodka and after a while demanded to sleep with the "Jew woman," Shmuel's mother. Fortunately, Shmuel's mother heard the commotion and slipped out the back door. The policeman eventually tripped and fell asleep on the floor. During the night, the Englenders dragged the sleeping officer to the Kupershmidt house and pondered the dilemma. If they reported the policeman's activities, it would mean he would be punished or fired, surely resulting in ramifications for the Jews. A few days later, Shmuel's father was invited to the Kupershmidt house, where prominent community members, including Iser Midler, were eating lunch (with a bottle of vodka). The Polish policeman was there and asked for Shmuel's father's forgiveness. There, again, in the thick of the action, was my uncle, Iser Midler. More pieces to my family puzzle.

Of course, the villager I am most interested in is Iser Midler. Throughout the memoirs, the Midler name comes up within the ordinary business of a thriving community. Even when Shmuel lists the old home of the Christian Orthodox priest, he relates that the priest had taken over the Midler family property and built himself a beautiful brick house. "Andrea Simon, a member of the Midler family . . . photographed the new house and the old wing."

Although I learn few new family facts, I am still delighted to read a complete paragraph about my uncle: "He was one of the town businessmen and served as one of the five members of the board of directors of the Jewish community, . . . was the captain of the volunteer Fire Brigade. He was quite wealthy and was the head regional salesperson for Singer sewing machines. He also sold and repaired bicycles. . . . [The Midlers] had a fruit orchard in their garden. We used to sneak into the orchard and pick a few apples or plums."

Finally, through Shmuel's rich anecdotes and cartographical identifications, all these figures and objects coalesce. What emerges, maybe for the first time in my search, is what I had been looking for from the beginning—the forces and types of people that shaped my grandmother. What emerges is a replica of a functioning village, where actual living souls shopped, studied, bathed, worshiped, ate, slept, played, made love. What emerges comes from the title of the map, written in Shmuel's hand. It translates as "Volchin: As It Was." The map is signed by Shmuel, "Born in Volchin and saved from the Holocaust."

All these stories interweave through each other in strange and wonderful ways. Our roots may be tangled, but the main branch is far-reaching and strong. It extends from the Old World to the New, from shtetl to metropolitan city, from east to west, from one century to another, and across rivers and seas and oceans.

As I pull on the branch, there's a tug-of-war with tradition and tragedy weighing heavily on the other end. The branch is so long that it has snagged on tree barks, circling forests of decimated limbs; snaked through the rotted seepage of ghetto gutters; looped like camel humps over complicit shrugs; stuck in collaborator silence; dunked into freshly dug pits; and tripped over the polished leather boots of voluntary and often celebratory executioners.

Those particular sections are frayed and thinning. Somewhere along that continuum was a live wire, without the insulation of an outer shell. From that wire sprung five strands in graduating sizes, perfect for soldering into the main cord. Instead they were snipped. Each one hung down, fried from electrocution. In between the blackened tendrils were bits of charred flesh and bone shards, smeared with thinned blood. Five strands, each with a name: Iser Midler, Bashka Midler, Ida Midler, Sala Midler, Ester Midler.

All the way at the other end of the main branch, I feel the tug of my grandmother Masha. Her section is variegated: thick and cushiony at points, followed by miles of narrow peaks and valleys, as many as an erratic electrocardiogram. As she faced the vicissitudes of situational challenges, her earlier advantages gave her the arrogance to believe she could—and should—survive.

Somewhere further along the branch is my mother as a young child. This piece is so frail, it must have broken and been artlessly repaired with coiled wires. Though the branch grows stronger, there are sudden drops followed by more reparations and wild spikes; the irregular pattern continues as my mother searches for emotional restitution.

With a gentle drag at the cordlike branch, I take up some slack, wrapping it as loosely as possible around my wrist, as if it's a skein of wool and not a coarse and brittle substance. There's not much to gather before it tightens again, and I press what I can close to my breast. I'm almost at its end, almost at the point where I can throw it back and reel it in like a fishing line, but I'm cautious, too familiar with the false dips of colorful lures and the potential poison of rusty hooks.

I let it go for a while, and it embraces surprises in its path—the Kremers, Shmuel Englender, the Bars, Hannah Williams, Louis Pozez, Sara Sanditen, Lily Guterman, Rosanne Lapan—those whose wires caught on mine. The world—my world—becomes closer, tighter, easier to manage. It's ruled by nothing tangible, something elusive, something like . . . *bashert*.

Finally, I get to the end. It's easier to grasp than I imagined. There's a hole, and I look through a narrow tunnel. My vision inside is short-sighted, but the distorted perspective is clear as I hold it up to the light. My own disappointments show up in short and complicated twists, which appear from afar as one continuous bumpy connection. If I didn't know whose section this is, I'd guess it belongs to a person who has also managed to survive. But unlike those before her, this person did not lash out at the unexpected intrusions. No, this person kept her grief inside the network. This person survived by living in her head.

What began as a search for missing facts, for missing relatives, ultimately became a search for myself. Yes, the branch was long and tangled, but I found my end. As I shake it, another piece dislodges. It looks short, but it seems composed of a more modern and pliable substance and, if shaken hard enough, is even retractable. It can be pulled in a smooth, even line, much further than I can go. This is the cord of the future, the one I hand to my daughter.

During what became my final taping with Masha in 1980, I tried to get her to answer my questions. Her responses were more and more incoherent. Giving up, I ask on the tape, "Should I finish interviewing you?"

"I don't want somebody should have them," she says, suddenly alert. "You'll laugh at me, when I'll be gone."

I try to reassure her. I tell her while I may laugh with her, I'd never laugh *at* her. That her story will live on, that she will always be remembered.

I didn't know what she understood by this time in her life, but she became more interested in posing for my camera, ready with a coquettish wink.

Shortly thereafter, Masha suffered rapid and irrevocable setbacks in her mental abilities. She no longer had control over her bodily functions; she could not recognize familiar objects. She ate a raw onion marinated in orange juice, painted her hair with shoe polish, turned on all the gas jets. Obviously, she could not be allowed to remain in her home, even under the watchful eyes of friends and relatives. This fact was painful and hard for her family to accept.

Under professional advice, Masha's children decided to send her to a hospital, where she would be evaluated and eventually placed in a nursing home. Masha, her two daughters, and her Russian caretaker rode to the hospital. To ease the tension, the caretaker began to sing Russian folk songs. Masha soon joined in, remembering all the words and melodies as clearly as she had learned them 80 years before. While tears streamed down my mother's cheeks and her sister Sara clutched the steering wheel, Masha sang all the way to the hospital.

At that moment, my grandmother was not a woman with Alzheimer's disease, close to 90 years old. No, she was a young, beautiful girl, full of life, full of song. She was a Jewish girl in her beloved Volchin. She had the spirit of a survivor. And she was one of the last of her kind.

In the nursing home, Masha's deterioration was heartbreaking. She stole her roommate's false teeth, buried money in a flowerpot, and believed the solarium was her living room. Even toward the end, when she could no longer remember anyone's name, she flirted unabashedly with the doctors. She became docile and childlike, subject to irrational tantrums. Her senility robbed her of any previous duplicity or complicated thoughts. Her life was reduced to its basic functions, with little lapse into coherence. Perhaps she left life the way she arrived—stripped of any memory, with her inhibitions diminished—a naked, wrinkled, and lonely soul. But there is one major difference. During her journey, she left her memories.

When Masha was approaching old age, she found it difficult to associate with other seniors. Pride and vanity kept her from taking solace in her contemporaries' friendships. Her later years could have been full, without the bitterness of a strong woman unable to face a weakened body.

Masha's final irony was that she had to end her life among the very people she had resisted—the old and the sick. If she had had any wits left, she would have cursed God for her helplessness, for her ultimate humiliation.

Masha died in the nursing home in 1982. She was 89—or so.

When I close my eyes, I refuse to see Masha sitting in a dark room, mumbling incoherently amid the chatter of dribbling chins and soiled remains of yesterday's meals. I see Masha as the mistress of her home, entertaining her guests with amusing gossip and steaming onion rolls. I nestle under her arms, convinced of her agelessness, convinced that she will be here and the same forever.

My search continues. Whenever I think I'm finished with the material, I receive another gift in the mail. The archival sources need to be tapped further; much still remains there. I have written letters to the eyewitnesses Shmuel Englender interviewed in Volchin, asking if they remember more about the Midler family. While they are still alive, there is always a possibility something, someone, will trigger a memory, some paper will be found in some vault, some keepsake will be unearthed under some flowerbed.

If someone had asked me years ago about my lost Volchin family, I would have said that they were killed, probably shot, but we will never be certain. And, here I am, with so many facts, so many jumbles of memories.

From Yad Vashem, I have a form entitled "A Page of Testimony." The museum calls these forms "symbolic tombstones, intended to serve as a lasting memorial for the victims of the Holocaust." The descriptive page says that details beyond names and places provide a "personality" for an identity, otherwise lost in the coming generations. A note on the bottom reads: "Many names of Holocaust victims have not yet been recorded in the Hall of Names. In less than a generation, there may be no one living who personally remembers the victims. Please FULFILL YOUR OBLIGATION by registering your dear ones. Interview your oldest living relatives for details on the victims before it is too late."

On the testimony form itself, it explains the task of Yad Vashem: "To gather into the homeland material regarding all those members of the Jewish people who laid down their lives, who fought and rebelled against the Nazi enemy and his collaborators, and to perpetuate their NAMES and those of the communities, organisations, and institutions which were destroyed because they were Jewish."

Because they were Jewish.

On the bottom of the form, there is a quote from Isaiah: ". . . even unto them will I give in mine house and within my walls a place and a name . . . that shall not be cut off."

In my drawer of precious papers, I keep five pages of testimony. The names are already entered: Midler, Iser; Midler, Bashka; Midler, Ida; Midler, Sara (Sala); Midler, Ester. Most of the lines I can fill: family name, first name, sex, approximate age, birthplace, victim's mother, victim's father, permanent residence, wartime residence, victim's profession, death place, circumstances of death. I mean to complete all the lines, but I postpone the task. Some people in Volchin were shot before the massacre. Some may have been killed elsewhere, such as Brona Gora. It's still possible one of the Midlers was among those victims.

I have searched the Brest passport records for the Midler names, but it's only a partial list of those killed at Brona Gora. Some of Volchin's young adults were sent to Brest-Litovsk. It's still possible that one of the Midler girls was there. Though Hanna Kremer remembers hearing about Ida's protest and subsequent shooting in Volchin, I have heard many conflicting stories from eyewitnesses, including the number of Nazis and the number of collaborators. Though I believe that all of the Midlers died that day, September 22, 1942, in Volchin, I am not 100 percent certain.

I will wait a little longer. I may learn more. After all, I now know so much I didn't know before. I know that Iser was tall, handsome, good-natured. He was treasurer of the relief society, member of the community council, captain of the Fire Brigade, owner of bicycle repair/Singer sewing-machine shop, and business partner of Hanna Kremer's uncle. By village standards, he was wealthy. I know he was the type of man to inspire the remark, "Who didn't know Iser Midler?"

I know the Midlers had a lovely house, abutting a fruitful orchard and a garden. Their house was so lovely it was chosen as the residence of the police chief and headquarters of the village chief and the *Judenrat*.

I know the Midlers had a gramophone.

I know Bashka looked innocent and much younger than her years. I know Sala was best friends with Hanna Kremer, that she was short, pretty, and blond like her mother. I know that Ida studied at the Tarbut, the Hebrew high school in Brest-Litovsk; had an idiosyncratic and rebellious spirit; was tall, sturdy, dark-complexioned, and looked like a gypsy; had long hair—and eyes like mine. And I just know that little Ester was cute and lovable.

Yes, I will save these pages of testimony. I will wait a little longer. I want to be sure to include as many facts as possible. I want to record as much as their personalities as I can. I want it to be known in perpetuity that these people, once vibrant, once hopeful, once carefree, like you and me, these people, my people, were destroyed for one reason only—because they were Jewish.

I'm not ready to close the book on them—not yet.

June 22, 1998

It's fitting that I get an answer on this day, June 22, the anniversary of the German invasion of Russia and a year after my trip to Eastern Europe. It's fitting—or more likely, it's *bashert*.

I receive a response to the letter I wrote Anna Gagarina, the former classmate of Hanna Kremer. The letter, of course, is in Russian. It is neatly written, not one crossed-out word. The bold script seems to flow, filling two sides of a graph-paper sheet and half of another. I scan the lines as if, after over a year of receiving material in Russian, I'm now able to decipher some words. But the only thing I recognize is 1924, and I get excited, remembering that this is the birth year of Hanna Kremer and Sala Midler. Gagarina must be writing about them!

I wait patiently for the translation.

When it comes, my hands shake. Still standing, I tear open the envelope. I now hold answers to my questions. They may not be the definitive answers, but there is something on these pages I need to know. After greetings, the letter begins: "The Midler family I knew well. I remember Isaac; his wife, Bashka; and their daughters. The girls were pretty and nice. Ida and Vera Makarevich Shpagina went to school together. They were born in the same year. . . . I went to school with Sala. We were both born in 1924. Ester was younger and went to the same school. I remember them all very well."

At this point Gagarina mentions that Hanna Kremer went to school with Ida and Vera. But I know that Hanna was the same age as Sala, not Ida. Can it be possible that Anna Gagarina's memory has faded? Perhaps I should stop now. Perhaps I will only learn more contradictory information, information that will only be distracting and disturbing.

But I can't let one inconsistency deter me. I read on. Gagarina tells me about a windmill in Volchin that had been owned by Schmulke Zuprik, who was married to Fanya. They had a daughter named Riva and a son, Moishe. Riva, Gagarina says, was in her class. The Zupriks were good friends of the Midlers. Both families were taken to the ghetto.

These names are familiar. Zuprik must be the same name as Zufrik, the member of the *Judenrat.* Yes, this is the same man recalled by Volchin witness Pavlovich. This is the same man whose daughter, Riva, clung to her mother during the massacre.

Anna Gagarina also repeats this story. She says that when the younger Jews were taken from Volchin, Fanya hid Riva, so the girl remained in Volchin, only to be killed with her family. In Gagarina's version, Fanya hugged both her children (undoubtedly having hidden Moishe as well). They refused to undress and were locked in an embrace as they were shot.

When Gagarina received my letter, she went from Brest, where she now lives, back to Volchin. There, she visited Vera Makarevich Shpagina and a few other older villagers and showed them my letter. Their conclusion: "The Midlers were not killed in Volchin."

I can understand how people faint from startling news. "The Midlers were not killed in Volchin." This line goes through me so quickly, so piercingly, I almost grab the table near me for support. No, this cannot be. Not after a year and a half of research.

I can understand that Ida and perhaps Sala may have been sent elsewhere, probably to Brest, but I have consistently believed that Iser, Bashka, and Ester were killed in the village massacre. Now, if the villagers' conclusion is true, all my searching has been in vain.

When I was in Volchin, I thought, at least I was able to say my farewell to the Midlers at the mass grave. At least I was making some peace for my line of relatives. At least.

At least, I thought, they died together. At least, they died in their village, with their friends.

At least.

But now, now, everything is different. "The Midlers were not killed in Volchin." Where, where had they gone?

Maybe I was afraid of this all along. Maybe I was afraid that Iser and Bashka were too able-bodied to have been left in the village with the elderly, sick, and young children. Sure, they were probably shipped elsewhere. Sure, it makes sense.

Then again, maybe Gagarina and the other villagers are mistaken. There have been so many inconsistencies in my search. Maybe this is just another one.

There is more to the letter. I sit down. I don't trust my trembling legs. I reread that line again and then press forward: "The Midlers were not killed in Volchin—this I know for sure. People say that they were taken to labor camps, along with others. Ester was not taken; she was too young. Rumor has it that the night after her family was taken away, Ester was secretly smuggled out of Volchin into Poland, where she had some relatives. (I am not sure as to the exact name of the place—Botki, Bohki?) The man who took her to Poland was a very nice man named Korshenevsky. Unfortunately, he is already dead. His middle-aged son lives in Poland, and sometimes comes to Volchin. Vera Makarevich says that he told her that Ester was taken to Poland that night on horseback by his father. Nothing else is known of Ester's fate."

I stop for a second and catch my breath. Ester, smuggled out of Volchin by a man named Korshenevsky. This must be the same person who was appointed head of the village during the war. This must be the once-friendly neighbor (previously translated as Kuzshenyovsky) who assisted the Germans, the man Shmuel recalled in his memoirs. This man took Ester to Botki. Botki—I also know that name. I search my notes from my interview with the Kremers. There it is. Bashka Midler was from a little town between Volchin and Bialystok named Bocki. Mike Kremer had shown me the name on the map. This is a similar name to the town my Aunt Ray insists was the true birthplace of my mother. Yes, Bocki, this now makes sense. Perhaps Bashka's relatives were believed to be still there. Perhaps, Iser and Bashka sent Ester to them, to Bocki, where they thought she'd be safer than in Volchin.

And since no one in my American family ever heard from Ester, I can only assume that if she made it to Bocki, she was killed there or elsewhere. I put the letter down and consult my notebook, filled with research facts. There I find Bocki: "Southwest of Bielsk-Podlaski. Ghetto created in fall of 1941. Ghetto: 40 houses; about 750 Jews. Liquidated Nov. 2, 1942. During liquidation of ghetto, Jews were transferred to Bielsk-Podlaski, then to Bialystok, and ultimately to Treblinka." So it is Treblinka that may have been Ester's fate. Treblinka, the same probable destination as Hanna Kremer's immediate family.

There are nine lines left in Gagarina's letter and I am both eager and filled with dread. These contrary forces keep me unable to move for several minutes. Finally, I will my eyes to focus. Gagarina writes:

> Of the Jews who were taken from Volchin, none have returned, including the Midlers. I think that they were probably killed at Brona Gora. In Volchin, the Germans killed local children and the old people, and also some of the Jews from the village of Chernavchich, which is close to Brest.
>
> The Midlers' house was destroyed. Another house was built in its place, where other people live. Hanna Kremer's house stands to this day.
>
> This is probably all that I can tell you about what happened.

So maybe this is what the end must be. I read this section again. "I think that they were probably killed at Brona Gora." Two years ago, I had never heard the name. Brona Gora. Ironic, yes. *Bashert*, certainly.

"They were probably killed at Brona Gora," I repeat to myself. This is too much for me.

Brona Gora. Perhaps I had said good-bye to the Midlers after all. Perhaps, when I was standing in that huge forest, bending my head in overwhelming sorrow with all the others, I was saying good-bye to my own people.

But it's hard to believe—even harder to accept—that most likely, I'll never know.

Chapter 1

1. For specifics on these figures, see chapter 4.
2. In *Holocaust in Belorussia, 1941–1944*, Leonid Smilovitsky reports that between 1941 and 1959, the number of Jews in Belorussia fell from 1,000,000 to 150,000.

Chapter 3

1. Survivors of the Shoah Visual History Foundation is a nonprofit organization founded in 1994 by Steven Spielberg. It is dedicated to videotaping and archiving interviews of Holocaust survivors, eyewitnesses, liberators, and rescuers. In 2005, the Foundation merged with the University of Southern California.

Chapter 4

1. These figures are taken from Joram Kagan's *Hippocrene Insiders' Guide to Poland's Jewish Heritage* and from Paul Johnson's *History of the Jews*.
2. The *Encyclopedia of the Holocaust* estimates that at least 1,600,000 people were murdered at Auschwitz-Birkenau— about a quarter of all Jews killed during World War II—and *The Ghetto Anthology* states that the minimum number of victims at Auschwitz-Birkenau was 2,500,000.
3. Other Holocaust sources refer to this body as the "Extraordinary State Commission for the Investigation of Crimes Committed by the German-Fascist Invaders and Their Accomplices" and the "Extraordinary State Commission to Investigate and Establish War Crimes of the German-Fascist Invaders."
4. *Einsatzgruppe B* was responsible for killings in Belorussia.
5. The report also concludes that there was another area of mass execution near the village of Smolyarka, six kilometers from the Brona Gora station. Five mass graves were found

there, and an estimated 1,000 people were executed. The report contains the names of the perpetrators. The original documents are located at the State Archives of the Russian Federation in Moscow.

6. In the second area of mass graves, near Smolyarka, the committee found three pit graves. This section estimates that 3,000 "peaceful Soviet citizens" from Brest and nearby villages were killed in this area. The forensic evidence indicated that most of the victims were shot from a short distance. The third area, a kilometer northwest of the settlement of Malorita, contained nine mass graves. The committee opened two and determined that most of the victims were shot; some were buried alive. The number of "peaceful Soviet citizens" killed here was also estimated at 3,000. Besides these burial sites, the committee uncovered graves in the Brest prison yard, the Brest Fortress, and in other locations in Brest.

7. These included Pichmann and Gerik, SD (Security Service); Cibel, assistant chief of the SD; Franz Burat, regional Gebietskommissar; Franz and Pandikov, assistant regional Gebietskommissars; Dauerlein, chief of the Gebietskommissariat's police; Gardes, chief of the SS, Bereza Kartuska; Rode and Biner, chiefs of police, Brest; Hoffmann, chief of the First Police Precinct; Golter, Grieber, and Boss, assistants, First Police Precinct; Preizniger, chief of the Second Police District; Zavadski, chief of SD criminal police; and Ivanovsky, commandant of the criminal police.

8. Even before this illustrious time, in the 16th century, Volchin was owned by prominent townspeople. The section then reviews the attributes of the various owning families, leading back again to the Poniatowskis, who greatly improved Volchin's economic situation by increasing farmstead size, building seven mills, and, of course, rebuilding the Troisky Church. Volchin also had an orthodox church, which was damaged and renovated many times in its long history.

9. The next section from *Memory* tells the story of Estonian Vilgelm Kukhelbeker, a poet-Decembrist who studied with Pushkin and was famous for his courageous speeches, as well as his part in the 1825 uprising. After the rebellion, this famous man not only visited Belorussia but stopped in the town of Visoke on his flight from Russia to Poland.

Chapter 5

1. The accepted Polish spelling is *Wolkowysk*. According to the 1921 census, the town had a total population of 11,100, including 5,130 Jews.

2. Although the Visoke youth prepared for resistance and escape to the forest, their plans didn't materialize. According to Shalom Cholawsky's book, *The Jews of Bielorussia during World War II*, liquidation took place on November 2, 1942.

Chapter 6

1. Ivanovich is a patronymic often used by friends. His real surname is not identified. I later read about an Ivan Ivanovich Gents, who was a witness to the murders of 1,000 Jews near the village of Smolyarka in October 1942 (see chapter 8). There is no corroborating evidence that this is the same person.
2. Committee members are: Zlotovsky Vasuly Karpin, chairperson of the committee; Doctor Kolobo Boris Afnosevich, member of the committee; Sacharin Pumin Philipovich, vice-chairperson of Visoke-Litovsk City Hall; Yurchok Anatoly Dimitrevich, principal of Volchin School; Sinleko Nikolay Ivanovich, secretary, Visoke-Litovsk Communist Party; Sacharin Nikolay Yacovlevich, priest of orthodox church, Volchin; and Groshevsky Ivan Tripomovich, member of the committee of the surrounding area.
3. The *Gendarmerie* were rural police, similar to county troopers. The Russian word is pronounced *Zhandarmeria* and has been translated as "Gendarmerie," but it is more likely that Semenyuk was the head of the *Schutzmannschaft* (local police) because the *Gendarmerie* consisted only of Germans and a few ethnic Germans.
4. Others Semenyuk accuses are: Malyuta, regional chief; Ivan Pluteinyuk, assistant chief; Otto Adolph Vuit, who killed two POWs in Semenyuk's presence; Commissar Pavle; Felix Zhukovski, policeman; Major Rode, massacre supervisor; Petro Kesa, Semenyuk's assistant and a participant in executions; and Pavel Semenyuk (relationship to Vasily Semenyuk unknown), a windmill machinist, who also collected clothing from the executed Jews.

Chapter 7

1. Other sources give the date as the beginning of July.
2. A Brest government archive states that according to records dated March 20, 1937, 21,653 of the 52,024 residents of the Brest region were Jewish. Also according to the archive, the majority of the approximately 40,000 Brest citizens killed by Germans during World War II were Jewish.
3. According to the *Encyclopedia of the Holocaust*, Jews constituted more than 75 percent of Brest's population.
4. This is the date given by the *Courier* and the *Black Book*. Other sources, including the *Encyclopedia of the Holocaust* (as reported in chapter 4), attribute the atrocity to June 28–29.
5. A Brest archive report gives 16,873 as the number of Jews in Brest on June 5, 1942.
6. There is recorded documentation of underground organizations and signs of revolt in 94 out of 111 (85 percent) of western Belorussia's ghettos, work camps, and communities.

7. The men of Battalion 101 participated in every phase of the Erntefest massacre.

Chapter 8

1. Commission members included Arkady Ivanovich Tarasevich, chairman; Vasily Nikolaevich Bury, head of the Berezov District Executive Committee (DEC); Ivan Pavlovich Kashtelyan, representative of the partisans; and Comrade Kosar, representative of the people of Berezov.
2. The witnesses to these crimes included Ivan Ivanovich Gents, Ivan Stepanovich Gents, Andrei Ivanovich Levkovets, and Iosif Yakovlevich Kutnik.
3. Commanding the troops were Major Rode, chief of police, Brest District (until the beginning of 1944); Captain Biner, chief of police, Brest District (from 1944 until the German retreat); Lieutenant Hoffmann, chief of First Police District (PD), city of Brest; Officers Golter, Grieber, and Boss, deputy chiefs, First PD, city of Brest; Lieutenant Preizniger, chief of Second PD, city of Brest (until the beginning of 1944); Zavadski (German), chief of SD, criminal police; Ivanovsky (Polish), commandant, criminal police; Cibel, assistant chief of SD; and Gerik, SD, supervisor of executions.

Chapter 9

1. He adopted this shortened version of his last name, which to my memory was Hershkovitz.
2. For reasons of privacy and amnesia, the name *Schwanke* is fictitious.
3. Other sources report this number as 2,892.
4. The ghetto was actually liquidated on October 15, 1942.
5. The article claims that 100 such police companies decimated 400 villages and killed all inhabitants of at least 20 villages.
6. The 1921 census figures given in YIVO's *Image before My Eyes* are: total population of Brest, 29,533; number of Jews, 15,630; percentage of Jews, 52.9.
7. From the translation, it's difficult to reconcile the exact titles with those listed in the first section of the report or to perfectly match them to material obtained from other sources.
8. The date of this massacre matches that given in some sources, although others list the date as July 12 and report a larger number killed (see chapter 7).

Chapter 10

1. My translator interpreted the spelling of the names of those appearing in the videotape.

2. Sources differ on the number of Jews in wartime Brest and on the number of survivors. A *Brest Courier* newspaper article gives the total number of Jews as 36,000 (see chapter 7). Federation delegate Lily Guterman remembers 11 survivors, including herself.

3. Discrepancies in the date and number killed have been discussed in chapters 4, 7, and previously in this chapter. Other reports also state that such an execution was conducted on the outskirts of town.

4. Elsewhere in his book, Dean cites another source estimating that, "Between 1941–1943 . . . approximately two million Jews were killed within the May 1941 borders of the Soviet Union, primarily by shooting in pits close to their homes." As far as Brona Gora is concerned, the book presents a report from the Polish underground confirming "the active role of the local police" (including many Poles) in the liquidation of the Brest ghetto, including "finishing off" and widespread looting. It states that about 12,000 Jews from Brest were shot at Brona Gora. In addition, a *Gendarmerie* report states that 20,000 Jews were "resettled" in Brest on October 15–16, 1942.

Chapter 11

1. Though etched in Wolf's mind, this date is probably wrong. Although Treblinka I was set up as a forced labor camp in 1941, the first transports (from the Warsaw ghetto) for extermination arrived in the summer of 1942. Given Wolf's subsequent testimony, it seems likely the year "he never forgot" was 1942. Sources used in chapter 5 state the date as November 2.

2. There was another market, for horses and cattle, at the edge of town.

Books

Arad, Yitzhak, Shmuel Krakowski, and Shmuel Spector, eds. *The Einsatzgruppen Reports: Selections from the Dispatches of the Nazi Death Squads' Campaign against the Jews in Occupied Territories of the Soviet Union*, July 1941–January 1943. Trans. Stella Schossberger. New York: Holocaust Library in cooperation with Yad Vashem in Jerusalem, Israel, 1989.

Browning, Christopher R. *Ordinary Men: Reserve Police Battalion 101 and the Final Solution in Poland*. New York: HarperCollins, 1992.

Cholawsky, Shalom. *The Jews of Bielorussia during World War II*. Amsterdam: Harwood Academic Publishers, 1998.

Dawidowicz, Lucy S. *The Golden Tradition: Jewish Life and Thought in Eastern Europe*. Syracuse, N.Y.: Syracuse University Press, 1996.

Dean, Martin. *Collaboration in the Holocaust: Crimes of the Local Police in Belorussia and Ukraine, 1941–44*. New York: St. Martin's Press in association with the United States Holocaust Memorial Museum, 2000.

Dobroszycki, Lucjan, and Jeffrey S. Gurock, eds. *The Holocaust in the Soviet Union: Studies and Sources on the Destruction of the Jews in the Nazi-Occupied Territories of the USSR, 1941–1945*. Armonk, N.Y.: M.E. Sharpe, 1993.

Dobroszycki, Lucjan, and Barbara Kirshenblatt-Gimblett. *Image before My Eyes: A Photographic History of Jewish Life in Poland before the Holocaust*. New York: Schocken Books in cooperation with YIVO Institute for Jewish Research, 1977.

Ehrenburg, Ilya, and Vasily Grossman, eds. *The Black Book: The Ruthless Murder of Jews by German-Fascist Invaders throughout the Temporarily-Occupied Regions of the Soviet Union and in the Death Camps of Poland during the War of*

1941–1945. Trans. John Glad and James S. Levine. New York: Holocaust Library, 1981.

Garrard, John, and Carol Garrard. *The Bones of Berdichev: The Life and Fate of Vasily Grossman*. New York: Free Press, 1996.

Goldhagen, Daniel Jonah. *Hitler's Willing Executioners: Ordinary Germans and the Holocaust*. New York: Knopf, 1996.

Hoffman, Eva. *Shtetl: The Life and Death of a Small Town and the World of Polish Jews*. Boston: Houghton Mifflin, 1997.

Horn, Alfred, and Bozena Pietras, eds. *Insight Guides: Poland*. Rev. ed. Trans. Susan Bollans, Thomas Fife, and Ginger Künzel. Singapore: APA Publications, 1996.

Johnson, Paul. *A History of the Jews*. New York: Harper and Row, 1987.

Kagan, Joram. *Hippocrene Insiders' Guide to Poland's Jewish Heritage*. New York: Hippocrene Books, 1992.

Kurzweil, Arthur. *From Generation to Generation: How to Trace Your Jewish Genealogy and Family History*. Rev. ed. New York: HarperCollins, 1994.

Levine, Samuel, and Morris Gevirtz, eds. *Entertainment and Ball Given by the United Wisoko-Litowsker and Woltchiner Relief*. (*Yizkor* book, in Yiddish). New York: United Wisoko-Litowsker and Woltchiner Relief, 1948.

Lipilo, P. P., and V. F. Romanovskii, eds. *The Crimes of the German-Nazi Occupation of Belorussia, 1941–1944* (in Russian). Minsk: Belarus, 1965.

Noble, John, Andrew Humphreys, Richard Nebesky, Nick Selby, George Wesely, and John King. *Russia, Ukraine, and Belarus: A Lonely Planet Travel Survival Kit*. Rev. ed. Victoria, Australia, and Oakland, Calif.: Lonely Planet, 1996.

Petrashevich, A. L., U. I. Lemyashonak, B. V. Ulyanka, L. Y. Rakita, and R. Y. Lifshits, eds. *Memory: Kamyanetski Region* (in Russian). Minsk: Uradjai, 1997.

Roskies, Diane K., and David G. Roskies. *The Shtetl Book: An Introduction to East European Jewish Life and Lore*. Rev. ed. New York: Ktav, 1979.

Smilovitsky, Leonid. *The Holocaust in Belorussia, 1941–1944* (in Russian). Tel Aviv: Biblioteka Matvey Chornoro, 2000.

Weiner, Miriam, in cooperation with the Polish State Archives. *Jewish Roots in Poland: Pages from the Past and Archival Inventories*. Secaucus, N.J.: Miriam Weiner Roots to Roots Foundation 1997.

Periodicals

"Catastrophe" (in Russian). *Brestski Kuriyer*, October 9–15, 1997.

Funke, Phyllis Ellen. "Jewish Traveler: Minsk." *Hadassah Magazine*, December 1996.

Gross, Jan T. "Annals of War: Neighbors." *New Yorker*, March 12, 2001.

Haida, Gerd E. "The Massacre: What Really Happened in Kortelisy" (in

German). *Nürnberger Nachrichten*, January 24–25, 1998.

Katz, Dovid. "Begin's Cousin Preserves Jewish Memory in Brest." *Forward*, August 21, 1998.

Rosenblatt, E. S. "Jews in the System of Relations between the Ethnic Groups in Western Belarus, 1939–1941," (in Russian). *Belaruski historychny zbornik*, 2000, no. 13.

Zimak, Z. "The Brest Jewish Community before World War II." (in Russian). *Aviv* (Jewish Belarusian newspaper). 1997.

Archival Sources

Brest State Archive (Gosudarstvenny Arkiv Brestskoi Oblasti)

"Brest (Bronnaya Gora)," compiled under A. Terebun, director of the State Archive of the Brest Region, 1997 (in Russian).

"Brest Ghetto List, Administrative Department of the Municipality of the City of Brest, Book of Records of Distributed Passports, Started November 10, 1941, Ended June 5, 1942" (in Russian).

German Archives, Ludwigsburg

"Excerpt from Cessation Order of December 8, 1965, Regarding the Massacre in Brona Gora of October 15, 1942," issued by the district attorney's office in Dortmund, Germany (in German). 110 AR 2289/98.

"The Head of the Main Office in the German State of North Rhine-Westphalia, Dealing with the Mass Crimes Committed by the German National Socialists, at the Supreme District Attorney in Dortmund" (in German). 204 AR-Z 334/59.

Lore Museum of Brest Archives

"History of Brest," culled by Anatoli Yaroshchuk of Brest-Intourist (in Russian).

United States Holocaust Memorial Museum Archives, Washington, D.C.

"Acts, Protocols, and Interrogations of Witnesses, and Other Materials Regarding the Evil Deeds of the German Nazi Invaders against the Innocent Population of the Berezovsky District, Brest Province, 1945" (in Russian). RG-22-002M, reel 16, "Brestskaya oblast." Original records in the State Archives of the Russian Federation, Moscow (fd. 7021, op. 83, del. 9).

Extraordinary State Commission to Investigate Nazi Crimes Committed on the Territory of the Soviet Union. "Summary Translation of the Statement

Prepared in 1944."

Yad Vashem Archives, Jerusalem, Israel

"Document No. 8" (in Russian). Volchin, September 29, 1944.

"Protocol" (in Russian). Brest ghetto file M.41/500.

"Protocol 34" (in Russian). September 28, 1944. Docs. A and B. Prosecutor Grushevsky of Vysokovsky District, interrogating witnesses concerning Nazi crimes.

"The Testimony of the Former Commandant of the German *Gendarmerie,* Brest District, Vasily Timofeyevich Semenyuk" (in Russian). Motikali documents, recorded November 13, 1945.

Audiotaped Interviews Conducted by Author

Bronitsky, Dina. New York, April 14, 1997.

Brooks, Ray. Warren, Conn., July 6, 1991; New York, April 16, 1996.

Englender, Shmuel, Dov Bar, Esther Bar, and Drora Schwartz. Brest, Belarus, June 23, 1997.

Kremer, Hanna. New York, October 22, 1997; videocassette. New York, December 1, 1997.

Lew, Gerson. Warren, Conn., July 6, 1991; Woods Hole, Mass., June 14, 1997.

Midler (Miller), Masha. New York, 1978–80.

Simon, Norma. Warren, Conn., July 6, 1991; New York, March 30, 1997; Woods Hole, Mass., June 14, 1997.

Spindel, Sara. Woods Hole, Mass., June 14, 1997.

Personal Testimonies

Bar, Dov. "The Journey to Volchin" (in Hebrew). Written testimony. April 1998.

Englender, Shmuel. "The Summary of My Trip to My Hometown, Volchin, in Belorussia" (in Belarusian/Russian; translated into Hebrew and from Hebrew into English). Audiocassette. Interviews with eyewitnesses and others in Volchin. June 1997.

———. "Volchin Memoirs" (in Hebrew). Written testimony. April 2001.

Guterman, Lily, Rosanne Lapan, Paula Morgenstern, Louis Pozez, Sara Sanditen, and Judith Sears. Interviews by Jewish Federation of Southern Arizona. Videocassette. Brest–Brona Gora, Belarus, June 24, 1997.

Martynov, A. "Martyrdom of Kobrin's Jews, 1941–1944" (in Russian). Written testimony.

Martynov, A. "Requiem" (in Russian). Written testimony.

Sanditen, Sara, "Beginning of a Personal Journey." Written testimony. June 1997.

Williams, Ann [Hannah]. "A Journey to My Birthplace." *Oxford Menorah,* December 1995.

Williams, Hannah, "The Russian People of Volchin Telling Their Stories about How the Nazis Killed the Jewish People in 1942" (in Belarusian). Audiocassette. June 1993.

Other

The Brest Ghetto, Russian-language documentary. Script by Elena Yakovich and Ilya Altman, directed by Jonas Misavicius, 38 minutes. English version. Videocassette. Concordia Investments and Trusting Company, Iskussivo Studio, Belarus, 1995.

"Jewish Leadership Mission, Jewish Federation of Southern Arizona, June 18-28, 1997." Videocassette, 87 minutes.

"Opening of Holocaust Memorial Center, Brest, May 1995." Videocassette, 63 minutes. Translated from Russian.